W9-BZK-662

Single

SEXUAL CULTURES

General Editors: **José Esteban Muñoz and Ann Pellegrini**

SINGLE

Arguments for the Uncoupled

Michael Cobb

NEW YORK UNIVERSITY PRESS
New York and London

NEW YORK UNIVERSITY PRESS
New York and London
www.nyupress.org

© 2012 by New York University
All rights reserved

References to Internet websites (URLS) were accurate at the time of writing.
Neither the author nor New York University Press is responsible for URLS that
may have expired or changed since the manuscript was prepared.

Library of Congress Cataloging-in-Publication Data
Cobb, Michael L.
Single : arguments for the uncoupled / Michael Cobb.
p. cm. Includes bibliographical references and index.
ISBN 978–0–8147–7254–6 (hardback) — ISBN 978–0–8147–7255–3 (pb) —
ISBN 978–0–8147–7256–0 (ebook)
1. Single people. I. Title.
HQ800.C73 2012
306.81'5—dc23 2011052259

New York University Press books are printed on acid-free paper,
and their binding materials are chosen for strength and durability.
We strive to use environmentally responsible suppliers and materials
to the greatest extent possible in publishing our books.

Manufactured in the United States of America

C 10 9 8 7 6 5 4 3 2 1
P 10 9 8 7 6 5 4 3 2 1

In Memory of Will Munro,
who had us all dance, together.

William, it was really something . . .

Contents

Acknowledgments

If writing this book has taught me anything, it's that a single person doesn't have to be lonely, which matters because sometimes we'll each have to confront the worst heartbreak, in our own solitary way. When that happens, and when you need to literally regroup, you're lucky if you can see and embrace the wide world of friendship, interest, work, pleasure, and love that might just help you not collapse.

I wrote the majority of this book while one of my dear friends, Will Munro, fought and lost his battle with brain cancer. Often the book was my retreat away from the world of his sickness. At times I wrote it in hospital waiting rooms, or beside him as he slept. (So his influence, care, and spirit of collaboration tint all the sentences.) In all these moments, I was never without a group of the most impressive caregivers, friends, colleagues, acquaintances, strangers, and animals that could soothe the worst tragedy, the worst catastrophe.

In the world of work, the University of Toronto English Department and its students have had my best interests always at heart and have made teaching, research, and writing exciting. Who knows why they've embraced me so, but they're just the greatest. A few of the many need special mention (but, as before, I could just list the entire faculty and staff): Alan Ackerman, Alan Bewell, Elspeth Brown (an honorary English department member), Brian Corman, Jeannine DeLombard, Paul Downes, Andrew Dubois, Elizabeth Harvey, Antonette diPaolo Healey, Cristina Henrique, Linda Hutcheon, Daniel Justice, Deidre Lynch, Lynne Magnusson, Jill Matus, Alice Maurice, Naomi Morgenstern, Andrea Most, Nick Mount, Heather Murray, Mary Nyquist, Clare Orchard, Tanuja Persuad, Mari Ruti, Donna Sabo, Sara Salih, Cannon Schmitt, Dana Seitler, Paul Stevens, and

Sarah Wilson. Invaluable research support came from excellent graduate students: Christopher Trigg and Alexander Eastwood.

Outside the University of Toronto, audiences at several MLAS, ASAS, and numerous university campuses have helped make these ideas better. For kind invitations to deliver parts (in wildly different forms) of this book, and for the questions that followed, I must thank the faculty, students, and staff of the University of Chicago, the University of Colorado at Boulder, Cornell University, University of Guelph, the University of Illinois at Chicago, Indiana University, Napier University (Scotland), Queen's University (Canada), the University of Rochester, Rutgers University, the University of Utah, and Yale University. Terrific colleagues have supported this book since it was first an idea (hatched over a dinner in Berlin with my beloved mentor, Hortense Spillers, who must always be thanked): Elizabeth Anker, Ian Balfour, Lauren Berlant, Bill Brown, Debra Campbell, Joshua Chambers-Letson, Pete Coviello, Jonathan Culler, Ann Cvetkovich, Cathy Davidson, Carolyn Dinshaw, Elizabeth Freeman, Diana Fuss, Janet Halley, Ellis Hanson, Molly Hite, Greg Jackson, E. Patrick Johnson, Dana Luciano, Dwight McBride, Meredith McGill, Michael Moon, Tim Murray, Christopher Nealon, Jeff Nunokawa, Andrew Parker, Don Pease, Elizabeth Povinelli, Shirley Samuels, Mark Seltzer, Michael Snediker, Gus Stadler, Jordan Stein, Rei Terada, Kyla Wazana Tompkins, Ken Wissoker, and Christina Zwarg. Sara Guyer, Scott Straus, Scott Herring, and Shane Vogel went above and beyond the typical friendly, collegial support and encouragement, opening up homes, kitchens, and their mouths to make me argue more convincingly.

At NYU Press, I'm once again humbled by the support of José Esteban Muñoz and Ann Pellegrini, who have always included me in the fantastic conversations they inspire and orchestrate. Eric Zinner is the rarest of editors — smart, apprehensive, imaginative, supportive, and not willing to let you rest on your laurels. And if that weren't enough, his compassion and kindness make me hope that we'll always work together. Ciara McLaughlin has had the onerous task of keeping me on track and responding to all the intricacies of making a book a book, for which I'm thankful. The Press's rigorous readings provided by an anonymous reader, Emily Apter, J. Jack Halberstam, and Kathryn Bond Stockton literally made these odd arguments work. I'm in their debt, wishing that every reading of my writing could be so exacting, intelligent, and generous.

Speaking of Kathryn Bond Stockton, she and a few other Utah lovers need special mention. Much of this book's thought was informed by awe-inspiring vistas, which required a lot of hiking to reach. This beleaguered single boy was lucky because he was surrounded by a group of seriously impressive thinkers and outdoorswomen, who introduced him to the beauty of Utah's landscape. So thanks to Patriarch Kathryn, Wife Number One (Shelley White), and Wife Number Two (Lisa Duggan). "Number Three" hopes he'll always be there to help us get up and down those cliffs.

In the world of play, there's Toronto, a Queertopia of charming proportions, delicious coffee, dance nights at The Beaver, and Rec Room Karaoke at The Henhouse. I'm spoiled there by the best of pals: Jeremy Laing, Frank Griggs, Paul Paincurvo, Scott Treleaven, Alon Freeman, Robert Alfons, Kevin Ritchie, Maggie MacDonald, Jaime Sin, Margot Keith, Jowita Kepa, Catherine Clarke, Anthony Hill, Markus Ziegler, Oliver Husain, Graydon Sheppard, Shawn Micallef, Vanessa Dunn, Katie Ritchie, Jason Poisson, Shaun Brodie, Duncan Forbes, Brendan Jensen, David Phillips, Anthony Collins, Patrick Borjal, Owen Pallett, and my beloved pup Sebastian. In and out of the New York City region (a Toronto suburb of sorts), I have other mesmerizing-if-only-they-could-be-constant-companions: Kate Bolick, Karen Azoulay, Rattawut Lapcharoensap, June Glasson, Rosten Woo, and Hong-An Tran.

Finally, there's the Wolf Pack that surrounded Will Munro before, during, and after his illness. If you could have witnessed the care, the love, the grace, the improvisation, the heroism, and the support under the direst of circumstances, you'd never be cynical about people again. All of my respect and love and best wishes, for as long as I live, will be with Peter Ho, Lex Vaughn, Alex McClelland, Leila Pourtavaf, John Caffery, Luis Jacob, Zavisha Time, Margaret Munro, and Dave Munro. Everyone did so much for Will, who, in thirty-five too-short years, did so much for us, for Toronto, for queers, and for people everywhere who want to meet, talk, dance, do things, and care for each other. His impact cannot be celebrated enough. The book, and its spirit of generosity, is for you, William. I miss you every day.

Generous research support (and leave time) for this work came from the Social Sciences and Humanities Research Council of Canada. And portions of chapters appeared in *South Atlantic Quarterly, Western Humanities Review*, and *Utah Law Review*. I thank these journals for permission to include that work here.

Introduction *Bitter Table for One*

Je fermerai partout portières et volets
Pour bâtir dans la nuit mes féeriques palais.

[I'll lock up all the doors and shutters neat and tight,
And build a fairy palace for myself at night.]
      CHARLES BAUDELAIRE, "Paysage" ("Landscape")

The necessity for this book is to be found in the following
consideration: that the lover's discourse is today of an
extreme solitude.
      ROLAND BARTHES, *A Lover's Discourse*

One Is the Loneliest Number

On her deathbed, my grandma Jewell commanded me to do
something she (and the whole world) had been commanding
me to do my entire teen and adult life: find someone to love.
By "someone," she didn't mean friends, colleagues, pets, ideas,
beliefs, or things. She meant a "significant other," a person with
whom I could settle down, get married, have sex— definitely
share a life. This command, which I never could quite convince
her I was obeying, was always coupled with the following threat:
"Michael, you don't want to die alone!"

Of course, these comments were inspired by her faith in romantic couple love, proven by years of personal experience, especially as a woman traversing the twentieth century well before
second-wave feminism. Jewell had, at least from our perspective,
a terrific marriage to my dear grandfather, Joe: a 1930s romance;
a long and sentimental separation while Joe was a cook on a naval
ship in the middle of the South Pacific during World War II; the
adoption of an adorable blonde girl, with curls, whom they took
to Disneyland the year it opened; and so on. In fact, as would

be expected, many of my first contacts with the major historical events of the twentieth century were mediated through the love story of my grandparents: the Depression, a world war, the prosperous fifties, the rebellious sixties, and Watergate were all accented by familial vignettes that danced around Jewell and Joe's love. I can picture my grandpa saving money for a Depression-era engagement ring he couldn't afford so he could appropriately propose to Jewell. I wish I could have read the long wartime letters Joe wrote to my grandma after he, floating on the South Pacific, finished his daily chores as a ship's cook. I would have enjoyed witnessing Jewell and Joe's anxiety over their daughter's wild streak — a wild streak that would have tipped into sixties activism had it not been for the chance meeting of my buttoned-down father at a fraternity party her first year of college. I was repeatedly told about my staunchly working-class, true-blue Democratic grandparents' horror over my mother's voting Republican after her marriage, a horror that deepened after the scandalous revelations about Nixon's involvement in Watergate. For Jewell, her relationship with Joe (and all those people around this couple) was her way of understanding her place in the world, her history, which was both personal and public every time she returned to stories we knew almost as well as she.

Everyone, I think, uses such a personal filter. My grandmother's lived experiences of her gender most certainly also added to her sense of her marriage's worth. So it wasn't surprising that Jewell felt the supreme value of her couple — it worked for her; it made sense of her "everything." After they courted and decided to get married, my grandfather's promise, as Grandma liked to report to me, was realized: he had offered her "the world," and that's exactly what she received. Or, at least, that's their official story. There is no way of really knowing what went on between my grandparents when they were away from the eyes of those attached to, but still outside, their coupledom. I don't remember them ever touching, or kissing, or hugging. I never learned the history of my grandfather's first wife, or why that marriage ended in a bitter, estranging divorce. But that doesn't mean anything, really. Jewell's picture of her life and her relationship endures and charms.

So did the anguish she felt for the years she lived after my grandpa's death. Her pain took the place of Joe, and she could never mourn him fully. Or to be more precise, she could never stop mourning him. In a strong way, he continued to be her companion, but in a special, spectral form. It wasn't melancholy she was feeling.[1] It was the kind of feeling that animates, that drives, the couple. (But more on such feelings a bit later.) So her dying words were a plea *and* a threat: it was as if she were telling me, "Michael, living, loving, and world building are the kind of activities that require not only a witness but a close companion who helps you belong to the larger histories, worlds, and dynamics that compose a life worth living." You need another, a most Significant Other, in order to order the world.

Certainly grief and loss were in the air on Jewell's deathbed, and I could excuse the potential violence of her plea for my coupledom because it soothed her to urge me to get something like a wife (she refused to acknowledge, explicitly, my queerness), a wife who would, in predictable turn, get me a life. Grandma's words were a gift of love rather than an instance of nagging harassment. I also understood that she was vouching for the conventional wisdom about love and marriage: marriage is good because it is terrible to be single. In my head, I could immediately rattle off "proof" of its horrors: the scent of rotting vegetables and unused product portions drifting out of my fridge; the numerous wedding invitations with an "and guest" violently scrawled next to my name; the pitying glances of people saddened that I often have nothing of substance to report about a "love life" (and the relieved glee when sometimes I do have things to report); the sad knowledge that not even the commodity form often fits the single; and the perplexed utterances of wait staff asking me, "Just you?" This perpetual "Sex and the City panic" can, indeed, be partially blamed for driving people into increasingly legitimized forms of desperate Internet mate shopping on sites such as Facebook. Suddenly, the Internet is full of lonely and desperately available hearts, just waiting to be saved by a click of the mouse or a perfectly worded text message. Sitting by my grandmother's bedside, I realized that my cell phone had not rung for days.

Yet it's not the single's fault that single status is so reviled. Part of the reason being single is terrible is that it's been made into a mystifying condition, marked by failure, characterized by an almost unassimilable oddity despite its always threatening ubiquity. In her book that became the basis for the TV series *Sex and the City,* Candace Bushnell explains her main reason for creating Carrie Bradshaw and her other famous, glittering, fabulous New Yorkers: "Most of all, *Sex and the City* sets out to answer one burning question [about her unmarried female friends] — why are we still single?"[2]

That this is a question at all, *still,* nearly says it all. Singleness is now always figured as a conundrum, and, if all goes according to plan, a conundrum to be solved by coupling off, and as soon as possible. Bushnell answers her own question disingenuously: we're all single "because we want to be."[3] This is disingenuous because she and her characters can't stay that way — they can't sustain that desire to be single, which may mean they've never really had it. Bushnell got married, surely much to the relief of her friends, the year after the book was published, to the ballet dancer Charles Askegard.[4] And her fiction imitates her own life. The last two sentences of the book are separated by a space that was apparently just too upsettingly wide to keep apart over the course of the series and films: "Mr. Big is happily married. Carrie is happily single."[5] So I wish it were a surprise that Carrie and Big, after a protracted separation, marry in the first movie sequel. In fact, all the main characters are substantially coupled off and mostly married, at varying points for varying durations, as we progress through the years of these characters' sex-filled lives in the city. Sustainable coupledom becomes the point of this world, not singleness as a happy, thriving lifestyle choice.

Tellingly, a similar media zeitgeist around single women in cities, the *Bridget Jones* franchise, makes light of the strangeness of singleness that even Bridget, like Carrie, must overcome. In the first film when asked, at a dinner party of couples, why so many women are still single "these days," Bridget offers this famous response: "Because we may seem normal to you but underneath our clothes we're covered in scales."[6] Bridget does end up with

Sex and the City: These ladies are most concerned with coupling, any kind of coupling. Screen capture from *Sex and the City* (dir. Michael Patrick King, 2008).

the right man, of course. So perhaps there are no scales; Bridget was certainly teasing the couples about their compulsive need to couple everyone else off. But in the jest we might also hear that, like the nonexistence of scales, there are no *real* single people out there — they're all just waiting for the chance to find that special someone, sometime soon. Everyone is pre- or postcouple. No one is *really* supposed to be single.

At the time of these large-scale film and media renderings of the single girl (Carrie and Bridget), I began attaching the letter "s" to the LGBTQ abreviation (LGBTQs) so I could affiliate those who were "single" with the ever-elongating list of nonmajority sexualities that deserve more sustained attention, political interventions, and cultural investigations. I wanted (and still want) to provoke serious reflection on why "relationships" and "coupledom" were so unquestionably considered better than singledom. I wanted to inquire why there was always the demand to be oriented toward enduring, intimate relationships, especially since the single seemed (and still seems) like one of the most despised sexual minorities one can be. Bella DePaulo, in *Singled Out: How Singles Are Stereotyped, Stigmatized, and Ignored, and Still Live Happily Ever After*, helps unearth the persistent cultural, social, psychological, and affective biases that "singlism" inflicts on the uncoupled, defining a variety of prominent types and characterizations of singles (widows; bachelors; women desperate for children; frivolous, noncommitted gays, etc.).[7] But don't just take my or DePaulo's word for it (especially since, sadly, I'm not always single). At least in the West, we almost always slight the experience of those who remain uncoupled. Proof is everywhere, especially at the highest and most far-reaching levels of popular culture. In the fall and winter of 2008, for example, you could hear and watch, in almost every place, pop superstar Beyoncé Knowles's hit song, "Single Ladies (Put a Ring on It)," made viral on YouTube in a video featuring an engaging and athletic dance routine with Knowles and two female backup dancers.

The clip is an updated and radically altered version of Gwen Verdon's "Mexican Breakfast," choreographed by Bob Fosse in the sixties. The homemade digital parodies of the video from all over the globe, always a YouTube staple, proliferated at lightning speed — the dance was too good not to both learn and digitally record (especially with friends). Rap star Kanye West at the 2009 MTV Video Music Awards famously interrupted the singer Taylor Swift's Best Female Video Award acceptance speech to say that Beyoncé's video was more deserving: it was, according to West, one of the best videos of all time. Fox's *Glee,* a campy television hit about a school show choir, devoted an entire episode to recreating the video's dance moves, even going so far as to have an entire high school football team perform the routine on the field.

The song, after seven calls to "all the single ladies," offers a story with a fiercely worded message: a previous lover from three years ago is jealous that the singer of the song is "doing [her] own thing." He has no "right" to be jealous, Beyoncé's voice assures us, "Cause if you liked it then you shoulda put a ring on it / If you liked it then you shoulda put a ring on it / Don't be mad once you see that he want it / If you liked it then you shoulda put a ring

Beyoncé (and backup dancers), scaring all the single ladies into marriage. Screen capture from the video *All the Single Ladies (Put a Ring on It)* (dir. Jake Nava, 2009).

on it." The "it," one presumes, is the singer, who is the thing to be ringed. The implication of the ring is that the ex-lover should have married, or at least gotten engaged to, the singer.

So the story of "Single Ladies (Put a Ring on It)" is not really the story about single life: it's about a missed opportunity to be coupled in a sustained way — which sadly, might be all we ever really hear about being single. It's not even about glorifying the fun of being a single lady because all there is to say to all the single ladies (and, by proxy, the single men who are wondering if they should pop the question) is that something grave happens if you don't make couplehood stable and permanent: one day you might have to see the one who got away from you with someone else. Moreover, Beyoncé is not satisfied with describing jealousy she might provoke or announcing the man's loss of the right to possess her (it). There's a significant shift of tone during the bridge of the song, and we're treated to an even more confusing message — confusing because there might still be a chance for this reluctant-to-get-engaged ex: "Don't treat me to the things of this world / I'm not that kind of girl / Your love is what I prefer, what I deserve / Is a man that makes me, then takes me / And delivers me to a destiny, to infinity and beyond / Pull me into your arms / Say I'm the one you own / If you don't, you'll be alone / And like a ghost, I'll be gone." Not only does this single lady not want to be single, she doesn't even want to be with, as she puts it, the "man on my hips."[8] She wants her ex to acknowledge his desire for her; otherwise, she threatens, he'll be all alone and she will be "like a ghost" to him, tormenting him with his now tragic status.

Here's where Beyoncé's song is making more than a claim for the necessity of participating in the normative recognition of couples in the form of marriage (she's not arguing for the relative value of marriage; that's a value she's taking as a given). Marriage is never a real controversy, and she's not immediately concerned with the failure to reach that preferred kind of social status (with all its rights and privileges). Instead, she's putting the emphasis on how tragic it would be to remain single: it will get spooky if you don't keep engaging (literally) the couple, and instead of having the "It" girl, Beyoncé, you will have only loss. Her song helps train us to want the thing that hasn't worked before: the broken couple rather than the terrible status of the haunted, and most likely lonely, single. The song is very typical in its approach to all the single ladies: it chooses to highlight loneliness as a dimension of singleness that can and must be overcome by no longer being single. That's all we'll learn here; there's nothing more to see in the lives of the singles who dance all over the place.

Such pop commentary is fun to think about, but I'd hate for people to worry that in my desire to focus on the status of the single I'm rehashing a tired sexual liberation argument about the need to focus on what a single status often is thought to permit: sex without love; sex without a relationship; and sex without the imperatives of marriage.[9] I don't have any interest in developing yet another argument that vilifies those who make meaningful, often monogamous, commitments to a Significant Other. I don't even have the desire to promote the value of a free and available Beyoncé. Instead, I want to pursue, in this book, the figurative dynamics and stakes of singlehood, especially in a world slavishly devoted to the supremacy of the couple.[10]

Only the Lonely

Singles studies are starting to appear with greater frequency, but people have been obsessed with loneliness for millennia, and that's the emotion thought to belong most to singles. Thomas Dumm's recent meditation on the "existential situations" of the "souls of lonely people" helps us get beyond the typical trends in loneliness studies that "have been a constant feature of sociology and the political study of civil society" over the past fifty years.[11] He points out that these numerous inquiries into loneliness have typically investigated the effects of social alienation, opposed the work of developing the self to the work of developing social ties, and expressed concern about the disastrous impact on the individual's psyche of spending too much time alone. He particularly singles out *The Lonely Crowd,* by David Riesman, Nathan Glazer, and Reuel Denney, a tremendously influential book from the 1950s about three American character types that highlighted a new middle class so "other-directed" they could, oddly enough, feel only the loneliness-inducing sensations of shallow connection with others.[12] This sociological story about trends in community life usually characterizes as a threat to intimacy the increasing availability of multiple social situations and their resulting demands on the individual to become quickly socially adaptable to all sorts of new, if not fleeting, relations. Because of the overwhelming number of social opportunities encountered on any given day, individuals do not become "inward-directed" enough to develop the kind of character that would cherish and develop relationships and a sense of responsibility to such relationships over time. Intimacy, in this new world order, is thought to always be in peril, characterized by a fragility proposed by nearly every social development or interaction.

Almost sixty years later, we're still thinking about loneliness, single individuals, and crowds in roughly similar terms. While reviewing the significance of *The Lonely Crowd,* a contemporary writer sums up our revived interest and worry about new configurations of our shallow, and shallow-making, crowds, which are not-so-coincidentally emerging at the same time as the singles' "Sex and the City" panic. Instead of confronting busy urban streets full of "stranger-intimacies," we're now immersed in a "crowd" of new media, made possible by the supremacy of the Internet's proliferating forms of technological mass publicity, which are displacing and transforming all forms of information distribution and traditional broadcast and print media outlets.[13] We're not just surfing the flow of information; we're flooded by social networking opportunities, made more urgent and physically proximate by the ubiquity of cellular technology that puts a twittering and texting premium on social networking and intimacy creation and consumption. According to the columnist rants:

> It is apparent in many aspects of American society today that it is in fact a "lonely crowd." The ability to get along with most everyone, to be "normal," and to behave properly is essential for Americans at work, play, in traffic, in school, even at the mall. Response to the signals picked up by the inner "radar" while also needing to be friendly with everyone leaves little time for people to develop strong, lasting friendships as previous generations did. As the internet (a tool that can expand the inner "radar" to learn what people are doing around the world) has made the world accessible at the click of a mouse, people are also becoming more isolated for [sic] each other. The sheer flood of information incessantly incoming on the "radar" can make it difficult for individuals to have the same sense of self that an inner-directed individual would, which can lead to loneliness. All of these elements combined have factored into the current state of American society as a "lonely crowd."[14]

Whether or not this is the subtlest reading of Reisman et al., what we hear, over and over again, is a strong thesis that the crowd is a very lonely place, quite possibly because we can never relieve our loneliness by the shallow relationships that the techno-market has made so readily available even as it isolates people from each other. Relationships now have no possibility of depth because people are not developing themselves, and thus their relationships, enough. A major implication of these worries about the superficiality of social networking is that our selves aren't deep enough to be committed to another. Lurking within the logic of these worries is the notion that the development of a self has a particular goal: relationships with others. (Always overheard on daytime talk shows, "You've got to learn to love yourself so you can love others.") And more often than not, by "others," we mean "an," *and only just one*, Other.

Even our leaders can't help but characterize the crowd and its technologies as lonely. Barack Obama is the first U.S. president known to be addicted to smart-phone technology — he refused to give it up once he took office in 2009, perhaps because he ran the most socially networked and technologically advanced presidential campaign in history. But his BlackBerry also manifests a long-held drive for sociability that saturates his first autobiography, *Dreams from My Father: A Story of Race and Inheritance*. In this *bildungsroman*, Obama relentlessly pathologizes being alone, perhaps because his otherwise impressive and articulate memoir seems to have bought the lonely crowd thesis nearly wholesale. On page after page, despair is visualized as a scene of individuals who are forced into alienated postures and have not done the necessary introspection and self-development to correct such postures. Obama writes often about his own tormented search for meaning in life, and these scenarios usually take place in an isolation that distresses him. Lines such as these pervade the book: "The earth shook under my feet, ready to crack at any moment. I stopped trying to steady myself, and knew for the first time that I was utterly alone."[15] "It was like a bad dream. I wandered down Broadway, imagining myself standing at the edge of the Lincoln Memorial and looking out over an empty pavilion, debris scattering in the wind."[16] "I had tried to imagine this pale Englishman in a parched desert somewhere, his back turned away from a circle of naked tribesmen, his eyes searching an empty sky, bitter in his solitude. . . . The emotions between the races could never be pure; even love was tarnished by the desire to find in the other some element that was missing in ourselves. Whether we sought out our demons or salvation, the other race would always remain just that: menacing, alien, and apart."[17] "My mother was that girl with the movie of beautiful black people in her head, flattered by my father's attention, confused and alone . . . and perhaps that's how any love begins, impulses and cloudy images that allow us to break across our solitude, and then, if we're lucky, are finally transformed into something firmer."[18]

His worry over his loneliness, and the way that that feeling marks the world's ravenous emptiness, stirs up so much pathos and longing in him that his journey to the unknown side of his family, his father's side of his family in Kenya, seems necessary: Obama wants, desperately, everyone and everything to connect. His desire is consummately postpartisan. So the entire book prepares us for the final vignette: after reading over four hundred pages of his struggles with familial, personal, professional, and political quandaries, we're invited to the wedding of Obama to Michelle, who is responsible for "several improvements in [his] character,"[19] not least his improvement from a single, shallow person to a happily married one with a large, united, and connected family. Curiously, Obama doesn't dwell much on the ceremony, or even on descriptions of Michelle. Instead, he evokes a crowd that is no longer lonely, that can instead serve as his support, because his character has improved enough for him to value his relations, at least at his wedding. His description of the reception after the ceremony at Jeremiah A. Wright's Trinity United Church of Christ is replete with family feeling, resolving all the sad, fractured loneliness that throbbed through so much of his earlier story. "Everyone looked very fine at the reception, my new aunts admiring the cakes, my new uncles admiring themselves in their rented tuxedos. Johnnie was there, sharing a laugh with Jeff and Scott, my old friends from Hawaii and Hasan, my roommate from college."[20] It's not just that the occasion allows for family and friends to celebrate a couple's nuptials; the wedding allows for a crowd of desperate, lonely people to be *thought* of as substantively connecting. The setting is underdescribed because we all know what weddings are like. Obama does not have to articulate the depth and strength of connection that according to the lonely crowd theorists may no longer exist; instead he merely evokes important family alliances, describes his own gathering confidence, and finally asserts that, "for that moment, at least, I felt like the luckiest man alive."[21] Lucky, because he's found a wife, a life, and a family. As in a Shakespearean comedy, a marriage ends our tragic twists and turns, nullifying all the bad feelings of misunderstanding and misconnection that preceded it. Could you even imagine a president who could be elected if she or he were single?

But Obama's book is hardly alone in its expression of the lonely crowd thesis. (Symptomatically he even wrote a companion autobiography before the age of forty-eight.) So many books have appeared since, most notably *Bowling Alone: The Collapse and Revival of American Community* and *Loneliness: Human Nature and the Need for Social Connection,* that a thorough literature review would be impossible and, given the similarity of the authors' conclusions, might bore even the most patient reader.[22] Loneliness and loneliness studies are ubiquitous. Over the last few years of my research, I often recalled the snide description of correspondence from the lovelorn in Nathanael West's 1933 novella, *Miss Lonelyhearts,* about an "Aunt Agony"–style columnist who reads letter after letter about social isolation: "And on most days he [Miss Lonelyhearts] received more than thirty letters, all of them alike, stamped from the dough of suffering with a heart-shaped cookie knife."[23] Likewise, the number of examples of lonely singles I've received from colleagues, friends, interlocutors, and strangers while I was working on this book is staggering — and although so many are fine examples, taken as a whole, they start to feel cookie-cut for easy consumption.

If it weren't for West's snide comment urging me to get beyond the topic of the loneliness of singles, I would have found it too daunting to think about what else could or should be included in this book. Would an exhaustive account of centuries of muscular American individualism be required? Singleness must be shaped by the legacies of Emerson and Thoreau (and countless others). There could have been numerous *Walden*-esque witticisms about the trials of a life "alone in the woods, a mile from any neighbor, in a house" built by oneself. Certainly being single is a variation on being individual. Even Thoreau had to keep reassuring us that he was not too lonely in the woods: "I am no more lonely than a single mullein or dandelion in a pasture, or a bean leaf, or sorrel, or a horse-fly, or a bumble-bee."[24] I'm not sure if he can prove or commit too many pathetic fallacies in these comparisons. Such rhetoric betrays a sense that the question of his loneliness is still very much open, and something about individualism must be thought about as we consider the single.

My quick reference to Thoreau helps me express a hunch about what has changed in how we think of individuals in our time: the individual is now usually marked as someone alone, suspiciously without a partner. Even Dumm's smart *Loneliness as a Way of Life* crescendoes into heart-wrenching insights about grieving his wife's death from lung cancer.[25] His project and my own share similar impulses (the value of individualism in isolation) and authors (Arendt, Freud, Du Bois, among others), but we differ significantly because his critique of the discrediting of loneliness does not push the couple form from its primary perch. Here's what he says, exquisitely, about what the death of his wife means to him:

> My wife, as a thing, no longer exists, and hence is never again to be available *for me*, but through the fact of her irretrievable absence she is insistently, still sometimes overwhelmingly, available *to* me. Grief gives her a profound presence in my ongoing life; her ghost, even in its exhausted state, comforts me and frightens me. This is how she is real to me. In my long nights she is silent, I cry to her, I follow her through bizarre dreamscapes, and allow myself to miss her. As her presence as absence comes to be integrated into my life, I begin to lose her again; in her real absence she becomes a metaphor for my real loss of her — she becomes, as Emerson says, a part of my estate.[26]

This is a beautiful passage, with important sentiments to express, and in no way could these feelings not be true. My grandmother might have articulated something similar, though in a less philosophical idiom. Yet the loneliness of being alone is so often framed by the intense, lyrical loss of a loved one — if not *the* loved one, a spouse. I'd like to work with Dumm's insights about the useful existentialism that "thinking about being lonely" offers us. His wife's ghost, any spouse's ghost, will be, as we'll see, vivid and provoking to our understandings as well. So the different angle I take throughout this book is that singleness marks being alone in a nearly paralyzingly profound manner — so much so that individualism, the value of aloneness, can barely be thought unless we strip away the pathologizing dynamics of coupledom that attach to the individual a bitter affect we might call loneliness. What we'll discover is crucial: loneliness will not brand the single as much as aloneness does. A point this book offers: the contemporary individual is not lonely, just single — but this is not culturally recognized. So before we can even understand the individual's singleness, we have to understand the affective dynamics that layer onto the heart of the individual debilitating feelings that are generated by those who are not single: by the couple.

What I want to develop, polemically, are my serious misgivings about the miscasting of singleness as a terrible condition worth our pity and obfuscation, if not an addictive dance that will address but not describe "all the single" ladies and gentlemen. As DePaulo and anyone else who has thought seriously about single life already know, the problem of the single is not the actual, lived experience of people who find themselves alone as much as the feelings that deliberately foreclose our understanding of singleness because singles are *thought* to be lonely — and loneliness, as we're frequently reminded, has terrible consequences. To be blunt: I'm sick and tired of the single person being the avatar of the lonely crowd.

In John T. Cacioppo and William Patrick's recent study *Loneliness* we are reminded, yet again, of scientific "findings" that make you want to run to the nearest available partner and pop the question:

Social isolation has an impact on health comparable to the effect of high blood pressure, lack of exercise, obesity, or smoking. Our research in the past decade or so demonstrates that the culprit behind these dire statistics is not usually literally being alone, but subjective experience of *loneliness*. Whether you are at home with your family, working in an office crowded with bright and attractive people, touring Disneyland, or sitting alone in a fleabag hotel on the working side of town, chronic *feelings* of loneliness can drive a cascade of physiological events that actually accelerates the aging process. Loneliness not only alters behavior but shows up in measurements of stress hormones, immune function, and cardiovascular function. Over time, these changes in physiology are compounded in ways that may be hastening millions of people to an early grave.[27]

I can't help but think that Jones's "covered in scales" comment might not be off the mark if what these two writers say is true. Now's not the time to quibble with the rhetoric and findings of these researchers, especially since they've been finding their conclusions for so long. And I give them credit: they're careful to make sure that we understand that loneliness is not the same thing as aloneness; they're right to soon point out that "being miserably lonely in a marriage has been a literary staple from *Madame Bovary* to *The Sopranos*" (actually a literary staple for much, much longer than that).[28] But they can't resist prefacing their remarks with a prevailing notion that is considered axiomatic: "Married people, on average, are less lonely than unmarried people."[29] Maybe that's true. Maybe it's not. The truth doesn't matter because what we're rhetorically left with is a sense that social connection is absolutely necessary; that a menacing, debilitating feeling of loneliness lurks everywhere; and that, despite examples to the contrary, married people might be experiencing social connection more regularly, more healthfully. In the quickest of phrases, by describing marriage as an average, if not *the* average, experience of social connection, the researchers highlight the unmarried — and here I think Cacioppo and Patrick mean "single" rather than those who can't or won't be married even if they're coupled — as a heightened instance of alienation. And they recast marriage and coupledom, however obliquely, as kinds of relations that offer the greater chance of escape from the early grave of loneliness, a loneliness that is crowding us each time we look at our smart phones.

They're hardly alone in this assessment. Despite all the novelty of new social networks, there's still a very old-fashioned sense of what grounds people as social actors. For all the inventiveness of technology, it's strikingly hard to imagine the smooth functioning, if not the goods, of the social world without imagining the couple. This imagination, in turn, presents a powerful, if not compulsory, logic that dominates the manner in which we begin to even consider social interaction and connection, in any of its public forms (in old and new media; online or in physical, less virtual spaces where people gather). Moreover, this logic's corrosive effects play out in realms quite beyond the physiological or psychological impact at the level of the individual. Being single is not merely an individual's psychological or physical plight. There are huge political, social, and cultural stakes in dividing people up into those who are single and those who are not.

Those stakes belong to what is currently a very familiar terrain of family politics. I wrote a book on the Religious Right and homophobic hate speech in the mid-2000s,[30] so the nebulous category of "values voters" has been on my mind for some time. The cause of these voters was even further strengthened by the controversy and outrage over same-sex marriage — the plea for participation in state-sanctioned coupledom. "Values voters" are, for the most part, conservative Christians or political opportunists (even if they are not named as such) who profit, in many senses of the term, from patrolling and excluding those who can enter into official and state-sanctioned forms of intimate couple relating. Marriage, and same-sex marriage in particular, is serious political and cultural business, along with the other "values votes" issues that continue to have substantial clout in the United States (under any presidency, Democratic or Republican) — abortion, stem-cell research, affirmative action, health care reform. These are not wedge issues but central biopolitical concerns that ferociously animate our present and future politics.

Marriage, gay or not, and for that matter most forms of couple-dom, are at the heart of this political life. And those who are at its heart must have a heart: an openness to couple love and connection is increasingly considered prerequisite for personhood in a form of government (say, the U.S. government) that has striking resemblances to other totalitarian regimes of the last century.

For love, the putative emotion that relieves (or promises to relieve) loneliness, is not merely an activity one adds to a list of things that have to get done in this life. For many, like my grandma Jewell, it is not life's primary obsession but life it-self — life in which important feelings, work, and understandings are permitted to be accomplished because you have a witness. So if you belong to a couple, on sliding scales of social and legal legitimacy, you occupy a not-so-frivolous status. Laura Kipnis's saucy polemic *Against Love* puts love, and particularly the extensive work of love, in terms that can help us with what seems to be a long overdue critique of the couple form. She wonders, "Has any despot's [love's] rule ever so successfully infiltrated every crevice of a population's being, into its movements and gestures, penetrated its very soul? In fact it creates the modern notion of a soul — one which experiences itself as empty without love. Saying 'no' to love isn't just heresy, it's tragedy: for our sort the failure to achieve what is most essentially human. And not just tragic, but abnormal."[31] Kipnis is entirely right: you're not allowed to be without love; you're not allowed to be merely single — which is different from being pre- or postmarried/coupled, with designs on changing that nonimportant status by making your way into essential humanity *qua* the couple. There is, as Kipnis reminds us, "no viable alternative" in the "couple economies" that "are governed — like our economic system itself — by scarcity, threat, and internalized prohibitions" (23).

The critique Kipnis offers, although quite productive, turns on some familiar tropes that miss some crucial insights: "Why bother to make marriage compulsory when informal compulsions work so well that even gays — once such paragons of un-regulated sexuality, once so contemptuous of whitebread hetero lifestyles — are now demanding state regulation too?" (41). I appreciate Kipnis, a lot, but I'm afraid that the audacious and too-easy characterization of queers-gone-bad into the fight for wedlock does not take into account just how necessary the marriage form and its not-so-distant child, the couple form, are for intimate stability. And not only intimate stability: judicial, political, and cultural legibility that belongs to and exceeds official state regulation. People want to belong so they don't feel menaced by their isolation. And I'm convinced that the nation-state might very well want us to feel such desperate desires for belonging. If the fury over marriage and the increasing prestige of the "value voters" can tell us something, surely it is that for the United States, marriage and couples are foundational. In fact, they are the foundation upon which society is built — they are society's life support systems. From this vantage point, the American citizen is not a he or a she, but a "we" not "we the people" but "we the couple" (and a couple ideally with kids).

It's no accident that Hannah Arendt ended her magisterial *The Origins of Totalitarianism* with a discussion of terror and ideology that pivots on loneliness. People dismiss Arendt for all sorts of good reasons, yet they continue to argue with her for a reason: she can provide startling, smart formulations that help us refine our own new thoughts, even if we're not in complete or comfortable agreement with all her conclusions. And in what I take to be her masterpiece, she makes clear that totalitarianism, which relies on creating new and unpredictable order through terror-filled ideological forms of reasoning, requires that people lose their abilities, or perhaps their sensibilities, to be with others in generous and meaningful relations. She distinguishes between the capacity to be in solitude, which does not necessarily imply one is lonely, and the condition of feeling deserted, abandoned. The feeling of loneliness produces sensations of desperation that open one up to the cruel ideologies of totalitarianism — ideologies that produce compelling ideas, full of persuasive power, whose logics are much too consistent, much too able to misread the circumstances of the world, providing instead a paranoid "sixth sense." Let me quote, at length, one of the closing paragraphs of the book:

What prepares men for totalitarian domination in the non-totalitarian world is the fact that loneliness, once a border-line experience usually suffered in certain marginal social conditions like old age, has become an everyday experience of the evergrowing masses of our [the twentieth] century. The merciless process into which totalitarianism drives and organizes the masses looks like a suicidal escape from this reality. The "ice-cold reasoning" and the "mighty tentacle" of dialectics which "seizes you as in a vise" appears like a last support in a world where nobody is reliable and nothing can be relied upon. It is the inner coercion whose only content is the strict avoidance of contradictions that seems to con-firm man's identity outside all relationships with others. It fits him into the iron band of terror even when he is alone, and totalitarian domination never tries to leave him alone except in the extreme situation of solitary confinement. By destroy-ing all space between men and pressing men up against each other, even the productive potentialities of isolation are an-nihilated; by teaching and glorifying the logical reasoning of loneliness where man knows that he will be utterly lost if ever he lets go of the first premise from which the whole process is being started, even the slim chances that loneliness may be transformed into solitude and logic into thought are oblit-erated. If this practice is compared with that of tyranny, it seems as if a way had been found to set the desert itself into motion, to let loose a sand storm that could cover all parts of the inhabited earth.[32]

There are echoes in this passage of Thoreau's comment that "we are for the most part more lonely when we go abroad among men than when we stay in our chambers."[33] But Arendt is more visceral, more physical. The absence of connection, the absence of even having a connection with oneself, is the condition of loneliness, which makes one too much of a one, outside of re-lationships, mistrustful of everyone. And when one is made to feel lonely, one is prepared to endure a kind of "inner coercion" by permitting oneself to seek out a logic for why the world is barren, for why one has been abandoned. One is impelled to turn to a sharply insistent support system that will make one read the world ideologically, feel the world terribly, and thus become ready for — prone to join in — any kind of strong movement that totalitarian forces wish upon the masses.

It might sound odd that I would start thinking about totalitarianism's origins and the socio-psychological effects of terror as one method to think about the plight of the single. But if my queer theory training has taught me anything, it is that I should be vigilant about the rhetorics and politics of connection, especially intimate connection. And if there's no intimacy, no intimate connection, then what can one think? At first blush, what one begins to encounter among the lonely is not the absence of people but the sheer abundance of others. Arendt believes that "loneliness . . . [is] the common ground for terror, the essence of totalitarian government" (475). On this common ground we have an incredible crowd — an army of the lonely, too many lonely. And one of the primary logics of this ground is what is thought to be the ultimate antidote for the lonely: falling in love, coupling off, or simply the rubbing and touching of sexual contact. But this "being together" is one of the primary totalitarian logics that accelerate the feelings of alienation and dislocation. The loneliest of us are not necessarily those of us who are actually alone but rather those of us trying our hardest not to be alone — something with which Cacioppo and Patrick might very well agree. But Arendt goes further. She is shrewd when she reminds us that sometimes terror will not be so explicit; total terror will succeed in becoming the fabric of life, the bonds between humans who will be forced together so deeply. The "body politic," then, "no longer uses terror as a means of intimidation," for its "essence is terror" (468). This insight certainly clouds the conclusions of Cacioppo and Patrick (and nearly all others) who believe that we desperately need social connection. If social connection, often reflected in "the body politic," is a sense of terrifying loneliness, how can social interactions possibly alleviate rather than intensify loneliness?

So here's where Kipnis and I part ways: she wants to subvert the labor of love by ushering in a radical politics of adultery, with new and exciting (not dead or exhausted) loves perpetually on the horizon — a horizon of couples, if you will. I want to suggest that we think beyond the potentials of sex and sexuality in which Kipnis seems to have faith. I want to question what it means to be in any kind of close, intimate contact in an intimate sphere and a public sphere that are so intertwined as to be almost non-distinct.[34] I want to explore the much-too-close quality of "men [and women] pressing men [and women and other genders] together," and to assert that to indulge the couple form is to indulge the crowd. The lonely crowd thesis has been much too individually focused, much too inward looking, to be of much use in understanding a crowd that is repetitively figured as a couple. I wonder if by shifting the focus, by making the couple, rather than the single, the avatar of the lonely crowd, we can discover figures that are alone but not lonely, not menaced by the feelings of loneliness that push most of us into the couple, which is really the crowd, or the way we understand the public. I must stress that I'm not arguing for the value of individuation at the expense of meaningful connection and ethical responsibility toward others. I'm not even against couples, or love. Instead, I'm thinking about figures of the single, the alone, the isolated, that critique (but do not necessarily abolish) the couple as the default model of very significant relating that is at the core, the soul, the heart, and the mind of the United (and other) States. If anything, I'm hoping to take the burden of the whole world off the shoulders of the couple.

The Man Not of the Crowd

I use the word *figures* deliberately, for it reveals the major methodology of this book, one very much suited for our topic, the "problem" of the single that, as DePaulo phrases it, "has no name."[35] I am first and foremost a literary scholar who believes in the force of language, of the rhetoric we employ. So I want to explore the manner in which inventive usages of language make

possible, make intelligible, or obscure the political, social, cultural, aesthetic, and intimate worlds in which the dramas of the
single versus the couple play. Moreover, we're thinking about
types of people (single or not) that are characterized, manipu-
lated, and put into a hierarchy, in which the couple always wins
out. So much of this book will be about how relationship status
turns us into characters, into forms, that have dramatic impacts
on our lived experiences and self-understandings. Along the way,
we'll wonder if we could find another kind of character, or at least
find other kinds of characteristics, that could interrupt the steely,
totalitarian logics of the couple characters that not only interrupt
but also teach by their contrary example.

To be less abstract: taking Bushnell's stable of single ladies as a
case study, why do people play the conversation game of "Which
Sex and the City character are you?" You might be a Carrie, a Sa-
mantha, a Charlotte, or, if you're a bit dowdy, a Miranda (from
the earlier seasons). By thinking about this question, we inves-
tigate traits, passions, and interests that resemble those of the
characters on screen. All sorts of women and gay men have been
playing this game for years whenever they gather (Sacha Baron
Cohen's 2009 *Bruno* makes fun of this compulsion when he has
his flamboyantly gay character, Bruno, play this name game, un-
comfortably, with a bunch of very straight hunters around the
campfire). Bushnell's situational comedy features four strong
lead characters that are similar enough to belong to the same type
(affluent, white, urban, temporarily single lady). But each character has obvious, slightly individuating characteristics, offering
us her own quick but related catalogue of attributes that might
inspire all sorts of self- and group analysis, often over a fancy,
expensive cocktail.

Or a keyboard: I took the Facebook quiz that helped identify
which *Sex and the City* character I am by answering a short quiz
about my dating and sartorial preferences. Do I have an adven-
turous, daring sense of fashion? Or am I more sensible in dress,
wanting to be comfortable, expressing my unerring sense of se-
riousness? Is my perfect date a romantic evening starting with
flowers? Or might I prefer a date riddled with intense, intellectual

conversation? Or do I just want to have great orgasms? I'm sad to report that according to this quiz I'm a "Carrie" — not my favorite character, and I hate to think about why I came up as her rather than the smart and self-possessed Miranda. Sadly, what my mother told me years ago might be inanely true: I'm Carrie because I write about sex for a living. Let's see if this book, which is uninterested in sex, can prove her wrong.

Carrie or not, I'm concerned with figurative expressions of the single and the couple and with the logics that such figurations impress upon us. I do so not only because, as Thornton Wilder put it in the 1920s, "the whole purport of literature . . . is the notation of the heart."[36] I look to the expressive register in literature, film, art, television, music, architecture, history, law, psychology, and memoir because "inventive forms," as Kathryn Bond Stockton puts it, "are rich stimulators of questions public cultures seem to have no language for encountering."[37] Certainly, as I've said, there are examples of the single everywhere in public, but they are always obscured by the toxic, totalitarian prominence of the couple. The single tends to not have its own language, its own way to be articulate and understood. In fact, if I were writing a book on epistemology, say if I were to write something akin to Eve Kosofsky Sedgwick's *Epistemology of the Closet*, I might be able to pursue, fully, why the production of knowledge, "the contestation of meaning," the movement from ignorance to knowledge, is rarely filtered through any other analytic construction than an analytic devoted to the couple form — those axiomatic "pairings" Sedgwick identifies as crises of definitions, those crises that are "basic to modern cultural organization as masculine/feminine, majority/minority, innocence/initiation, natural/artificial, new/old, growth/decadence, urbane/provincial, health/illness, same/different, cognition/paranoia, art/kitsch, sincerity/sentimentality, and voluntarity/addiction."[38] Dialectics, encounters, face-offs, and conversations tend to be formally thought of as a relation between two (and rarely, especially now, one). True/false: we must wonder, even at the level of definition, why there are always two sides to every story. Why not three, or more? Or fewer? As we'll see, the creation of knowledge, the movement from ignorance to insight, often requires the formal register of a couple, which does, I think, much to obscure how to even think about the singularity of singles.

Many of my poststructural and queer theoretical insights are obsessed, for good reason, with intersubjectivity, with the definitions and ideas we create through our relations with others, especially as we use language, interact with tradition, and make ourselves legible to ourselves and each other. We are taught to be wary about inflated individualisms, with muscular forms of self-understanding and valuations that insist on hierarchy and subjugation in order to possess and wield power, often unethically and ruthlessly. For collectivity, community, minorities, and all sorts of oppressed and repressed knowledges are devalued when we think of individuals in this way. So much work, then, rightly tries to account for others, for difference, for those who have suffered or have been stricken or obscured from analytical records, not to mention excluded from adequate political representation and protections. My own academic position as a professor of queer theory in an English department certainly wouldn't exist if the academy had not seen the need for queer theoretical work to exist alongside work on authorial "geniuses" such as Shakespeare and Milton (among many others). I'm a student of queer poststructural theoretical axioms; I owe my livelihood to them. This knowledge work is in many ways ethics driven, which means it's worried about the proper relationships we should have in a world that often does not treat its actors properly, humanely, or peacefully. But what I worry about now is how we've perhaps become too suspicious of singular beings as we've been working with the subjugated knowledges of others. I wonder if the epistemologies that we're creating with our focus on the "Other" when we structure the knowledge of difference might actually help some conservative forces. Judith Butler circles around this quandary when she writes in her book *Precarious Life* about Levinas and his perplexing concept of the "Other's" face, which, far from being a human face, relies on the figurations of a human to insist on a kind of philosophical humanization of an "Other" being who should not be harmed, should be allowed at least to live, and has a precarious existence that should not be terminated. As she explains Levinas's major ethical figuration, she rightly sees that the "political scene" is distorted because in that scene "there are always more than two subjects at play." But in Levinas (and numerous others) we reduce the political, ethical engagement because "we begin by positing a dyad."[39] The face of the Other, which produces at least initially a coupling, disciplines our imaginings as an interaction between two, which matters even as Levinas and Butler complicate the picture (and make nuances that are crucial). Foundationally speaking, I think we tend to understand by way of a very conventional kind of interrelational dynamic, which can then make even the most progressive, ethically charged work deeply conservative along one structural axis: the intellectual world this work elaborates insists on theories that belong, in some fundamental ways, to the uninterrogated supremacy of the couple.

Certainly, I'm deliberately overstating the case, but I do so to snap us out of imagining a couple at the beginning of our most ethical, most relational thoughts. To help overcome the hyperbole that is the couple form, I look to invented, literary figures that can split apart that very steely way of ordering the world, perhaps breaking open the possibility that even the lonely intimacy of pairs cannot contain what can and might occur if the single were ever able to insist on its value, on its meaning that isn't lonely as much as it is, quite simply, valuable on its own.

Of course, I'm not the first literary critic to crowd the couple into a lonely corner.[40] Leo Bersani and Ulysse Dutoit do as much when they generate subtle readings from Jean-Luc Godard's 1963 Le mépris, a French New Wave classic about the interrelated dynamics of a couple and that couple's relation to the film industry. Rather than try to explain the psychological or social reasons why the film's couple breaks up in mutual contempt, Bersani and Dutoit try to do away with the easy knowledge one might construct out of the film's dynamics of intimate relating. So they isolate figures that are isolating themselves from one another — characters that confuse rather than explain, characters that refuse to be fully expressive, that refuse to bring any knowledge out of the closet of their selves. They read Godard's film about the catastrophe of the modern couple as an opening up of deep questions about the ontology of the couple form, about the kinds of possibilities and impossibilities that one finds in the couple form, indeed multiple kinds of couple forms, that will not be ever fully understood using typical, conventional forms and figures of intimacy. Bersani and Dutoit fixate on the lonely and alienating images of the characters in Godard's film — who have "lost the levity of imaginary being" — not to offer a story about relating gone wrong but to offer something like a cautionary tale that has enormous relevance: the failure of coupledom is a result of the couple's attempts to be too real, too understood, and too explained — in other words, too comprehensive in its scope.[41] Bersani and Dutoit, following the film's visual and formal cues, thus urge us to remember that we have a "responsibility *not to be*," that perhaps the couple's loneliness would not have had to be so catastrophic: "By potentializing their relation *while they are in it*, they would have left their condemned coupledom and given to each other the freedom to reappear, always, as subjects too inconclusive, too multiple, too unfinished, ever to be totally loved."[42]

I appreciate this kind of couple critique very much, especially since it can be optimistic about the possibility of relating in ways that go beyond the ideological constraints of any relating we are coerced to assume. But I'd like to situate my very unruly, often inconsistent object of inquiry — the single — in another take on the aesthetic register. For the aesthetic often offers, as the solution, more intimacy, more special and secretive knowledge that resists generic communication. Marked by the negative, it extends an understanding that close by plenty hides. While arguing about the couple formation, Bersani and Dutoit also argue something quite revealing: "To aestheticise our relation to the past is not to remove ourselves irresponsibly from it, but rather to live in proximity to it."[43] I couldn't agree more, which makes me nervous. The aesthetic, especially when it is erotic, always seems to give us so much freedom. A literary closeness, if you will, provides for a kind of intimacy that has the capacity to escape typicality and convention; it's often the solution we find at the end of our critiques, which doesn't make them any less correct. Sedgwick's infamous analysis of masturbation and Jane Austen, providing another example of a literature that redeems intimacy as a closely felt experience, finds that "*Sense and Sensibility* . . . can succeed in making narrative palpable again, under the pressure of its own needs, the great and estranging force of the homo-erotic longing magnetized in it by that radiant and inattentive presence — the female figure of the love that keeps forgetting its name."[44] Something about the erotic in the aesthetic inevitably conjures up the intimately felt, the palpable, which seem to always resist the more negative forces that surround sexuality. This is very local, however inarticulate, knowledge and/or feeling. And although I always find such gestures simply alluring, I want to arrest my own patterns of thought, for a bit, and think about Arendt's critique of totalitarian loneliness, which is really a critique of a forced intimacy that we always seem to welcome because loneliness terrifyingly keeps us up at night.

So I have a major, isolated, single figure — a figure of nonrelation — that helps give an important perspective on this crowd and its emotions. Walter Benjamin, who first inspired me to read Baudelaire, allowed me to see that within Baudelaire's very sad and lonely verses there were crowds. Benjamin writes of crowds to initiate a series of reflections about the never-ceasing conflict between the mass and the person and, more importantly, how the conflict makes the poet (or a person) a mass, or a mess ("a traumatophile"), who is nevertheless forced to offer some kind of statement about the modern age's effect on imagination, memory, feeling, perhaps even sexuality. What we discover is that one's contact with the crowds of modern life puts into crisis what Benjamin elsewhere calls "aura," the "unique phenomenon of distance, however close it may be."[45] There is the "desire of contemporary masses to bring things 'closer' spatially and humanly, which is just as ardent as their bent toward overcoming the uniqueness of every reality by accepting its reproduction."[46]

Here Benjamin's insights resonate with those of Arendt (who introduced his work to English-speaking readerships) when she argues that "by pressing men against each other, total terror destroys the space between them" (466). Men (and women and others) pressed together are given generic and needy totalitarian ideologies that feel like support, but such support takes away space, the possibility of distance, thereby giving us a strange twist on what feels like a remedy for the terrible, everyday sense of dislocation and alienation we are made to feel. People are pressed to be together in order to eliminate the space between them. Modern life domesticates distant things; shocks of novelty that a crowd might excite (in either negative or positive ways) in the modern human are absorbed, mechanized, defended against. I'll put it like a pedestrian: the individual is crowded, but not in a good way. And more relevantly to the matters I have at hand: people are crowded with couples, but not in a good way. Closeness has come at the expense of distance.

Perhaps a poet, or some other kind of observer (maybe even Godard), might get us out of this condition, but characteristically, Benjamin, and for that matter, Baudelaire, doesn't provide us with any clear indication. Instead we're given these sentences of Baudelaire's: "Lost in this mean world, jostled by the crowd, I am like a weary man whose eye, looking backwards, into the depth of the years, sees nothing but disillusion and bitterness, and before him nothing but a tempest which contains nothing new, neither instruction nor pain."[47] There's really too much touch, too much pressing, for the speaker to be truly moved or excited. The banal contact of the crowd has dulled his senses. He is weary, not deeply disturbed. We're left with a tragic Baudelaire, betrayed by allies, an artist who, according to Benjamin, "indicated the price for which the sensation of the modern age may be had: the disintegration of the aura in the modern experience of shock."[48] Instead of distance, we have proximity — intimacy, but an intimacy that refuses to acknowledge the shock and awe of connection. Even the *flâneur* cannot have the appropriate perspective on the world that no longer lets a shock be a shock. He or she cannot have the perspective because there is no more space; all is crowded, especially the public, which is full of couples absolutely everywhere. "We know that the iron brand of total terror," writes

Arendt, "leaves no space for private life and that the self-coercion of totalitarian logic destroys man's capacity for experience and thought just as certainly as his capacity for action" (474).

In my most ambitious desires, I'd like the work I'm doing now to give us back some space, some crucial distance in the world of pressed men and women (and other genders). I want to explore an "aesthetics of distance" rather than intimacy. I'd like to figure out a way to remove loneliness from the condition of modern life by bringing back a perspective not unlike that of the *flâneur*, who looks for more than the relief of loneliness in the shocks of the crowd's sociality, who looks for that special something or someone.

In the following pages I want to describe how the couple form, the logical leap away from loneliness, is one major method of making the "body politic" full of terror. So I start with an investigation that traverses the ideology of the couple — which is distinct from the myriad intimate relationships that are often the most important relationships in people's lives. I have to interrupt the steely, enduring logic of the couple, strip away some of its more toxic emotional restraints, and offer up some proposals for how to think about people who are not only in a couple. Much more than loneliness helps the couple reign supreme.

I'll be presenting a variety of emotional themes that correspond with the predicament of being single and coupled these days — the affects, cultures, laws, and politics that are cultivated and stirred when one is single — and I'll organize these themes under these headings of feeling: "lonely," "impossible," "alone," and "empty." I'll do this in order to carve out an idea of singleness that is not about the pitied status of being exiled or excluded from the land of couples. Moreover, I'm refusing to typecast the single by drawing on a set character list. I'm not particularly interested in versions of the single as the free and uncommitted bachelor who eschews or escapes intimate attachments and duty; nor am I immediately concerned about the single as someone who has lost a love (the widow, for instance); I'd like to avoid the assumption that single life is either masturbatory or celibate, especially if masturbation is now what provides, as Thomas Laqueur asserts, "an experience of self-esteem or self-love, a form of personal autarky that allows each of us to form relationships with others without losing ourselves."[49] It's not that any of these ideas of single experiences is bad or bankrupt, especially masturbation; I just want to avoid typical assumptions about single life, which is so quickly posed as the exact opposite of coupledom and then lauded as freedom from attachments like wedlock, and often a freedom that resists normalization. In fact, I want to suspend questions of sex, sexuality, and courtship to open the possibilities of other questions about what it means to be single, to be in solitude, with no immediate sexual/relational prospects, or the couple's narrative and historical belonging, in sight. Singleness is currently not compatible with a society in western Europe, North America, and probably other locations that wants people to feel desperate, lonely, fearful of death, and ready for toxic forms of sociality.

Giorgio Agamben understands the politics of relationship in the West and thus often says provocative things about relating. He helps us here because at various points in his work he's trying to think through the impossibility of nonrelation. More specifically, he's concerned with those who are lonely, abandoned, and thus deeply bound to "sovereignty and constituting power." He provides an antidote: "thinking ontology and politics beyond every figure of relation."[50] It's one of those ideas that are maddening, especially if one wants to relate, and especially if what Freud says is true: "In the last resort we must begin to love in order that we may not fall ill, and must fall ill if, in consequence of frustration, we cannot love."[51] But we must remember that Agamben is not being literal; his analyses of ontologies and politics are often invested in figurations, especially figurations that go beyond what we've been bound to for too long: figures of relation. He's challenging many ethics that are caught in Levinas's coupled emphasis on the Other (or in much continental philosophy's insistence on the Other), but not in order to further aggrandize an autonomous and empowered self. He's not advocating that we abolish relationships or neglect significant others. Instead, he's critical of the manner in which certain postures toward others — an other — have the toxic effect of binding one's being to destructive, totalitarian, sovereign forces.

I want Agamben's brief statement about thinking "beyond," or after, figures of relation to be a starting point for thinking (not necessarily living) the "beyond," and specifically the "beyond" that isn't blocked or locked by the politics and knowledge of intimacy that is always prefigured by the couple. I want to think about the isolated figures of the "single" who are misconstrued as lonely and pathetic figures but who are actually much more. They may not be lonely — they may just want to be antisocial, or they may just want to relate to others outside the supreme logic of the couple, which has become the way one binds oneself to the social, otherwise known as the crowd. To think in such a manner is a potentially massive project: for instance, I could think about the status of single people in marriage, property, corporate, and tax law; I could trace the intellectual, political, and cultural history of single types such as the Bachelor, the Widow, the Celibate, the Priest, the Bitter Queen, the Masturbator, the Nun (always wedded to Christ — she has a ring on it), and so on; I might also explore the philosophy of the "Enlightened," rational subject from Rousseau onward, especially its expression in the sublime solitudes of Romanticism; it could become necessary to analyze the development of the psychoanalytic concept of the ego; I'd perhaps even think about alienated labor and its impact on value in Marxist thought; I'd want to figure out how chattel slavery and racial logics further crowd the many into the One; and I could also be compelled to wonder how sex and gender difference could be nonrelational.

But this book cannot even attempt such an exhaustive investigation (I'm hinting at all the books I hope others will one day write). I can't even begin to trace a history of the dynamics I see at play in the examples that have captured my attention. As Arendt assures us, loneliness is a feeling that is starting to become a universal feeling, so a project of such scope would be useless. In other words, there are innumerable ways to write this book, so my work is an attempt — a form of speculative thoughts on the single, offered to inspire conversation and consideration. I could be neither an empiricist here nor a historian: so much of the force of couples culture, and singles' resistance to it, happens in the more fantastical, expressive, and psychological registers of experience rather than the known (or soon-to-be-known) world of facts. As a literary scholar, I'm offering readings of the figurative language of singleness as it traverses the literary objects, film, television, art, landscape architecture, legal cases, nature writing, popular culture, philosophy, and psychoanalytic criticism that surround us. My book is polemical (a "camp polemic," as Kathryn Bond Stockton dubbed my method), idiosyncratic, and, appropriately, singular: I'll guide us, in the first two chapters, through the lonely and impossible affects of the couple that purposely block insights into what can happen to the world when one is permitted to be single. Then, in the last two chapters, I describe the possibilities offered by the perceived aloneness and emptiness of the single's desolate state of being.

I couldn't resist starting the first chapter, "The Inevitable Fatality of the Couple," with Arthur Hiller's iconic 1970 film, *Love Story*. Written by a classicist, it brings us to 1970s Harvard to watch the courtship and then death of a couple so we can learn that a couple in love is a couple that always must face each other's death, as well as their relationship's extinction. Hiller's film rehearses a story of love (and its totalitarian grasp) that is straight from Plato's *Symposium* — a speech made by Plato's Aristophanes, often adapted since its first appearance (a recent adaptation is John Cameron Mitchell's *Hedwig and the Angry Inch*). This ancient logic keeps our couples' stories classic, highlighting the macabre sense of loneliness that encircles and limits any couple, leaving the two participants to consider the precariousness of each other, fixated on a very intimate kind of death. In some close readings of this film, Freud's *Civilization and Its Discontents*, Virginia Woolf's *Mrs. Dalloway*, and Anne Carson's *Autobiography of Red,* what begins to take shape is the sad realization that for all the promise of a great romantic affair, replete with enduring charm and appeal, what you actually develop when you fall in love is a relationship that is anxiously marked by its mortality, its fragility. A double, contradictory logic of the couple starts to come into view. The greatness of your love, the way it gives you the world, might actually give you so much less. So we learn that a classical moral persists in our present: the couple is the punishment for your struggle to be a great individual. Hands off immortality: your supreme insights will be taken from you if you become too full of yourself. So rather than being a consolation for loneliness, love divides couples into people who thus become their own antiheroes, foiling their own great strivings, keeping themselves corralled in a small, lethal place with just one other person. The lasting, durable couple is really a relationship that kills you quickly, kills you softly, as the song goes. These insights, these secrets, are hard to hang on to because there are other consolations that the couple form is purported to provide: the impossible survival of the death that the couple brings right to your bed — eternity. This survival in the couple relies on a rhetoric of the afterlife, on a conception of time that outlasts death, by way of the proliferation of heirs, of family, that will give you posterity in this life and in the next (if you're inclined to think there's life after death). So the second chapter explores what turns out to be another terrible feeling, prompted by the deadly affects described in the first chapter: the feeling of what I think is impossible — an eternity in life, made possible by an erroneous idea of a couple that won't ever die and is exempt from time.

Chapter 2, "The Probated Couple, or Our Polygamous Pioneers," claims that the strategy for survival, or at least the appearance of survival, in your couple is the notion that you can live forever in an eternal life that will never ever cease. I start by looking at some last wills and testaments and some probate cases from Utah, a region of the United States that is extremely devoted to couples and the residue that couples often leave behind: children. On this frontier, we'll read wills from Norman Mailer's *The Executioner's Song*; the revelations of the founder of the LDS Church; an episode of HBO's hit family drama about polygamy and Mormonism, *Big Love*; some late nineteenth-century probate cases in Utah that had to be resolved by the U.S. Supreme Court; wedding vows that sound like death vows; and Marx's descriptions of commodity fetishism. We look at these objects so we

can see how the succession of property connects people across
the divide between the living and the dead, reifying people into
couples (even couples within plural marriages) that insist there
are literally no deadlines of lasting consequence. As we read wills
and think about a person's last wishes, we understand that official
recognitions of couples, often through marriage, are no longer
contracts that exist until "death do us part." From wills (or from
probate courts that decide what happens if there is no will), we
learn about much more than who gets what: we learn about how
a family is the couple's desire to be able to endure forever, in spite
of a love that is, as we understand in the first chapter, riddled
with its inevitable death. The deathly feelings of the couple create sensations of loneliness, which in turn provoke the need for
an eternity that is hard to trust (especially since the couple feels
so fragile) and inspire awful affects of doom and wrongness or at
least anxiety. Surely there are other feelings and dynamics, but
they necessarily exceed the scope of my small, polemical book.
(And don't worry about what I'm not showing you here; just
look for yourself at the "richness" of the lover's grim landscape.)
In this bind, couples need a scapegoat. Enter: the single, the really lonely and really impossible one, whose very existence must
be stricken from the official record of a couples culture but who
must remain near enough to be the worse alternative to all the
bad affect of being in love: those poor singles — they must be
so much unhappier in their empty, lonely existences. The couple
thus defeats itself by worrying itself to death and beyond. And
the projection of defeat onto the single is the couple's collateral
damage — the couple's terrible gift to those who are single.

So in chapter 3, "The Shelter of Singles," I attempt to imagine what might be impossible: what the single might be when
not being suffocated by the bad affect the couple displaces
onto it. I'll suggest how the single might be a status that also
relieves (rather than always displaces) these affective pressures
of deadly fragility and impossible endurance. Oddly, the single
need not be the couple's scapegoat and can instead be its savior.
So in this chapter, I read the mass public sphere as a debauched
public that is too frequently understood or accessed through a

totalitarian couple form, one that disseminates a lonely and impossible feeling that kills even an option for identification with something like an abstract mass of many unidentified individuals. The couple, not the abstract individual, transforms how we might conceive of our appeals to the public. Instead of thinking of self-abstraction as something that belongs to publicity and its public sphere that is peopled with couples, I want to suggest that self-abstraction, or the emptying of self, often occurs at home, or at least in a house, maybe the only private place where you can maybe find someone alone, utterly single. That's the condition in which we find the unmarried, uncoupled narrator of Ralph Ellison's *Invisible Man*, who is, as I'll show, a character desperately resisting the dynamics of the couple and its standardizing and totalitarian force by retreating into his famous hole. In this hole, surrounded by the walls of what Ellison describes as a forgotten nineteenth-century structure, "a kind of no man's land," we begin to understand something hard about singleness: there is no way to tell the story of the value of the single except as that which has been completely blocked from our critical vision by the couple. The single has been made invisible by the overwhelming projection of the couple form's feelings of loneliness and impossibility onto the single. The single, then, can be considered a figure of inscrutability, upsetting the intimate forces of conventional public coupling by insisting on something like a large structural blockade. The single has been rendered negative, and we have to figure out a way to work with its invisible abstraction.

This discussion sets up my contribution to the increasingly important readings of Herman Melville's nineteenth-century story "Bartleby, the Scrivener," the enigmatic single whose tagline, "I'd prefer not to," I'd like to revise in this chapter as "I'd prefer not *two*."[52] Bartleby remains resolutely single and won't reveal anything personal or private. He's rapt in thought, wrapped and shielded in his own reverie. We'll watch as a single figure such as Bartleby strands us in place, fixing us in an isolated figuration that makes us feel the relief of an emptiness that is not cramped with the terrible affective trappings of couples. In other words: the single can be a figure that offers us not only a private room but room, roominess, as opposed to the crowded touch of the couple.

The narrator of *Invisible Man* and Bartleby aren't the only archetypes, and the single need not be fixed in an enclosed space. I'd hate for anyone to think that singleness is the condition of being stuck in a kind of internal emptiness, impenetrable by anyone on the outside. Singleness is more than an abstraction of a state from which the awful affect of the couple has been stripped away. In fact, the hiding place behind the walls is only a pedagogical retreat from the public culture: we must encounter that culture, but not always (eternity is not part of the single's story). What awaits the stranded single on her reemergence is not only the negativity that hides what's on the inside but something much more like a wide-open world, a world that doesn't have to shrink. The world can swell with potential. The single, indeed, isn't only the refusal "not two."

So the final chapter, "Welcome to the Desert of Me," breaks down the doors of the hideouts of these major literary figures. The single, I think, can teach us to open ourselves up to the world of isolation and distance, which might give us, not eternity, but something not so outside of time and impossible to achieve. The single can teach us how to be alone — "all one," as the word *alone* etymologically suggests. And the journey of the single is an ancient one, a path of mystics or those seeking immortality. It might be a story of a great individual, or of a great talent, that can aspire to great heights and insights — but it's a story anyone can access. And it's a story that seems different from the awful versions of individual mastery that dominate others and accrue power through violence, coercion, carelessness, and ignorance. The single can be a very democratic figure, especially if she or he strips away the ideology that it must always "take two."

So I end this book by recounting details about a hike I did in the Utah desert in order to frame the tales of some very special, isolated people who have all been deserted, who have all, as the title of the chapter suggests, trekked into an arid, unoccupied landscape. They've gone to the contemplative desert (that is both literal and figurative) because they were broken by couples, or at least couples culture: Morrissey, Georgia O'Keeffe, and Agnes Martin. I present very slim accounts of their lives and work in this chapter as parables (rather than exhaustive biographies) to point to the valuable perspective that the single presents to a world cramped with couples. Morrissey, one of the most iconic singles of my generation, twists and turns in the desert for no reason, refusing you any access to his intimate life. Georgia O'Keeffe, marketed and restrained by Alfred Stieglitz, would have to flee him for New Mexico to be alone in order to make abstract art that now commands extraordinary mass appeal. And Agnes Martin, an umbrageous lesbian, escaped New York's Abstract Expressionist scene in the late sixties for a plot of land near Taos and a life of solitude painting grids. I offer these historical figures not as individuals who've hurt the world by insisting on the value of the single's solitary experience (and yes, one doesn't have to be single literally to have the sensations of the single life). Instead, they have in their ways striven for an old-fashioned absorption in producing "great" things — and great *things* rather than "great" but divided, dividing loves. Their great things have an ethical value — a value that values others and that might very well exceed any chastened mode of being that the requisite couple's love plot has laid out before us. And something about the desert — in its literal and figurative dimensions, its geographical specificity, or its troping qualities (isolated, deserted, outside the realm of humans, etc.) — helps some extraordinary moments happen to these singles. The desert inspires them to make something (art, ideas, work, action, whatever) that strives toward what Arendt, Dickinson, Plato, et al. suggest as the audacious project of self-extension (and not self-reduction, as in the couple): they strive to achieve their own approximations of "immortality."

Perhaps another way to think about what I'm trying to say is to think about something that is hard to do with others: sleep. Carson, in "Every Exit Is an Entrance (A Praise of Sleep)," tells us about her earliest memory: a dream of a green living room that she knew well, with everything in its place, but that, in her dream, became radically different from, if not distant from, her commonplace understandings of the space: "Inside its usual appearance the living room was as changed as if it had gone mad." Because her youth did not permit concepts of madness to help her explain the dream, she described her encounter with the uncanny evocatively: "I explained the dream to myself by saying that I had caught the living room sleeping." She elaborates: "For despite the spookiness, [the] inexplicability . . . of the green living room, it was and remains for me a consolation to think of it lying there, sunk in its greenness, breathing its own order, answerable to no one, apparently penetrable everywhere and yet so perfectly disguised in all the propaganda of its own waking life as to become in a true sense something *incognito* at the heart of our sleeping house."[53] This kind of perspective, this kind of distance, this kind of vista, is not just another gesture of defamiliarization we bring to so many of our critical questions. It's a form of thinking that isolates. And it's about a comforting, not menacing, form of isolation — a form of not being "answerable" to the propaganda of our "waking lives," enabling, one hopes, to give what an isolation free of loneliness could ideally give, according to Arendt: the capacity to be productive and creative even as humans are being forced into an "impasse . . . when the political sphere of their lives, where they act together in the pursuit of common concern, is destroyed."[54] Further, this retreat from the ruins of the public sphere and into isolation might produce some very important kinds of immortal dreaming — for perhaps, even the single, at a conceptual remove, can put away for one night some of that proximity, that lonely terror, that greedy eternity, and get a bit of much-needed sleep.

1

The Inevitable Fatality of the Couple

O happy dagger.
WILLIAM SHAKESPEARE, *Romeo and Juliet*

their heart grew cold
they let their wings down
SAPPHO, fragment 42, Anne Carson's translation

Killing Me Softly

As I suggested in this book's introduction, couple love is an ideological apprenticeship in loneliness — a loneliness so upsetting
that it's often displaced onto singles. But if you don't believe me,
pick up a book. Watch a movie. Listen to a song. Or spend any
amount of time wondering about the person you love that you
can't live without. And then think about all the lonely hearts out
there that seem to have it worse. In this chapter, I'd like to indulge
in some lonely words about what it means to be in love, or, more
precisely, in a love that is predicated on the supremacy of the
couple — a form of love that insists that the whole world should
be created, sustained, or connected by a relationship with just
one other person. This kind of intensity makes a relationship an
impossible thing to sustain, perhaps explaining why so many relationships are destined for failure. At hand is an appeal to ancient
forms, with eternal and immortal words that fill our heads with
perhaps the most deadly of myths.

Let's first briefly go to the movies. A classicist educated at
Harvard, Erich Segal, wrote a story called *Love Story*, which
became a New York Times best seller and the number one box
office attraction of 1971. Barbara Walters, on television, helped
launch its best-seller success by claiming that she couldn't
put the book down even though she had been crying all night
reading it. And thus the author was a frequent guest of talk

shows — not the most likely early career of a then Yale classics professor.[1] In the early seventies, my parents' generation wept throughout the melodramatic film adaptation (directed by Arthur Hiller) of the story of two people, a preppy Harvard "hockey jock" (played by Ryan O'Neal) and a will-die-too-soon Radcliffe music student (played by Ali MacGraw). Its imprint on popular culture, both as a narrative and as a movie with a very recognizable theme song, persists to the present. Never far from an exaggeration, Al Gore, over a decade ago, proclaimed that he and his wife, Tipper, were the models upon which the story was based. His claim was only partially true: Tipper was known to the author but was not a source of inspiration for the Jenny character. Al Gore and Tommy Lee Jones (who had a small role in the film) were amalgamated into the character of Oliver Barrett IV, according to a 1997 *New York Times* interview with Segal, who had met them both while he was on a 1968 sabbatical at Harvard.[2]

When I watched this film after having seen the book throughout my childhood, unopened but cherished on my mother's bookshelf, I felt some odd forms of awful affection for the buildings of Harvard. Much of the movie feels like one big montage honoring that ancient American institution, which seems to radiate so much charm and value that the buildings themselves can stand in for the monumentality of falling in love, even if we're not quite sure why the film's characters like each other. But it's too easy to mock and disagree with the film. It has a contagious and enduring logic that deserves our attention. It teaches you about the couple's inevitable fatality; it prompts you to want this kind of devastation.

To do as much, *Love Story* showcases what you need to do in order to enroll in this lonely school of coupledom, and nowhere more clearly than in Jenny's hospital deathbed scene. Oliver, who has just returned from borrowing money from his father to pay for Jenny's ineffective medical treatment, is left alone with Jenny to share the couple's last words. Jenny does something few dying people do in these iconic scenes of morbid sentimentality:[3] she asks Oliver to hold her, "really hold" her, by lying "next to her,"

Love Story: Deathbed. Screen capture from *Love Story* (dir. Arthur Hiller, 1970).

thereby requiring him to enter her deathbed. It's her final request. The way this tender scene is shot is crucial: the frozen posture of the embracing couple is illuminated by an eerily beautiful light — the camera hovering at ceiling height, just to the right of the bed, so we can watch, from above, Oliver holding a supine Jenny, their cheeks touching. This shot visually recalls the first bed scene of their romantic love; by being similarly lit and shot from a similar vantage point, it invokes parallels between the sex-bed, where they consummate their love, and the deathbed, which punctuates and defines their love. This view is an exemplary view of the couple.

After Jenny dies, Oliver leaves the bed, the hospital, and the awaiting family members. The ending shots are the same shots that began the film. The opening: there is a pan over Central Park, tilting down and tightening focus onto a lonely Oliver, sitting, turned away from the camera, looking off to the right, refusing to focus on the skating rink where he was recently skating for Jenny's final moments of amusement (she's too sick to join him but has always loved watching him on the ice). Oliver has taken

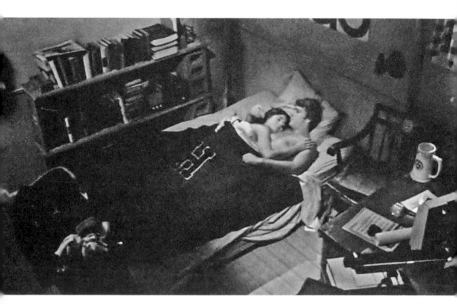

Love Story: Sexbed. Screen capture from *Love Story* (dir. Arthur Hiller, 1970).

the place where Jenny was sitting (although we won't realize this substitution until the film's conclusion), so his lonely seat, as he stares out over an empty winter scene (with no Jenny in sight), is a reminder of what he has just lost. Then we hear Oliver in a voice-over, interrogating the point of the love story that's about to be told: "What can you say about a twenty-five-year-old girl who died? That she was beautiful and brilliant. That she loved Mozart, Bach [we hear a slight, bemused chuckle in Oliver's voice], the Beatles, and Me." Sadly, these are the most salient details of this too-short life, and the movie barely deepens a sense of her qualities or her passions. That's not the point of this love story. It's not a story of a particular girl. Hiller wanted this story to be a "universal story." So rather than drench us in deep detail or complex character development, the film relies on camera movement, the Harvard setting, and the musical score to *not* tell the story of a particular life. The story, instead, is about the loss, which might go by the name "couple." We are made witnesses to a fatal relational dynamic between *two* people (dead Jenny and lonely Oliver, the "me" who can be as beguiling as Mozart, Bach, and the Beatles).

According to the sociologist Georg Simmel, "A dyad . . . depends on each of its two elements alone — in its death, though not in its life: for its life, it needs *both*, but for its death, only one. This fact is bound to influence the inner attitude of the individual toward the dyad, even though not always consciously nor in the same way. It makes the dyad into a group that feels both endangered and irreplaceable, and thus into the real locus not only of authentic sociological tragedy, but also of sentimentalism and elegiac problems."[4] Simmel does not mean, here, that we always die alone (even though we probably do). He's making a comment on the anxious form of attachment that marks couples quite differently than other groups (say groups of three or more people). The durability of the couple obviously requires the life of both of its members — the life of the couple is a shared activity by both parts of the dyad. But the death of one of the members brings about not only the death of the member but also the death of the couple — the group of the couple ceases to exist if one of its members dies (unlike any other group composed of three or more people). So deep feelings of morbid and moribund desperation encircle this group formation, and this quality generates a panic that also makes the group (the couple) feel unique — only if *this one particular person lives* can my relationship, my group, endure.

So the couple becomes a "locus" of "sentimentalism and elegiac problems." And *Love Story* is a hyperbolic illustration of such a locus: the love plot begins and ends with death, and we're forced to be haunted by a sense that despite all the beauty of Oliver and Jenny, in montage, making snow angels in Harvard's stadium, the angel of death is closely hovering. A quiet, desperate, and upsetting feeling pervades the dyad because it knows that it's always considering death and dying: one wrong move, one accident, one untimely diagnosis, and the relationship (as well as one of the members of that relationship) will end. And, to be honest, both parts of the couple will eventually cease. So the other's death will certainly point the way to your own. Dyads, indeed, are always dying.

When Oliver and Jenny marry (as all good couples should), they use some verses from Elizabeth Barrett Browning and Walt Whitman as their wedding vows. While they stand up together, in their modern, nondenominational ceremony, the camera does something it hasn't done yet in the film: it circles the couple completely, just as Jenny finishes quoting, "A place to stand and love in for a day, / With darkness and the death-hour rounding it." As the camera rounds it, the couple stands, and it's positioned as a necessary, circular creature, encircled by death. Certainly many ancient myths, poems, ideas, novels, and films serve as the couple form's moribund foundation. But since a classicist made up this story, one might think about one of the most famous love stories in antiquity's canon: Aristophanes' speech in Plato's *Symposium*, in which we are treated to a rounding off of the couple, and a dire account of division, death, halving, and thus not having, which makes couple love a desperate thing to embrace. This speech has its hands all over love, and innumerable examples of a couple's wholeness, roundness, and eternity owe their emotional clichés to Plato's caricature of Aristophanes (a contemporary iteration of the myth formally orders the sentimentality of John Cameron Mitchell's *Hedwig and the Angry Inch* [2001]). Here's what Aristophanes contributes to the symposium, a religious story about what it means to fall in love: "First you must learn what Human Nature was in the beginning and what has happened to it since, because long ago, our nature was not what it is now, but very different. There were three kinds of human beings, that's my first point, not two as there are now, male and female. In addition to these, there was a third, a combination of those two."[5] Much can be and has been said about the queerness of this etiology of sex difference, but rather than fixate on sex difference (or sex sameness), I'm more intrigued by the menacing effect of becoming two (rather than three).[6] See, we have in this myth strange human creatures that were made up of four legs and arms, two faces, and one head, and "each human being was completely round" (25). These round things were raucous and crazy, and as a group they were a threat to the gods that needed to be punished: "In strength and power . . . they were terrible, and they had great ambitions"

(26). To curtail their power, their aspirations for immortality, Zeus had to cut the singular, round beings into two and issue an enduring threat: "But if I find they still run riot and do not keep the peace . . . I will cut them in two again, and they'll have to make their way on one leg, hopping" (26). Hence, one becoming two is an act of division that is the basis of human control. These three kinds of creatures, which together could pose a threat to the gods, are cut apart and mesmerized by a logic of divisions, a logic of two, a logic that really does divide and conquer.

It wasn't enough for Zeus to cut them down to halfsize. He's a bit of a sadist, and he forces them to fixate on that cutting, their coupling: "As he cut each one, he [Zeus] commanded Apollo to turn its face and half its neck towards the wound, so that each person would see that he'd been cut and keep better control" (26). Control means making the one and the many into halves, with wounds, wanting desperately to have:

> Now since their natural form had been cut in two, each one longed for its other half, and they would throw their arms about each other, weaving themselves together, wanting to grow together. In that condition, they would not do anything apart from each other. Whenever one of the halves died and one was left, the one that was left still sought another and wove itself together with that. Sometimes the half he met came from a woman, as we'd call her now, sometimes it came from a man; either way, they kept dying. (26-27)

Coupling is a form of constant dying in this scenario, and even Zeus eventually "takes pity" and adjusts their bodies so that they can at least get somewhat closer (usually through the act of sex). But this searching for your lost half never ceases. Human nature is kept in line by this pitiful condition. No matter how you slice it, you're alone, desperate to find your other (better) half, or, if you've found your other half, desperate to stay and grow and die together.

Plato has Aristophanes dress this wound obsession up with a now-so-familiar-it's-so-cliché sentiment. He imagines Hephaestus offering "all the good fortune that you could desire" (29): "I'd like to weld you together and join you into something that is naturally whole, so the two of you are made into one. Then the two of you would share one life, as long as you live, because you would be one being, and by the same token, when you died, you would be one and not two in Hades, having died a single death" (28). Why this option is "good fortune" eludes me, but it permeates the ancient story of romantic coupledom that is both an original curse of being too strong as one, and life's great destiny as something awfully divided: to die, reamalgamated, together as one, in Hades. To become well rounded, in fact, to become round again, requires that you first be halved, then prompted to find that ripped-off half, and, once finding it, be forced to enter into a deathbed in order to become whole. An impossible thing, wholeness, especially since Hephaestus doesn't usually show up to help any of the desperate couples I've met on this earth. No one really gets to share a life marked for death so unified.

After the marriage scene in *Love Story*, the camera never circles, fully, any character or object again in Hiller's film. The camera movement is still often dramatic but is purposefully used to punctuate the half-ness of any character's unity. We witness moments when Oliver is shot by a semicircular movement of the camera. Oliver walking down busy, but lonely, New York City streets after he's discovered that Jenny is dying. Oliver in the locker room, without Jenny, trying to talk to friends (but sad to be separated from Jenny). In fact, it's always lonely Oliver, who is shot in a semicircular sweep of the camera that emphasizes the roundness of couples that have been divided into two. Watch this scene: Oliver (and not Jenny) has been informed of Jenny's death prognosis; he is terrified of what he knows will come. The morning after he's been told (and after he's been instructed not to mention the disease to Jenny), Oliver wakes up after a night of sex with his dying wife. We have a cut to Oliver, chest uncovered, in bed. It is dark, but Oliver's face is lit, and near the center of the frame is a clock. We hear its loud clicking while we watch Oliver stare at the ceiling. The camera comes closer and then moves in a semicircular (and not fully circular) way toward him, as if to hug or kiss him. The clock keeps ticking. His eyes widen, and the alarm clock goes off. He blinks and looks toward the clock. Then the shot is cut, abruptly, and we're meant to experience some disquiet; the camera is ripping the dying couple apart here. There is a sudden shot to the other side of the bed, this time from the back, and the light is suddenly much brighter. Oliver reaches over and turns the alarm off. He looks over to the side where Jenny should be, but she's not there! Oliver is as alarmed as the alarm clock just was (Is her time already up? Is she already dead?); he lifts his head and torso quickly from the pillow and calls out Jenny's name urgently, with panic, as the camera continues to focus on his pillow, showing an empty bed. He keeps calling her, and then there is a cut to an already awake Jenny walking into the bedroom, urging him to get out of bed.

The halving of Oliver serves to underline the loneliness of Oliver; it's a constant in the film. He starts out the film in a pathetic posture on the bleachers after Jenny has died; we then have the tale of well-rounded Harvard love that we know in advance is tragically ripped apart by Jenny's death; we have Jenny's deathbed scene, where the couple clutches each other into her death; and then we return Oliver to his single (but now elaborately tragic) status as someone who has loved and lost. The huge appeal of this kind of love story might be pedagogical: even if you end up as lonely as Oliver does at the end, at least he has a love story to tell. At least he's trying to make something big and everlasting like a marriage work. Sure, it's hard work, and it even provokes tears and heartache. Perhaps we're also meant to learn that Oliver's kind of loneliness is an inevitable punishment for striving to round himself out by loving another. The pathetic quality of Oliver becomes a kind of encouragement: we don't want to be in that position, that place of loss (even if our choices will lead us there nonetheless). But we have no reason to expect that Oliver will stay lonely and alone in that park forever. After all, he falls in love very easily (at least with Radcliffe women), and he has the appeal of Jenny's love of him (and the Beatles) to prove it. There's always hope in the couple he has had and might still make in the future.

"Love," writes Plato, "is the name for our pursuit of wholeness, for our desire to be complete" (29). It's supposed to be a source of sustaining optimism. Yet in the next breath, Plato has Aristophanes remind us that this pursuit, this love, is also a reprimand: as I've been explaining, the gods were punishing the strong creatures by inflicting terrible acts of division — dividing beings and then making them couples again. Love, indeed, will tear us apart, again (and again).[7] But this pursuit of your other, better half is not merely a refusal of or rebuttal to the original punishment. It's a desire that has been implanted in us by an ideology of the couple that will help us cleave together in a lonely and deadly way. It's a terrible twist that even Plato's Aristophanes can't make entirely sanguine:

> Long ago we were united [as amalgamated beings] as I said; but now the god has divided us as a punishment for the wrong we did him. . . . So there's a danger that if we don't keep order before the gods, we'll be split in two again, and then we'll be walking around in the condition of people carved on the gravestones in bas-relief, sawn apart between the nostrils, like half dice. We should encourage all men, therefore, to treat the gods with all due reverence, so that we may escape this fate and find wholeness instead. And we will, if Love is our guide and our commander. Let no one work against him. Whoever opposes Love is hateful to the gods, but if we become friends of the god and cease to quarrel with him, then we should find the young men that are meant for us and win their love, as very few men do nowadays. (29)

Now Aristophanes is leading to his proclamation that we can, through the pursuit of love, achieve wholeness; Love will "restore to us our original nature, and by healing us, he will make us blessed and happy" (30). But as he describes this poetic pursuit, he still can't forget why humans are in their sorry state: their pursuit of love has been originally caused by their "original nature." So to get back to wholeness, we must achieve that wholeness in a more chastened spirit by honoring and obeying the ruling gods, who would have no problem getting out the hatchet again.

Love cannot make you big and grand again; wholeness, after being torn asunder, can be restored only if "Love is our guide and commander." There is a totalitarian imperative here to try and dwell within the punishment of love. We can't have anyone be hateful and oppose the gods by rejecting love (and love, here, means striving for your one other half). Love does not mean, as the most famous and untrue line in *Love Story* proclaims, "never having to say you're sorry." Instead, it means having to always say sorry to your commanding gods — the same gods that apparently have no problems shrinking the human world by chopping people into couples that then must cling and die together. The alternative to love is staying in the place of a pathetic Oliver, sitting alone on the bleachers, "not moving on." And we all know what happens to singular beings that defy the will and stature of the gods.

The moral of *Love Story* and Aristophanes' speech: Love discourages your own greatness, your own immortality. That's its problem. It promises durability, only to deliver, fatally, a lonely realization that the couple is always and only temporary. The couple shrinks the possibilities of this world (and the next, if there is one) by insisting on the division and death it brings. But it is the group you are always supposed to belong to; there is no way to be, other than with one other one. So in the next sections of this chapter, I need to unravel the bundled, contradictory logic of the tragic state of couple affairs with the help of Sigmund Freud and Virginia Woolf and thereby lead us, in the last section, to a poetic-fictional "account of oneself," in Anne Carson's *Autobiography of Red,* that is actually an account of the tragedy of falling in love. We'll begin to see that a love story reveals a modern variation on the classical tragic flaw: the hubris of the chastened couple, which peoples the world with a deadly but useful loneliness, much to the pleasure of the ruling gods.

Shrunken Religion

Freud knew both love and the classics. And for all his sacred skepticism, he grasped the ancient stakes involved in preventing couples from achieving immortality. Immortality — religion's theme — is for Freud a global concept. It's the large world outside the ego. At the beginning of *Civilization and Its Discontents*, he tries to define religion (just a few years before the totalitarian rise of the Third Reich). A friend's response to his earlier critiques of religion inspires Freud here to talk about religion as a grand, "peculiar feeling which he [his friend, Romain Rolland] himself is never without, which he [Freud] finds confirmed by many others, and which he may suppose is present in millions of people. It is a feeling which he would like to call a sensation of 'eternity,' a feeling as of something limitless, unbounded — as it were, 'oceanic.'"[8] Although Freud confesses that he does not find such grand sensations in his own self, he nevertheless can see what his friend means, and to help him make his point, Freud quotes Christian Dietrich Grabbe: "If I have understood my friend rightly, he means the same thing by it as the consolation offered by an original and somewhat eccentric dramatist to his hero who is facing a self-inflicted death. 'We cannot fall out of this world.' That is to say, it is a feeling of an indissoluble bond, of being one with the external world as a whole" (11-12).

It would be difficult to refute these assertions; it would be difficult not to see these sentiments articulated in many of the world's religions, so Freud risks being obvious. His intentions in a book about the way civilization makes people unhappy (primarily through the death drive, in a deadly and combative couple with Eros) are hardly about rigorously defining the dynamics of religion, so I might be looking in the wrong place for a theory of religion. But the manner in which Freud starts his book about the triumph of the death drive, in which he starts to think about religious feeling as oceanic feeling, as the desire to be connected, deeply and extensively, to the world, helps orient us in considerations of why some of the most costly battles to stay grounded in the world are religious battles, whether those battles exist at the level of the psyche or the level of the external world. Freud helps us consider something that we need to consider when we think about religious sentiments: questions of scale, of measurement, and how those scales affect our most intimate loves (are we big and whole, or small and divided?). If religion is an oceanic, global feeling, then its aspirations to largeness, fullness, and, most pointedly, the annihilation of isolation (through religion, we feel connected) have important consequences. So why, according to Aristophanes, are couples excluded from immortality — made so secular, so grounded?

To put the problem another way: religion is *the* problem of "greatness." Or at least the way Freud names "greatness," which makes "religion" more of a rhetorical register in which large, sweeping emotions can find some kind of language, some kind of philosophical idea. So religion's greatness is a standard of measurement, perhaps what Freud calls a "false standard of measurement" (10), that we rely on nonetheless, even if we don't believe in its power. And what makes the greatness of "religious" feeling a false standard is that it obscures; it, too, can fall into the "danger of forgetting how variegated the human world and mental life are" (10). But perhaps more pressing than its mysteries is something I can never fully understand when reading Freud on religion: Why should the feeling of belonging to greatness, to the oceanic world, be thought of as bad to have? Even if you're not a religious person, why wouldn't you welcome a gushing, enormous emotion of endless connection?

I need to tell you this: "religion," much like our world, is shrinking. It's not that secularization has won and that rationality is triumphant over faithful feelings. Surely the extreme potency of fundamentalisms in the East and the West should reassure us that faith matters, terribly. But religion's great feelings have become, in some sense, impotent. Or at least they've come into an awful relationship with something decidedly antireligious, or to use Freud's scale, something much smaller. That something might be called love (or at least the love of two). Plato's gods liked to make humans smaller in their loves. Characteristically, Freud wants us to see how developments in the world correspond with the developments of the modern psyche — a modern psyche that is on the defensive, shielding itself from the terrors (and the potentials) of the world:

> Originally the ego includes everything, later it separates off an external world from itself. Our present ego-feeling is, therefore, only a shrunken residue of a much more inclusive — indeed, an all-embracing — feeling which corresponded to a more intimate bond between the ego and the world about it. If we may assume that there are many people in whose mental life this primary ego-feeling has persisted to a greater or less degree, it would exist in them side by side with the narrower and more sharply demarcated ego-feeling of maturity, like a kind of counterpart to it. In that case, the ideational contents appropriate to it would be precisely those of limitlessness and of a bond with the universe — the same ideas with which my friend elucidated the "oceanic" feeling. (15)

We should linger here, perhaps longer than Freud (who resolves the greatness one may want to feel by describing religious connectedness as an intangible consolation). I would like to think about the interior coupling, "the side by side" coupling that Freud produces inside the ego: the "shrunken," religious ocean of the primary ego-feeling matched with its sharply demarcated counterpart — the ego-feeling of maturity, which is not so free in its ability to feel connected. With this couple we have a comparison, which measures and evaluates. On one side we have everything, on the other very little; we used to have an unbounded quality where now we have the tight, frustrated limits of the ego.

It is this relationship that reduces, that shrinks, religion's greatness. Or, to be more precise, it is this couple that helps Freud (and numerous others) make religion's grandeur seem like a "limitless narcissism" that is really akin to "infantile helplessness" (20-21). The maturity of one position, although fraught with all sorts of sources of unhappiness, is still more workable and understandable than a religious attitude that is "wrapped in obscurity." That is, the feeling of everything provides us with too much that can't be known — it has no boundaries. Freud thus sees the ocean of religious feeling as something that must be put into a relation with boundedness. Religion must be shrunk by its coexistence with that which is not religious: hard divides, well-defined distinctions, things that are knowable. Something about the coupling of religious feeling with maturity (which we learn is always battling disappointment) casts the oceanic in a negative light. Infants who are helpless must eventually learn how to feel like adults, or, to put it sharply, to learn how to feel sad. Such greatness is belittled by a contemporary condition that will always bind one. Through that binding, that coupling, religion is cast as an unknowable feeling that must be gotten over. That feeling is a very lonely one, and with or without religion, one needs to be careful, lest one "fall out of this world." Through the comparison, religion ceases to be great. Instead, we're instructed to feel secular, and thus depressed, solitary, and unable to do what religion promises: connect to everything. In other words, through the coupling of religion and ego, religion becomes what religion is not: a small, sharp, unhappy feeling.

It's telling that the "false measurement" Freud needs to accomplish this transfer is a couple. For couples always make one feel lonely and needy. Couples make one feel very small, stranded, and without a proper outlet for all our capacious waves of emotion. Couples shrink the world, contain the world, and paradoxically, have the ability to make one feel without a world (because what if the known world cannot understand your own, unknowable one?). Couples teach us that as we grow up in the world, we, and all our oceans of feeling, must only be cut into two.

The Clock Strikes Two

Virginia Woolf often echoes Freud. In 1925, she gave us a perplexing sentence, also about religion, and also, however obliquely, about couples, in her modernist novel *Mrs. Dalloway*. Here's something Clarissa Dalloway thinks in one of her waves of thoughts: "There was something solemn in it [watching an old lady in her private room] — but love and religion would destroy that, whatever it was, the privacy of the soul."[9] Although there are immediate reasons why Clarissa is frustrated by both love and religion at this point in Woolf's masterpiece, these words continue to perplex me beyond the narrative explanations that are presented in the novel about a deadly, post-World War I day in the lives of characters in London trying to make sense of catastrophes big and small, global and very local. In fact, in the final chapter of my book, we'll return to the character that casts Clarissa off into this meditation: a single woman in love with Clarissa's daughter, Miss Kilman, dressed in a mackintosh coat. But for now, I wonder what constitutes this privacy of the soul and why love and religion should be posited as its enemies, especially since love and religion both seem to belong to the domain of privacy (where our loves are most sacred and legal) and the soul (because religion has frequently been considered the soul's chaperone). Both experiences are very unsettling, and Clarissa certainly is disturbed by so much, especially by the affection she feels for her family members, for lost loves, for parties and flowers, and for the chimes of Big Ben's clock. Moreover, in private, much psychic work on love and religion can be performed, explored, sorted, and worked through. But this kind of privacy, this privacy of the soul, is special — it is essential because it reveals some very large-scale insights.

Soon, Clarissa hears Big Ben strike the half-hour:

> How extraordinary it was, strange, yes, touching, to see the old lady (they had been neighbors ever so many years) move away from the window, as if she were attached to that sound, that string. Gigantic it was, it had something to do with her. Down, down, into the mist of ordinary things the finger fell making the moment solemn. She was forced, Clarissa imagined, by that sound, to move, to go — but where? Clarissa tried to follow her as she turned and disappeared, and could still just see her white cap moving at the back of the bedroom. She was still there moving about the other end of the room. Why creeds and prayers and mackintoshes? when, thought

Clarissa, that's the miracle, that's the mystery; that old lady, she meant, whom she could see going from chest of drawers to dressing-table. She could still see her. And the supreme mystery . . . was simply this: here was one room; there another. Did religion solve that, or love? (127)

Perhaps we, as if also struck by the great sounds of Big Ben, can understand that this form of privacy is hardly a sad retreat (Clarissa is a voyeur, sharing in this moment, and she feels not at all lonely). The isolation produces an extraordinary insight: it's a "Gigantic" sound or feeling that gives us, not connection or easy relation, but separation. Two rooms — "here was one room; there another." Clarissa is not relating but observing. She calculates, understands, and reinforces the distance. And the "supreme," perhaps "large," mystery is simply that we can be alone; that we can have separation from the separation that is a deadly, daily reminder of a godly punishment; and that grandness might be felt in this condition rather than smallness. Perhaps, then, we're ready for the wide, open oceanic world rather than just one other person.

So here's the culprit that destroys privacy: not love *or* religion but the conjunction of love *and* religion, the combination of the two — or perhaps just the concept of "two." In other words, *and* is a terrible word sometimes. Although Woolf wonders, "Did religion solve that [mystery]," the clause is quickly followed by another clause, its menacing partner: "or love?" Tellingly, Big Ben, in its immense singularity, is thwarted by its own upsetting partner just as Clarissa attempts to answer her question:

Love — but here the other clock, the clock which always struck two minutes after Big Ben, came shuffling in with its lap full of odds and ends, which it dumped down as if Big Ben were all very well with his majesty laying down the law, so solemn, so just, but she must remember all sorts of little things besides — Mrs. Marsham, Ellie Henderson, glasses for ices — all sorts of little things came flooding and lapping and dancing in on the wake of that solemn stroke which lay flat like a bar of gold on the sea. Mrs. Marsham, Ellie Henderson, glasses for ices. She must telephone now at once. (128)

Two clocks, two minutes apart, two feelings, two repetitions of the same series ("Mrs. Marsham, Ellie Henderson, glasses for ices") all reinforce the *formal* terror of two, of couples, of Big Ben and the other clock, which destroy privacy and remind Clarissa of all her obligations other than the important reflection she has accomplished alone, in another room, watching her neighbor, feeling supreme. Read again this vague, imprecise pronoun reference that Woolf draws into relation with the second clock "with its lap full of odd and ends," "which it dumped down as if Big Ben were all very well with his majesty laying down the law, so solemn, so just, but *she* must remember all sorts of little things besides" (emphasis mine). Is the second clock Clarissa? Or is it just Clarissa trailing off from one thought to the next? In either case, the privacy of the soul, just one soul, has been, as we quickly learn, "Beaten up, broken up by the assault of carriages, the brutality of vans, the eager advance of myriads of angular men, of flaunting women, the domes and spires of offices and hospitals" (128). The advent of another clock, another term — an Other — makes privacy public, makes the mighty less mysterious, and produces a kind of oceanic feeling different from the one Freud wonders about; this feeling is "like the spray of an exhausted wave" (128). So the almighty scale of One has now become crowded with small "trifles," with so much anxiety, with so much lowly or small feeling, with so much, that both love *and* religion cannot keep separate one room from the next. The almighty scale of One is alarmed by two. And the greatness of the mystery has been made tiny and irrelevant as it has entered into the tyranny of two things: not just one room separated from another, but the anxious, lonely feelings of the love of two. Clarissa, after all, is most nervous at this point about her husband.

Woolf is telling us that conjunctions are terribly anxious. She's telling us about couples, married or not. And she's telling us that they've done something bad to the condition of being single.

Religion coupled with love renders being alone an impossible condition. Love is what kills religion because it relies on the comparison, the supreme importance, of a deadening two, making worldly greatness oh so very small. So we should try to disentangle religion and love, or at least the conjunction of the two. By doing so, we'll help release love and religion from their conventional, couple-bound definitions, thereby opening up meaning to something larger than any love, or any specific religious tradition, might even imagine.

You, Monster

We'll read more about *Mrs. Dalloway*, and specifically Miss Kilman's singleness, at the end of this book, but I want to turn to a love story that poignantly illustrates the dynamics of coupledom articulated in *Love Story*, Freud, and Woolf. This story, however, will end unpredictably, so I will also be required to return to its pages in the final chapter of *Single*. The story is about Geryon, who was the monster of Erytheia slain by Herakles (a.k.a. Hercules) in his tenth extraordinary labor, and he is the mythical figure that the poet Anne Carson, another classicist, uses to frame and explain her poetic novel ("novel in verse") *Autobiography of Red*, which she labels "a romance." In her updated version of this mythical story, she imaginatively translates the fragments of a poem about Geryon by the ancient Greek poet Stesichorus to give some kind of shape to the struggles of a young queer boy who must cope, as we all must cope, with what it means to be a "brokenheart."[10] The boy in her story is named Geryon, and he, too, is a red monster (or at least he feels like he's a red monster). He also falls in love with an older boy, aptly named Herakles. And like all love stories, their romance is short-lived. Herakles raids Geryon's small and special world, eviscerating our red monster, leaving him alone, with intense feelings of emptiness.

The effects of this romance, the implications of what it means to fall in and out of love, especially a love considered "wrong," are huge: this story of love and loss, we immediately know, reveals something about immortality, which is why Carson uses an ancient myth, and also why she starts the romance with an Emily Dickinson poem:

> The reticent volcano keeps
> His never slumbering plan —
> Confided are his projects pink
> To no precarious man.
>
> If nature will not tell the tale
> Jehovah told to her
> Can human nature not survive
> Without a listener?
>
> Admonished by her buckled lips
> Let every babbler be
> The only secret people keep
> Is Immortality.[11]

What might this secret of immortality be? Is the secret love? Is love immortal? Is this why Carson uses this poem to introduce her own attempt to tell a story about two queer boys in love? Certainly, we often consider our loves in mythical terms. We often make love feel endless — it is our opportunity to say words like *forever* and *always.* Rarely, I think, do we express term limits when falling for another: we don't hear or say, "I will love you for five months," and so forth. Volcanoes, smoldering and unbearable passion, myths about monsters and strong men, and the secrets of God are part of the literary repertoire close at Carson's impressive hand. But she's not merely dressing up a banal story of a relationship in the clothes of the epic, the geologic, and the religious, thereby making the ordinary extraordinary. She is working with questions of varying scale: large volcano; small loves; large secrets of God; and "buckled lips" that might be big or tiny. As I mentioned above, questions of scale (is it a large or small feeling?) are questions we often bring to those two related and confused feelings: love and religion, which are feelings that force us to consider that which really produces a pervasive disquiet: Are you alone? Who will kiss you? Lava? Literature? God? Or, sadly, *no one*? And you can't be kissed forever, so then what? Will you find your other half? As Carson asserts, while describing her two boys: "Up against another human being one's own procedures take on definition" (42). So love compares you to someone or something else. What will you be like after the comparison, the coupling? The question then becomes, after our experiences of religion, after our experiences of love: What are you like alone? Are you big (like religion)? Or are you so very small (like the frustrated ego)?

Geryon, who is a mythical and therefore "religious" being, is frequently rendered in terms of smallness: in the fragments, there's a persistent reference to his size. For instance, "Are there many little boys who think they are a / Monster?" (12). Or the softness of Geryon's perspective is emphasized by his status as a child: in the section called "Geryon's Parents," the fragment reads, "If you persist in wearing your mask at the supper table / Well Goodnight Then they said and drove him up / Those hemorrhaging stairs to the hot dry Arms / To the ticking red taxi of the incubus / Don't want to go want to stay Downstairs and read" (10). We have similar moments of small pathos in the story of the boy monster: outside a schoolhouse, Geryon, as a very young child, without the aid of a brother, waits, "motionless," hoping someone from his kindergarten class will show him the way inside, which he does not yet know: "He did not knock on the glass. He waited. Small, red, and upright he waited, / gripping his new bookbag tight / in one hand and touching a lucky penny inside his coat pocket with the other, / while the first snows of winter / floated down on his eyelashes and covered the branches around him and silenced / all trace of the world" (25). Geryon is poised to stay small, by which I mean he's about to fall in love, which will destroy that large "religious" feeling, replacing it with a relationship requiring the elegiac problem of division and death.

Geryon starts to create his autobiography soon after he also learns his own little lesson of separate rooms. In this world of the monster, where "the red world And corresponding red breezes /

Went on" (14), Geryon is deeply curious about separation, and he learns an important word:

> The word *each* blew towards him and came apart on the
>   wind. Geryon had always
> had this trouble: a word like *each*,
> when he stared at it, would disassemble itself into
>   separate letters and go.
> A space for its meaning remained there but blank
> The letters themselves could be found hung on branches
>   or furniture in the area.
> *What does* each *mean?*
> Geryon had asked his mother. She never lied to him.
>   Once she said the meaning
> it would stay.
> She answered, Each *means like you and your brother each*
>   *have your own room.*
> He clothed himself in this strong word *each*.
> (26)

Like Clarissa, Geryon appreciates that there can be two rooms: that there can be something like privacy that gives one perspective and distance away from the immediacy of a split self-in-love. But a terrible expression of brother love (or brother hate) destroys this kind of separation: Geryon is forced to share his room with his brother once his ailing grandmother moves into the family's house. He must disrobe that "strong word *each*" and become naked and vulnerable. His brother then couples with him, exchanging sex for marbles, for kindness, and Geryon acquires a skill all too common once one's soul has been violated, or simply loved, by another: he splits the world, and Geryon "thought about the difference / between outside and inside. / Inside is mine" (29). No longer breezing everywhere, his expansive, religious feelings — his internal redness that covers the earth, his "red pulse" — contract, and he starts to write his autobiography, and "In this work Geryon set down all inside things / particularly his own heroism / and early death much to the despair of the community. He coolly omitted / all outside things" (29).

The loss of separation of the world, brought on by the sexuality of his brother — the first experience of a couple, the first experience of something like love — inspires Geryon to imagine his own death — the impossibility of immortality, or divinity, or just that oceanic feeling. In his autobiography, he sets down the "facts" that will, in some senses, be the script of his adolescence and young adulthood:

> *Total Facts Known About Geryon.*
> *Geryon was a monster everything about him was red. Geryon lived*
> *on an island in the Atlantic called the Red Place. Geryon's mother*
> *was a river that runs to the sea the Red Joy River Geryon's father*
> *was gold. Some say Geryon had six hands six feet some say wings.*
> *Geryon was red so were his strange red cattle. Herakles came one*
> *day killed Geryon got the cattle.*
> (37)

Geryon asks and then offers answers to the most pertinent question about his facts: "*Why did Herakles kill Geryon?*" "*. . . Got the idea that Geryon was Death otherwise he would live forever*" (37). The mythical, the religious, being is hunted by Herakles, who wants to live for eternity. The desire for endless time, the desire for forever, is not just the desire of the forever young. In order to dilate time indefinitely, Herakles must kill Geryon. Herakles becomes the figure that brings death and destruction to Geryon by way of a relationship that will die, as all relationships eventually die. If to love means one has to kill, however metaphorically, one's most significant other, why love in the first place? Can't Herakles just ignore Geryon and all his red cattle? Why did Geryon decide that Herakles has this idea? Might this be the major idea of the couple? It's a pursuit for endless time, "the big time," the "Big Ben" kind of time, but through a very callous form of attention.

So if what we learn over and over again in film, in Freud, in poetry, and in fiction is that the words "I love you" are a death sentence, a bizarre logic can be grasped: our loves will last forever only if we overlook a thing our bodies share — our bodies will die. The "procedure that takes on definition" in a fine romance is that one's own mortality is emphasized — one's bounded limits of a body become gruesomely apparent. So we can't find eternity in a loved one. But we can ferociously cling to the version of the myth that we can. Suddenly, love is, as a very wise woman sang over a quarter century ago, "a battlefield."[12] And what seems to be the source of the conflict is once again the question of scale that will produce the kind of meaning and significance that will make you feel big or small, round or split in two. Can you exceed the limits of time if you fall in love? The small answer: no.

So no wonder Geryon, after he falls for Herakles, who he's predicted will want to kill him, thinks to himself, "Love does not / make me gentle or kind" (42). Here's an exemplary vignette capturing the tone and quality of their togetherness:

Herakles makes
a low sound and moves his head on the pillow, slowly opens
    his eyes.
He starts. *Geryon what's wrong? Jesus I hate it when you cry.*
    What is it?
Geryon thinks hard.
I once loved you, now I don't know you at all. He does not
    say this.
I was thinking about time — he gropes —
you know how apart people are in time together and apart at the
    same time — stops.
Herakles wipes tears from Geryon's face
with one hand. *Can't you ever just fuck and not think?*
        Herakles gets out of bed
and goes into the bathroom.
Then he comes back and stands at the window a long while.
        By the time he returns
to the bed it is getting light.

Well just another Saturday morning me laughing and you
    crying,
he says as he climbs in.
(141)

Love is something hard to feel forever, and it typically inspires
questions about what it means to be both separate and together.
Do I really love this person? Still? Geryon used to love Herakles,
but now he claims to not know him at all. And if you care to
notice, there's an almost neurotic concern with menacing singularity in this one moment in time: Herakles wipes Geryon's
tears with just *one* hand; Geryon "*once*" loved Herakles; the pronoun "they" does not appear, and instead we relentlessly have the
names of *each* boy; and "he," "me," and "you" assault the dyad.
This couple is a couple of threatening ones.

But then there's also the concern with time and timing: the
phrase "*at the same time*," written in italics, is literally stopped
by the word "stops," in normal script, so we can read the line as
both Geryon's meditation on "time" that he does not finish as
well as the suggestion that time "stops," which matches (or couples) the previous words in normal script (before the italics):
"he gropes" and then he "stops." This play with the italicized
and nonitalicized words recalls the words that initially describe
their first encounter, their love at first sight: "they recognized
each other like italics" (39). And certainly these two, who are
figured as persistently apart in their togetherness, cease to connect, which might always be the condition of their relation:
"*Well just another Saturday morning me laughing and you crying*,"
which resonates with another zinger of a line Carson treated to
us when their love first misfired years before: "Not touching /
but joined in astonishment as two cuts lie parallel in the same
flesh" (45).

Such moments of aesthetic arrest, of arrested lonely time,
bring us back to the desire for eternity and the murder that
Geryon thinks Herakles must perform so they will forever lie cut-
in-two in "the same flesh." But we must not think that Geryon's

fantasies about why Herakles must kill him in order to live forever are the same thing as that secret of Jehovah: immortality.
Herakles, according to Geryon's imagination, seems to require
something more akin to what Hannah Arendt describes as "eternity," which is in distinct contrast to the concept of "immortality." This distinction between eternity and immortality is crucial,
and it will be one that guides all of my readings here. I'll be illus-
trating these dynamics throughout the book, but for now I want
to divide those distinctions between those who are coupled and
those who are single.

In reference to the insights of antiquity that she always seems
to glamorize, Arendt explains that the "experience of the eternal, which to Plato was *arrheton* ('unspeakable'), and to Aristotle
aneu logou ('without word'), and which later was conceptualized
in the paradoxical *nunc stans* ('the standing now'), can occur only
outside the plurality of men. . . . Politically speaking, if to die is
the same as 'to cease to be among men,' experience of the eternal
is a kind of death, and the only thing that separates it from real
death is that it is not final because no living creature can endure
it for any length of time."[13] The eternal is the wish that can't make
it into language, into relating and relation: it is time standing still,
"the standing now," which has no word that is speakable and no
way to capture, measure, and express something as bewildering
as a relationship. It's an odd kind of time, which kills time, and
which is not available to humans except as a seductive idea. In
a way, it drives the time of the death drive into the hierarchy of
the couple, which requires a paradoxical strategy of the idea of
survival in something that is not at all possible. Time stops for
no one truly living. So to try and make something eternal, to
try and make a loving relationship eternal, requires an image of
death that Geryon repetitively imagines Herakles inflicting on
him. That way, Geryon can have the Herakles that stands in front
of him now (the standing now) forever rather than arrive at that
grim horizon: the future when Herakles leaves him all alone. The
couple form is what Geryon cannot let go (for even when Herakles has abandoned him, Geryon is described as "a talented boy
with a shadow side" [72], always trailed by the ghost of his lost

love, shadowing his talents): Geryon wants his couple to last forever and make a world that is, as we see, crowded not with people
but only with lonely emotion of one other one that restlessly allows himself to barricade himself within a claustrophobic narrative of death. As one of the fragments predicts, "Geryon walked
the red length of his mind and answered No / It was murder And
torn to see the cattle lay / All these darlings Geryon And now
me" (10). Eternity is couples' time, which gives one no time, gesturing only to fantasies of greatness that aren't actually there. No
oceans here. Just the slaughter.

But myths and epics are about those who are heroic and those
who strive to be like the immortals that make the "red breezes"
of the world blow. And immortality is the secret of God we're really trying to rescue from the eternal clutches of the couple form.
"Immortality," explains Arendt, "means endurance in time, death-
less life on this earth and in this world as it was given, according to Greek understanding, to nature and the Olympian gods"
(18). Immortality belongs to the gods; in fact it's not even really
available to humans, who are defined in large part by mortality.
But that does not mean immortality is not a necessary human
concern: immortality encourages. "The task and potential greatness of mortals lie in their ability to produce things — works and
deeds and words — which would deserve to be and, at least to a
degree, are at home in everlastingness, so through them mortals
could find their place in a cosmos where everything is immortal
except themselves" (19). It's a very brazen kind of response to
the gods that would prefer to cut us apart and keep us small by
rending us in two. Immortality, unlike eternity, *can* exist, at least
as a place, a goal, in the cosmos, permitting one to have a sense
of "endurance in time" rather than impossible evasions of change
outside time. Immortality, counterintuitively, sets up the possibility of mortality heading toward greatness.

Nevertheless, we sidestep, by walking side by side, our immortal, single selves, perhaps because we're striving for something
more like the couple's eternity (dead, together). I think, however,
we should consider striving for something larger, perhaps something more solitary. But even before we can begin to explore that

elusive "secret of immortality," we have to dwell for a bit more on the couple's obsession with eternity in the next chapter. And doing as much requires a detour to what couples often make happen: families, larger extensions of the couple form that still swarm our feelings of loneliness with an obsessive worry about a kind of death that is thought to not be final. A death that hopes to be blunted by sheer numbers — additions to the couple by marriage and procreation. A death that seems like the only option for all of our lives as we clutch, in our beds, on to our other halves.

And naturally, that detour takes us to Utah.

2

The Probated Couple, or
Our Polygamous Pioneers

Death sets a Thing significant
The Eye had hurried by
Except a perished Creature
Entreat us tenderly

To ponder little Workmanships
In Crayon, or in Wool,
With "This was last Her fingers did" —
Industrious until —

The Thimble weighed too heavy —
The stitches stopped — by themselves —
And then 'twas put among the Dust
Upon the Closet shelves —

A Book I have — a friend gave —
Whose Pencil — here and there —
Had notched the place that pleased Him —
At Rest — His fingers are —

Now — when I read — I read not —
For interrupting Tears —
Obliterate the Etchings
Too Costly for Repairs.
EMILY DICKINSON

The Family's Romance

Couples are not alone in the grip of loneliness's totalitarianism.
Couples often create and leave a special residue, which marks
their endurance in time: children, relatives, and all sorts of relations that stick to the dyad ("she has her mother's nose"; "his
name will live on"). Couples are the building blocks of family,
and as such they are inextricably wed to the thought of family, to the thought of any member of a family. To understand a

family, you need to start with the couple. Or perhaps a number of couples.

First I have to confess: families terrify me, and not simply because I came from one. Nor is it simply the case that the family terrorizes queers like me because it and its "family values" are the dominant institution of sexual and political regulation in North America.[1] There is something much more lethal in these relationships of terror. So on hand are two documents — one religious, one legal (although we can almost effortlessly argue that these categories are enduringly tangled) — that will start this chapter about the kind of couple's terror that animates the family. They are odd examples, about odd lovers' families, so I quote them at enormous length.

EXHIBIT A:

Selections from Section 132 of the Doctrine and Covenants of the Church of Jesus Christ of Latter-Day Saints:

1. Verily, thus saith the Lord unto you my servant Joseph, that inasmuch as you have inquired of my hand to know and understand wherein I, the Lord, justified my servants Abraham, Isaac, and Jacob, as also Moses, David and Solomon, my servants, as touching the principle and doctrine of their having many wives and concubines —

. . . .

4. For behold, I reveal unto you a new and an everlasting covenant; and if ye abide not that covenant, then are ye damned; for no one can reject this covenant and be permitted to enter into my glory.

. . . .

19. And again, verily I say unto you, if a man marry a wife by my word, which is my law, and by the new and everlasting covenant, and it is sealed unto them by the Holy Spirit of promise, by him who is anointed, unto whom I have appointed this power and the keys of this priesthood; and it shall be said unto them — Ye shall come forth in the first resurrection; and if it be after the first resurrection, in the next resurrection; and shall inherit thrones, kingdoms,

principalities, and powers, dominions, all heights and depths — then shall it be written in the Lamb's Book of Life, that he shall commit no murder whereby to shed innocent blood, and if ye abide in my covenant, and commit no murder whereby to shed innocent blood, it shall be done unto them in all things whatsoever my servant hath put upon them, in time, and through all eternity; and shall be of full force when they are out of the world; and they shall pass by the angels, and the gods, which are set there, to their exaltation and glory in all things, as hath been sealed upon their heads, which glory shall be a fulness and a continuation of the seeds forever and ever.

20. Then shall they be gods, because they have no end; therefore shall they be from everlasting to everlasting, because they continue; then shall they be above all, because all things are subject unto them. Then shall they be gods, because they have all power, and the angels are subject unto them.

.   .   .   .

30. Abraham received promises concerning his seed, and of the fruit of his loins — from whose loins ye are, namely, my servant Joseph — which were to continue so long as they were in the world; and as touching Abraham and his seed, out of the world they should continue; both in the world and out of the world should they continue as innumerable as the stars; or, if ye were to count the sand upon the seashore ye could not number them.

31. This promise is yours also, because ye are of Abraham, and the promise was made unto Abraham; and by this law is the continuation of the works of my Father, wherein he glorifieth himself.

32. Go ye, therefore, and do the works of Abraham; enter ye into my law and ye shall be saved.

33. But if ye enter not into my law ye cannot receive the promise of my Father, which he made unto Abraham.

34. God commanded Abraham, and Sarah gave Hagar to Abraham to wife. And why did she do it? Because this was the

law; and from Hagar sprang many people. This, therefore, was fulfilling, among other things, the promises.

35. Was Abraham, therefore, under condemnation? Verily I say unto you, Nay; for I, the Lord, commanded it.

36. Abraham was commanded to offer his son Isaac; nevertheless, it was written: Thou shalt not kill. Abraham, however, did not refuse, and it was accounted unto him for righteousness.

37. Abraham received concubines, and they bore him children; and it was accounted unto him for righteousness, because they were given unto him, and he abode in my law; as Isaac also and Jacob did none other things than that which they were commanded; and because they did none other things than that which they were commanded, they have entered into their exaltation, according to the promises, and sit upon thrones, and are not angels but are gods.

38. David also received many wives and concubines, and also Solomon and Moses my servants, as also many others of my servants, from the beginning of creation until this time; and in nothing did they sin save in those things which they received not of me.

39. David's wives and concubines were given unto him of me, by the hand of Nathan, my servant, and others of the prophets who had the keys of this power; and in none of these things did he sin against me save in the case of Uriah and his wife; and, therefore he hath fallen from his exaltation, and received his portion; and he shall not inherit them out of the world, for I gave them unto another, saith the Lord.

EXHIBIT B:

A Last Will and Testament of Nicole K. Baker, reproduced in Norman Mailer's *The Executioner's Song*

TO WHOMEVER IT MAY CONCERN:

I, Nicole Kathryne Baker — have a number of personal requests I would desire to have carried out — in the event that I am at any time found dead.

I am considering myself a strong, logical, and totally sane mind — so that which I am writing should be taken serious in every respect.

At the time of this writing I am going through a divorce from a man named Steve Hudson.

By my standards — the event of death should dissolve all ties with that man and the divorce be carried through and finalized AT ALL COSTS.

I wish to legally be returned to my maiden name which is Baker. And have none ever acknoledge me by any other name.

My daughters birth certificates states her name as Sunny Marie Baker, even thoe, at the time of her birth, I was then legally married to her father — James Paul Barrett.

My son's birth certificate states his name as Jeremy Kip Barrett. Because I was at that time still married to James Paul Barrett, who is not Jeremy's father.

Jeremy's father is the late Alfred Kip Eberhardt.

So Jeremy does have legal grandparents by the last name of Eberhardt who may wish to be notified of his whereabouts. They are residing in Paoli, Pennsylvania, I think.

As to the care custody and welfare of my children — I am not only desiring but demanding that the responsibility of them and any decisions concerning them — be placed directly and immediately into the hands of Thomas Giles Barrett and Marie Barrett of Springville, Utah.

If the Barretts so wish to adopt my children — they have my willing consent.

If they wish to place the responsibility of one or both children into the hands of another responsible party of their choice — they again have my willing consent.

That is of course — until the children are of legal age to make their own choices.

I have a pearl ring in hock in the bowling alley in Springville. I would really like for someone to get it out and give it to my little Sister — April L. Baker.

Also I have made arrangements for a sum of money to go to April's mental health problem. My mother should not spend that

*money for anything other than to pay a good Mental Hospital for
helping April back to her sanity.*

*Now, as the decision as to what should be done with my dead
body — I ask that it be cremated. And with the consent of Mrs.
Bessie Gilmore I would have my ashes mixed with those of her
son — Gary Mark Gilmore. To be then — at any future convenient dates scattered upon a green hillside in the State of Oregon
and also in the State of Washington.[2]*

Both documents are documents about couples' love, death,
and families. Both documents are also about Utah. And Utah is a
state strenuously marked by its devotion to families, a devotion
that seems peculiar even in a nation enthralled by its cherished
fidelity to making families. "The Mormons who fled to the sanctuary of the mountains, and the converts who joined them later,"
writes Wallace Stegner, "were the kind of people who naturally
have large families, and they lived in a time and part of the world
where large families were normal. But add to their normal fecun-
dity the ambition of Brigham Young to people his whole empire
with industrious Saints, the pressure he put on people to be fruit-
ful and multiply."[3] Whether or not we can agree that large families
are "natural," Mormons certainly have a unique take on families.
The Utah family, "Utah's Best Crop" — as signposts throughout Mormon country were reported to have advertised under
"pictures of chubby rosy children" — generates much national
anxiety.[4]

But it wasn't merely the largeness of Mormon families that
made them seem so noteworthy; it was the sexual and marital
practices of this frontier society, Brigham Young's "ambition,"
that inspired the most tried, tired, and salacious commentary.
That is, it was polygamy — with large numbers of unconvention-
ally reared folk — that got people talking, almost as soon as the
church gained notoriety in its early days in the mid-nineteenth
century. Polygamy is hyperbolic family making, rendering in
sharp relief what happens when the couple form can be dupli-
cated within a family.

Utah's best crop: children, the residue of the couple. Photo of popular vintage postcard, circa 1903. Photo by author.

Mark Twain mocks this fascination in his travel narrative about going West during the Civil War:

> And the next most interesting thing is to sit and listen to these Gentiles [that Twain is hanging out with in Salt Lake City] talk about polygamy; and how some portly old frog of an elder, or a bishop, marries a girl — likes her, marries her sister — likes her, marries another sister — likes her, takes another — likes her, marries her mother — likes her, marries her father, grandfather, great grandfather, and then comes back hungry and asks for more. And how the pert young thing of eleven will chance to be the favorite wife and her own venerable grandmother have to rank away down . . . in their mutual husband's esteem, and have to sleep in the kitchen, as like as not. And how this dreadful sort of thing, this hiving together in one foul nest of mother and daughters, and the making of a young daughter superior to her own mother in rank and authority, are the things which Mormon women submit to because their religion teaches them that the more wives a man has on earth, the more children he rears, the higher the place they will all have in the world to come — and the warmer, maybe, though they don't seem to say anything about that.[5]

I don't want to diminish or mock the history of sexual violence and abuse that adheres to the practices of polygamy (as well as monogamy) in the Beehive State. I cite Twain's comedic critique only to show off how part of polygamy's difficulty is the extraordinary, often absurd and lurid, attention repetitively paid to this marriage practice (the protectionist rhetoric still seems to be in circulation today). Picking on polygamy is hardly novel. Famously, the Republican Party Platform of 1856 declared "that the Constitution confers upon Congress sovereign powers over the Territories of the United States for their government; and that in the exercise of this power, it is both the right and the imperative duty of Congress to prohibit in the Territories those twin relics of barbarism — Polygamy, and Slavery."[6] There were numerous sister-wife narratives, which were generically similar to slave narratives. Harriet Beecher Stowe, for example, wrote a preface for Fanny Stenhouse's *Tell It All: A Woman's Life in Polygamy*, describing polygamy as "a slavery which debases and degrades womanhood."[7] And the prohibitionist Frances E. Willard went further, writing, in an introduction to *The Women of Mormonism: Or the Story of Polygamy as Told by the Victims Themselves*, "Turkey is in our midst. Modern Mohammedanism has its Mecca at Salt Lake, where Prophet Herbert C. Kimball speaks of his wives as 'cows.'"[8] There was even a silent film hit in 1922, H. B. Parkinson's *Trapped by Mormons*, featuring Mormons' savage capture of women in an attempt to satisfy their insatiable appetite for wives. It would not be difficult to link these various discussions of "Mohammedanism" to the current fret and fear stirred by Islam in the American imaginary today.

But instead of charting such a genealogy, I want to leave aside this critique, which is indebted to the explicit worry about the sexual practices of polygamists, and argue something from another angle. I want to suggest that perhaps what makes Utah families so troubling, so terrorizing, for so many is not so much the polygamous difference, not really the politics of traditional versus nontraditional marriage contests, especially since even polygamist families still rely on the dyad — each of the wives marry the man, so he has multiple dyads supporting his celestial family. What I think troubles us is what Utah families highlight about most families: a strenuous devotion to conceptualizing the couple's family as a death-making enterprise in the Latter-Day Saints' imaginary, one with a major elegiac problem that haunts and shadows sacred and nonsacred forms of family law. This problem is not merely Mormon; it belongs to most couples. And this problem hinges on a human right that marks ghostliness: the right of inheritance. But I'm getting ahead of myself.

Both documents I started this chapter with (the revelation of Joseph Smith and the last will and testament of Nicole Baker, girlfriend of notorious killer Gary Gilmore) are about the future of relationships, or how the families that the couplings make possible cope with a future that necessarily contains death — a death that, as we learned in the previous chapter, is figured by the couple form that cuts people into two. And even if polygamy adds others into the mix, there are always the illustrative dynamics between the couples within the crowded marriage. (The first marriage, for instance, has a modeling importance and hierarchy that cannot be ignored even with the additions of more wives.) Smith's revelation charts how one can, through the proper and moral kind of family, achieve a permanent place in the highest heavenly existence in the celestial order of the Mormon afterlife: one gets to the choicest afterlife by the best kind of marriage practices — plural marriage.

Baker's will (which she later has to amend once she realizes that she hasn't properly distributed her property, just her family) is about how she sees her family enduring after her desperate and unsuccessful suicide attempt (an attempt to be with her convicted killer in eternity since they couldn't be together on this earth). Most striking, after she has "arranged" the custody of her children (tangled in all sorts of marriage, ex-marriage, and ad hoc familial arrangements), urged that someone get her ring out of hock, and provided a small sum of money for the cost of her sister's mental health care, Nicole directs the disposal of her and Gary's remains. She wants her ashes mixed with Gary's; she wants to be with him in death since they can't be with each other in life; and she wants those ashes scattered in two states on the edge of the North American continent. This is Nicole's vision of what her future might be: an "everlasting" blended and scattered connection to her unmarried partner. Divided. Dead. But together.

Let's put aside the obvious judgments. Let's put aside any frustration we might have with a young mother who abandons her children and family for a lethal love with an abusive serial killer (who has helped devise this botched suicide pact, in part because he'd rather see Nicole dead than with another lover). Let's also put aside whether we agree with Smith's revelations about the "new and everlasting covenant" of marriage, or if we're angry that he violates his first marriage vows secretly, but "prophetically," by entering more couple relationships by the holy marriage practices that he invents to sanctify his marital infidelities (or that he comes to understand by prophecy, depending on your beliefs about Mormonism). Instead, I want to think of these two "exhibits" as examples of why questions of inheritance prey upon our imaginations about what constitutes a family.

Although Smith's revelation is not necessarily a will, it mimics the legal instrument that Nicole was trying to write. Mailer includes a letter Nicole wrote right after the will, underscoring the connections between a suicide note and a last will and testament (written under the influence of a particular religious understanding):

> Well, all will be clear and right just know that i love you all today and i will love you always.
>
> Please try also not to grieve for me — or resent Gary.
> i Love him
> i made my own choice.
> i'll never regret it.
> Please Love my kids always, as they are part of the family.
> Never hid truths from them.
> When any of you need me, i will be there to listen for i and Gary — and yourselves — are all part of a wondrous good understandin God.
> May this parting bring us closer in Loveing, understanding and expecting of one another.
> i Love you All
> Sissy[9]

Albeit written in a less formal manner, Nicole's letter essentially emphasizes the main points of her will: take care of my kids; I love you all; and Gary and I will be together. By ending her suicide letter with theological insights into the nature of love and family, Nicole, not particularly religious as an adult, seems to parrot the ambient understanding of family togetherness that permeates the Utah she inhabits. And as we think about her letter, listen to the forty-sixth part of Smith's revelation: "And verily, verily, I say unto you, that whatever you seal on earth shall be sealed in heaven; and whatever you bind on earth, in my name and by my word, saith the Lord, it shall be eternally bound in the heavens." In rapid succession, Nicole is sealing her fate, sealing her will, and sealing her bond with Gary in a manner that she hopes will bring her difficult, fractious, and unruly family into stronger relation. Love, for Nicole as for many others, will be for always. It is her *will*. It's God's *will*. Death gives us this inheritance. And death, as we've seen, is the feeling that stirs couples to employ all sorts of strategies for an impossible survival.

The Haunting

This odd optimism in Smith and Baker brings us to the heart of the couple: Is there a way to endure in our relations past death? Is there a way to survive the fatal couple? How can we have, or at least distribute, "forever"? And why are couples and the families they make supposed to be the place where we can seemingly negotiate these hopeful wishes? An area of law that helps me think about these questions is, of course, the realm of probate. Wills, trusts, estates are jurisdictionally specific, so it's difficult to theorize about them. But I'm going to try because it seems to me that the question of who gets your property after you die is, as Nicole's will illustrates, not simply about giving real or personal property to people you want. The right to transfer property reveals the particular role that the devisee or legatee occupies in the life of the testator. And not just the role (lover, brother, sister, mother, father, friend, dog, etc.), but also the quality, if not quantity, of the emotion or concern one can express as a parting wish, as a way of continuing to influence the lives one has left behind. Any Jane Austen novel certainly can reveal as much.

Nicole remembers her hocked pearl ring not simply because of the value it might have but because it could be a source of revenue that could help treat the mental difficulties of her sister, whom she loves. It's a material form of continuing to contribute to the quality of her sister's life. But the posthumous transfer of property is not only about the acquisition of certain monetary or chattel windfalls that could ameliorate (or provide for) some of life's expensive circumstances: my own grandfather, Joe, gave me a silver ring, made out of a 1942 dime, that he had made during the Second World War on a boat in the South Pacific. It might literally be worth a dime, and it certainly cannot pay for something substantial. But its sentimental value is forged into its silver in a way I can't forget. It's also the only "thing" of his that he once wore that I now own. He loved me enough to make it a piece of his legacy, and I, as his grandson, am his legatee. Our bond is formally recognized and represented by the property he gave to me.

In either case, pieces of property (Nicole's pearl ring, my grandfather's dime ring) have characteristics of a relative's regard, and the transfer of property, moreover, transfers parts of the testator (his or her emotion, wealth, attention, intention, even characteristics) to the inheritor. Oliver Wendell Holmes Jr. kept circling around this very issue when arguing about succession of property after death in his study of the common law. While detailing various ways other legal histories have dealt with the transfer of property after death, and while teasing out the particular and sometimes baffling manner in which an estate's executors and heirs assume the "*persona*" of the deceased, Holmes makes clear that the law treats them "as if they were one with him [the deceased], for the purpose of settling their rights and obligations."[10] He describes this function as a "fictional" function, which "shadows" specific facts from a long developmental history of common-law jurisprudence and even affects the laws "dealin[g] with the living."[11] But this fiction of transferring one's persona along with one's property to people who remain after one's death is not inconsequential. On the contrary, these legal fictions are the terms of art that help make possible what Marx famously says the commodity (which can be property, among other "things") does in the kind of industrialized nation that Holmes is writing about: the "mysterious character of the commodity-form . . . reflects the social characteristics of men's own labour as objective characteristics of labour themselves, as socio-natural properties of these things."[12] Commodities, property, start to resemble and reflect the social relations of people — social relations that become "the fantastic form of a relation between things."[13] Perhaps more interesting for our discussion is that the legal fiction of inheritance, the shadowy transfer of property and the deceased owners' persona to survivors, extends Marx's fetish idea beyond the social relations of the living. Succession and transfer open up the social relations of the commodity fetish to relations with the dead. In other words, a will can keep us carrying on and on with the dead in our alienated social worlds, never failing to make things play out relations between people, and thus with ghosts.[14]

So we're haunted by the property willed to us — the line of succession's solidification of social relations by the transfer of property after death. And even if you don't have a will, or if there is property that is intestate because it's not covered by a will, the line of succession closely follows the path of a ghost, if not a law, of familial affiliation, which begins with two people. For example, in the 2008 Utah Code's Section 75-02-103 we can read about what happens to intestate estates if there is both no will and, perhaps more grievously, no spouse (the easiest and most automatic line of succession in most probate jurisdictions, often not requiring a testament). What happens is a relentless, nearly commonsensical quest for a blood heir that follows the deceased coupling, no matter how distant:

75-2-103. Share of heirs other than surviving spouse.

(1) Any part of the intestate estate not passing to the decedent's surviving spouse under Section 75-2-102, or the entire intestate estate if there is no surviving spouse, passes in the following order to the individuals designated below who survive the decedent:

(a) to the decedent's descendants per capita at each generation as defined in Subsection 75-2-106(2);

(b) if there is no surviving descendant, to the decedent's parents equally if both survive, or to the surviving parent;

(c) if there is no surviving descendant or parent, to the descendants of the decedent's parents or either of them per capita at each generation as defined in Subsection 75-2-106(3);

(d) if there is no surviving descendant, parent, or descendant of a parent, but the decedent is survived by one or more grandparents or descendants of grandparents, half of the estate passes to the decedent's paternal grandparents equally if both survive, or to the surviving paternal grandparent, or to the descendants of the decedent's paternal grandparents or either of them if both are deceased, the descendants taking per capita at each generation as defined in Subsection 75-2-106(3); and the other half passes to the decedent's maternal relatives in the same manner; but if there is no surviving grandparent or descendant of a grandparent on either the paternal or the maternal side, the entire estate passes to the decedent's relatives on the other side in the same manner as the half.

(2) For purposes of Subsections (a), (b), (c), and (d), any nonprobate transfer, as defined in Section 75-2-205, received by an heir is chargeable against the intestate share of such heir.[15]

The property of someone dead must haunt the family tree as it hunts for a living person it can be possessed by. We could say that property's relational itineraries connect and fortify the family's story, which we could also call a ghost story, or a love story, obsessed with the couple's death. And all these heads of a family, all the "by heads" (per capita) who survive the decedent, not so subtly remind us that the couple is the default set of social relations that must be remembered and honored by the distribution of property. Sure, the equitable division of wealth between individuals is the explicit point of the law, but those individuals are found only within the realm of couple, then familial, relation, and specifically relations that are descendants, not yet decedents. This line of inheritance makes sense historically (families and the division of property by a long history of estates, common law, and other models of households throughout the history of law),[16] but one question needs to be asked, even now: Why? Are your family members really the ones you want to inherit your wealth, land, rings, lamps, or love? If your spouse is still alive, in Utah, is she or he a legal spouse? We don't have to be Mormon or in Utah or even religious to be affected by the implications of the code. I must confess: I've not made a will yet (I'll get to it, someday). If I don't do it, my house, pension, life insurance, even beloved pet might end up in the hands of my wealthy, Mitt Romney-loving parents who don't need or won't appreciate the money or the love or sentiment I'd perhaps prefer to transfer to my friends (or dog). Perhaps I'd like to continue relating to people other than my legal family after my death, in substantial ways. Surely, this predicament is my fault. But why is family the default when there is no will, or when there is property not covered by the will? What kind of insidious priority does this code, and do the laws of probate more generally in a myriad of jurisdictions, keep assigning to the family? Is the family really the most important kind of social relation one should always have? And what particular force do these compacts between the living and the dead have in sustaining and protecting the couples that made the families we make?

All in the Family

In 1891, the U.S. Supreme Court decided *Cope v. Cope*, a case about whether the Territory of Utah would be promoting and protecting the institution of polygamy by acknowledging the right of inheritance of an illegitimate child (George Cope).[17] The facts of the case were relatively clear: Thomas Cope fathered the child with his second plural wife, Margaret, who did not have the legal status of wife because that status belonged to Janet, his lawful first wife. He died without a will. Who, then, was automatically entitled to a share of the estate? Or to be more precise, given the obsessive logic of the couple and family in matters of succession: Who belongs to this family, and does a second coupling still loop us back to the first — the original, initial marriage? The probate, district, and territorial supreme courts eventually concluded that George was not an heir, citing various laws and strategies that had been put in place to discourage the practice of plural marriage, particularly the 1862 Anti-Polygamy Act of Congress, which had taken effect before the death of Thomas Cope. From this legal vantage point, George, quite simply, did not belong to

Cope's family. We could have only one legitimate couple here, and thus only one legal family.

But there were several questions for the Court because an 1852 statute of Utah allowed "illegitimate mothers and their children [to] inherit in a like manner from the father."[18] Normally, probate matters are left to the "state's cognizance," but this law, which would not necessarily be so prickly in another jurisdiction, obviously put in place legal mechanisms to provide for all the heirs of polygamous families, honoring the father's wishes to be able to achieve a celestial status, an eternity, for his first wife by marrying more wives and producing more heirs that would make the family line long, extending through, if not rendering irrelevant, time. But the 1862 statute fashioned some gray areas that were (and are) compelling: "all acts and laws which establish, maintain, protect, or countenance the practice of polygamy" were annulled, but could the 1852 statute definitively be said to promote and protect polygamy?[19] Certainly, in other jurisdictions, the 1852 statute could be read more innocently. The Court thinks out loud: "But while it is the duty of the courts to put a construction upon statutes which shall, so far as possible, be consonant with good morals, we know of no legal principle which would authorize us to pronounce a statute of this kind, which is plain and unambiguous upon its face, void by reason of its failure to conform to our own standard of social and moral obligations."[20] So it's hard to determine whether the 1862 act applies to a law when one has to read into the law the way it is responding to the "peculiar state of society" "existing at the time this act was passed, and still existing in the Territory of Utah."[21] In fact, after a variety of lines of thought, the Court concludes that if the 1852 statute "had been passed in any other jurisdiction, it would have been considered as a perfectly harmless, though possibly indiscreet, exercise of legislative power, and would not be seriously claimed as a step toward the establishment of a polygamous system."[22]

Subsequent acts of Congress, designed to prohibit and punish polygamous practices (especially the "Edmunds-Tucker Act"), kept returning to a nagging issue that made many of these issues about Congress versus state control a bit moot: for example, the Edmunds-Tucker Act contained an odd provision stating that the disinheritance of illegitimate children (the reversal of the 1852 statute supposedly shielding plural marriage arrangements) need not apply to any illegitimate children born within twelve months of the act. This inconsistency of application was obviously a practical solution to a problem inhering in this inheritance quandary: Should the modification of probate law in Utah punish those who had no control over their polygamous circumstance? Should children be stigmatized by an onerous challenge to territorial laws originally put into place to protect them from their ever-recoupling parents? Another, more crass, way to put it: Don't children in a patriarchal society such as the United States — who are the literal residue of a coupling — always remain tied to the father and his desires to provide for his heirs, if not his memory and salvation? The Court decides:

> Now if it had been intended by the act of 1862 to annul the territorial act of 1852, fixing the inheritable capacity act of 1852, why did Congress in 1882 recognize the legitimacy of children born of polygamous or Mormon marriages prior to January 1, 1883? Or why, in the act of 1887, did it save the rights of such children as well as of all others born within twelve months after the passage of the act? The object of these enhancements is entirely clear. Not only does Congress refrain from adding to the odium which popular opinion visits upon this innocent but unfortunate class of children, but it makes them the special object of solicitude, and at the same time offers to the parents an inducement, in the nature of a *locus penitentiae*, to discontinue their unlawful cohabitation.[23]

The lack of punishment of children, then, is considered an "inducement," in the form of allowing the parents to withdraw from their illegal marriage contracts and to choose, instead, the cessation of criminal cohabitation. Get out of your excessive marriages now, or your children will suffer. So the Court reversed the lower court's decision, making George an heir.

But it's not enough to say that *Cope* was decided in its way because the Court didn't want either to further stigmatize children or to use the children's potential inheritance as an incentive to get people out of plural marriages. Part of what makes *Cope* a fascinating problem for me is not necessarily the jurisdictional issues, or the questions about whether illegitimate heirs have valid claims on an estate, or even the persistent moral bias in the Court's consideration and condemnation of plural couplings. Instead, what is striking is the manner in which the probate claims of children from unconventional families provoke an intense rhetoric of emotion that enables the Court to contradict its (and the lower courts') position on the inheritance of polygamy. Polygamy's outlaw status is perhaps not as disturbing as what might happen when even the right of familial belonging, of indexing the sanctity of any kind of coupling, is denied to this "innocent but unfortunate class of children."

Moreover, children are not the only ones at risk. All couples and their families are at risk when there is a death. Death makes the Cope legacy endurance seem so fragile (even the *Cope v. Cope* title of the case demonstrates the division of the family), so upsetting, that reasonable jurists let a disturbing familial emotion get the best of them: "But it may be said in defense of this [1852] act that the children embraced by it are not responsible for this state of things, and that it is unjust to visit upon them the consequences of their parents' sins. To recognize the validity of the act is in the nature of a punishment upon the father, whose estate is thus diverted from its natural channel, rather than upon the child, while to hold it to be invalid is to treat the child as in some sense an outlaw and a *particeps criminis*."[24]

In this "state of things," we're immersed in Marx's relation between things, which is a relation between various family members, following the primary relation between a husband and wife, a relation that becomes adversarial when we have to think about the validity of a law that was intended to preserve the couple's influence as a family across generational lines and, in the Mormon worldview, the line between life and death. In the Court's reading of the legal quandary of a polygamous probate, we have either parents or children punished, and the legal distribution of things is also preserving the "sinful" qualities of polygamous actions. There is a sinful crime here, and no matter which way one divides it, someone, if not everyone, in the family is going to have blood on their hands.

But why is it "unjust" to "visit upon 'the children' the consequences of their parents' sins"? These consequences are really there only when the question of inheritance must be settled by a hostile court, one that doesn't believe that this family should exist in the first place — a court that has a moral position that adds "odium" to this family (and its class of children). So another way to think about this family's sinfulness is to implicate the Court in making the family so fragile, in mining that terror of moribund emotion that I argued defines the anxiety and fragility of the couple, an elegiac problem that mediates how we can even consider or understand all relations between people. The Court is making this generational issue an issue of sinful consequences by pulling apart the family when it revisits the question of whether probate statutes can protect the polygamous family. In this way, the Court is functionally similar to the plural parents, who can choose to be polygamous or not: it has a choice to make about how to connect the kids to not only inheritance laws but also the long vitality of the family structure that those laws about death enable. The rhetorical leaps of logic that eventually let the children (and the Cope family) off the hook in the decision reveal something curious: the Court authorizes, even protects, George Cope's relation to his father by giving George part of his father's estate; in a way, it condones polygamy (at least for a while) because it respects any kind of coupling (multiple or not) aiming for posterity, if not eternity. The sins of the father or Court be damned! It's much worse to tear the children away from their deceased parents, the couple that made them from scratch, even if other couplings in the marriage may be diluting the status of the child's parents. It's terrible to tear the children away from something everlasting and eternal, but thought to be terribly fragile: the couples, the families, that we want to make forever, especially as we look forward to our deaths. Because of the children's necessary link to the parents that made them, even criminal couples can be permitted, in certain circumstances, to endure. And this is a kind of crime in which even the Supreme Court can participate. The couple form always seems to hover, celestially, above the law.

The Sealing

The reason why we can put up with all sorts of familial criminality is that we're worried about the couple's durability, even if we're not part of a Latter-Day religious schism. We're worried, I think, about the way the couple so inevitably dies as we age, change, and move in the world. Assaulted by such moribund insights, one might worry that an everlasting eternity may not really be in the offing. So I'm convinced that something about Mormons, and their polygamous legacies, puts into sharp relief a concern with the afterlife, and we don't have to be living in 1891 for our national worries about polygamy to be ignited. Indeed, every so often (some people say every ten years), the nation remembers its polygamists, and inevitably controversies erupt over their place and meaning in American society. Currently, we're living in one of those moments. Why? We have here at least five culprits: same-sex marriage; the war on terror (with whiffs of Islamophobia that recall early condemnations of polygamy); the failed first presidential candidacy of Mormon ex-Massachusetts governor Mitt Romney; TLC's hit reality television show *Sister Wives*; and HBO's *Big Love*. I want to focus, here, on the last culprit. If I were writing a different kind of chapter, I could just explain how *Big Love,* appearing during a moment of increased political attention to same-sex marriage, mines the theology, history, and culture of polygamists in order to allegorize the struggles of queers who are interested in family, in marriage rights, and in the dynamic clash between religious belief and homosexual practice. The show's creators, Mark V. Olsen and Will Scheffer, both openly gay, have produced a remarkably sensitive portrayal of polygamy, often drawing parallels between queers' struggles for rights, respectability, and prominence within the United States and polygamists' struggles for rights, respectability, and prominence within the larger Mormon culture. Of course, there are differences between queers and the Fundamentalist Latter-Day Saints (and *Big Love*'s concern for polygamists is not an endorsement of a patriarchal, often abusive culture that pushes the limits of what many would consider acceptable instances of sexual and marital consent). But allegories are not identities. By green-lighting this show, HBO enabled people once again to look at a queer region of the United States (remote Utah, specifically what was once known as Short Creek but is now known as the border towns of Colorado City, Arizona, and Hildale, Utah) that gives rise to a story of nontraditional family values (but a story that has quite a long, transhistorical history) that is also the tale of America's inability to either ignore or embrace sexuality in all of what Gayle Rubin would call the acceptance of "benign variation" of sexual practice.[25] What marks this "raid" on polygamists as different from earlier raids is a very conservative epoch in what now counts as family values: soon after *Big Love*, Warren Jeffs, the leader and prophet of the FLDS, was promptly put on the FBI's Ten-Most-Wanted List, captured, tried, and convicted of assisting in the forced marriage and rape of a teenage girl; Anderson Cooper spent weeks in southern Utah reporting on this private underbelly of the Utah desert; hundreds of Mormon fundamentalist children were ripped away from their families in the FLDS compound in Texas in 2008; and marriage traditionalists were putting even more emphasis on the definition of marriage as a union between *one* man and *one* woman.[26]

But nontraditional sexuality or familial arrangements can't be the entire source of America's anxiety about Mormonism. In the terribly important case of *Reynolds v. U.S.* (the opinion delineating whether polygamy can be a religious belief worth protecting), a long historical overview about polygamous practice reveals something the majority opinion felt the need to cite in its condemnation of how the Mormon Church had brought an "odious" practice of non-European people to the West. The "ecclesiastical courts" of England, in charge of punishing polygamous offenses up until the time of James I, were deemed the most appropriate venue for the "trial of matrimonial causes and offenses against the rights of marriage, just as they were for testamentary causes and the settlements of the estates of deceased persons."[27] Certainly the relationship between marriage and probate law in ecclesiastical courts is important in the history of Western jurisprudence; but in the quick histories that the Court often trots out in its opinions, nuanced historical evidence does not usually appear in great abundance. So this rhetorical addition of the probate detail is striking because the questions at hand in *Reynolds* are not, at face value, necessarily probate questions. Instead, the Court was concerned with (among other things) the proper constitution of grand juries; the proper way of empanelling jurors; the proper admissibility of testimony; and whether polygamy was a practice that could be protected by the right to religious freedom. But by referencing ties between the history of marriage regulation and the history of probate regulation, the Court seems here to respond, however unawares, to the questions of death and celestial marriage that preoccupy not only the Mormon faith (as we've seen) but also all marriages, if not all couples, that must negotiate the difficulty of making sense out of a hope for an eternity together while facing and feeling the dreadful pragmatics of the couple's death. Something about Mormonism reminds the Court that marriage law and death law might also be in their own anxious, eternal marriage. And our fears about this link can even make the Supreme Court, as we just saw, participate in and support the continuance of the couple at the expense of laws that might threaten the family's promise of a multitude and wealth that would guarantee eternity. More generally, something about religion is important here; why else, at least historically, would an ecclesiastical court be the best place to adjudicate matters of marriage and death?

When Marx was introducing his "mysterious" concept of commodity fetishism, his analysis was rhetorically religious. In the section entitled "The Fetishism of the Commodity and Its Secret," Marx writes, "A commodity appears at first sight an extremely obvious thing."[28] Of course, it's not so obvious, and Marx attempts to work against simply thinking about the utility of a commodity. He wants us not to be so oblivious about our relationships with the commodities, things, and property that are circumscribing this odd world. He assures us, "But its [the commodity's] analysis brings out that it is a very strange thing, abounding in metaphysical subtleties and theological niceties."[29] To begin to make his point, Marx introduces what becomes his famous table, an object made of dead wood, which almost begins to dance:

> It is absolutely clear that, by his activity, man changes the forms of material in such a way as to make them useful for him. The form of wood, for instance, is altered if a table is made out of it. Nevertheless the table continues to be wood, an ordinary, sensuous thing which transcends sensuousness. It not only stands with its feet on the ground, but, in relation to all other commodities, it stands on its head, and evolves out of its wooden brain grotesque ideas, far more wonderful than if it were to begin dancing of its own free will.[30]

To illustrate his assertion about all the "theological niceties," Marx rushes into a fantastical description of something both physical and metaphysical, a table on its head, spinning out "grotesque" and "wonderful" ideas. He gives us a sense of this table, an idea that is literally turned on its head, haunted by its abilities to be possessed by some kind of life, by using religious terms and ideas. The table transcends its sensuousness by becoming, in a very strange way, religious — Marx takes a "flight into the misty realm of religion. There the products of the human brain [a 'wooden brain'?] appear as autonomous figures endowed with a life of their own, which enter into relations both with each other and with the human race."[31] Dead things, we're led to imagine, come alive in the religious idea; "the products of the human brain" become animate, entering into all sorts of social relations. And for some reason Marx calls this process "religious," perhaps not only because he believes the religious to be the realm that transcends the limits of sensuousness but also because it's a realm where one can imagine more readily dead things interacting as if

Couples hover celestially over the world. Screen capture from "Take Me as I Am," *Big Love* #2.11 (dir. Jim McKay), 2007.

they're alive. It's in the afterlife, many of us hope, where we find the dead alive. So in the realm of probate, which worries about how things and people will relate, we have a curious form of morbid optimism — the will of our loves, and the property we possess, exchange, and transfer, can live on and on. Our inheritances, which always require our families (headed by the couple form), are hopefully our religious salvations.

To imagine these abstract ideas, let's look at some scenes from HBO's *Big Love*.

After having acclimated viewers to the shocking circumstances of a plural marriage lifestyle over most of its first two seasons, the show began to delve more into what we might call the various curiosities (to a non-Mormon audience) of Mormon culture and history that come from the fundamentalist version of the faith, which has not abandoned the principle of plural marriage. The scenery and setting in Utah smack of traditional Americana; indeed, the rise of the Mormon religion and the settlement of

Utah have been termed by many a truly American story: Mormons are often considered, as Harold Bloom famously stated, a quintessential American religion, mirroring Western expansion and featuring the "authentic religious genius" that was Joseph Smith.[32] Yet what often fascinate us are the aspects of this milieu that seem mainstream but aren't quite. The history, faith, rituals, and theologies of the Church of Jesus Christ of Latter-Day Saints are not well known to a general audience (at least weren't well known before *Big Love*), so the allusions to the particulars of the Mormon worldview — the oddities that seem out of place in the American heartland — become the points of agitating contact that might compel us to wonder: Why are these Mormon differences both entertaining *and* disturbing? The Mormons' relation to death is one of these compelling almost-oddities.

Specifically, the penultimate episode of season 2, "Take Me as I Am" (dir. Jim McKay), is about the complexities of becoming and unbecoming "sealed," of being coupled (or not) in an eternal way, which then provides the glue that will hold the whole family together. In this installment, the first plural wife, Barb (played by Jeanne Tripplehorn), reaches out to her estranged, LDS mother, Nancy (played by Ellen Burstyn), who has ceased to be in contact with her daughter once she became an apostate from the Mormon Church by following the principle of plural marriage. Upon reading in the newspaper that her liberal (for Mormons) mother, a widow, is about to be remarried to Ned (played by Philip Baker Hall), who has recently lost his wife, Barb yearns to be in contact. For Barb, who has become increasingly ambivalent about her choice to add wives to her marriage over the run of the show, her mother and sister are part of not only a family she misses and loves but also her once "normal" LDS lifestyle. So when Barb learns that her eldest son, Ben (played by Douglas Smith), has made a "testimony" for the principle of polygamy himself (and starts to date identical twin daughters whose main ambition is to marry the same man), Barb experiences a crisis, questioning whether her choices have doomed her children to the same kind of anxiety and ambivalence she feels in her own religion. She seeks out her mother, who agrees to take Ben away for the summer (where he can witness monogamous behavior modeled for him and thereby have, according to Barb, a choice in his marital destiny). She also convinces her mother to let her children (and eventually, reluctantly, her) attend the wedding reception.

Once Barb and her children arrive at the wedding, Barb's sister, Cindy (played by Judith Hoag), quickly explains an interesting marital dynamic circulating around the nuptials of Nancy and Ned. Ned, apparently, has made it a condition of their wedding that they be "sealed in the temple," a coveted benefit allowed to worthy LDS members who have satisfied the requirements of their faith: in a temple that has recommended them and granted them access, the ritual of sealing is performed, ensuring that their marriage will be indissoluble not only throughout life but, in the words of the ceremony, "for time and all eternity." Being "sealed" together is a fascinating concept, especially because it involves some difficulties that this episode economically emphasizes. The "heavenly father's" "new and everlasting covenant" of marriage uses sealing as a way to attain a strong spiritual and social foundation that will protect and guide the salvation of all the souls within the Mormon family that become attached to the initial couple. But this sealing also is thought of as a way to continue spiritually and physically in the afterlife. The specifically Mormon qualities of this concept have to do with the idea that this kind of family attachment will lead, if all goes well, to the celestial kingdom (as opposed to the lesser terrestrial or telestial kingdoms). As printed above, Doctrine and Covenant 132 states: "And if ye abide in my covenant, and commit no murder whereby to shed innocent blood, it shall be done unto them in all things whatsoever my servant hath put upon them, in time, and through all eternity; and shall be of full force when they are out of the world; and they shall pass by the angels, and the gods, which are set there, to their exaltation and glory in all things, as hath been sealed upon their heads, which glory shall be a fulness and a continuation of the seeds forever and ever." In other words, one can become a god in this heavenly realm, but only if one marries, and marries well. Moreover, in the earlier teachings of the Mormon Church (the current teachings of the fundamentalists) one should ideally also be married, be sealed, to multiple wives, making the family a family of multiple couples, bursting at its seals with its generous multiples.

So here's the problem with Ned *and* Nancy, and listen to how the people sound in the following descriptions (especially since the things we typically seal are *things* — letters, jars, safes, doors, etc.): if Nancy is to be sealed in the temple to Ned, she must be "unsealed" to Barb's father first. But because LDS is a patriarchal religious tradition, Ned is not required to be unsealed from his first wife, Vera, in order to be also sealed to Nancy. Ned's children are angry, both because Nancy is "liberal" and because, as Cindy puts it, "Ned's children don't want Ned to share Vera in the afterlife." So a polygamist quandary moves into the nonpolygamist's ever after: Should Ned be sealed to more than one wife forever? The fact that this predicament is even a real possibility speaks not only to a gray area in the Mormon Church's claim that it no longer practices polygamy but also to the fact that a whole foundational, heavenly cosmos that guides so much of the Mormon worldview, the possibility of "celestial marriage," is eternally braided into the principle of plural marriage. Doctrine and Covenant 132, because it's a holy understanding, cannot be expunged from the sacred texts of the Mormon faith; so polygamy is not only a big part of the Mormon past (an odd, embarrassing practice of the church's founding fathers) but also very much a part of the Mormon future — the afterlife, with countless souls, sealed, unsealed, and multiply sealed to various family members. To put this theological worldview (which mirrors a probate worldview) more succinctly: in order to have a future beyond death, you need a family committed to marriage. Or, if you have no family with an upright, righteous couple, you have no future.[33]

But the episode's writer, Eileen Myers, is only in passing critiquing the church and its possible hypocrisies around the principle of plural marriage. What is more important is the showcasing of the potential complications that one finds in the sealed eternities of these families trying to live like gods forever on the basis of their patriarchs' marriage practices. Eternal salvation has a dizzying array of configurations, much like the present world. So even when you marry into an eternal life after death by way of a faith like Mormonism, there is no guarantee that you will be resurrected in the celestial kingdom as you had hoped. *Big Love* does a remarkable job, I think, in pressing upon us that such deathly concerns are not the occasional musings of a religious people that has faith in an afterlife. There is such a bracing distress about one's salvation that the whole concept of an afterlife saturates the Mormon outlook (and ours the more we watch *Big Love*). The eternal is not just the desire of an isolated soul hoping to get to heaven: it's fundamentally a couple's desire, where the faithful are eager to have their beloved family members sealed to the couple, forever.

So when circumstances require that Barb leave her mother's wedding celebration, we're treated to a heart-wrenching moment in which a daughter who desperately loves her mother is ripped apart, literally unsealed, from her because of the divergent theological takes on how one is to live the historical revelations of the Mormon Church. As Barb stands on a threshold between her polygamous family (where she is the first, and thus most important, sister-wife) and her prepolygamous family (where she is just an offspring), she tearfully pleads for a relationship that could put aside the pressing concern about eternity that is keeping these two family members apart. Barb: "I don't know if I'll see you in the afterlife. If you'll be with Daddy, or Ned, or if I'll be with you, or Bill [her husband, played by Bill Paxton]. But I know, at the very least, I just want to see you in this life." The two then hug, regretfully, before Nancy refuses to console her daughter. Nancy: "This is your one, big test." Barb shakes her head; Nancy turns, and returns to the wedding that Barb can no longer attend. Barb stares after her mother, then slowly looks back at her large, waiting family, and this scene dissolves into the episode's last scene, where she returns to her marital bedroom with Bill. Nancy will not agree to Barb's proposal to be concerned only with their relationship in the current life. Emotional intensity and sincerity

Mother wonders if daughter will be with her for eternity, which requires the right kind of marriage. Screen capture from "Take Me as I Am," *Big Love* #2.11 (dir. Jim McKay), 2007.

aside, Nancy has been entrusted with a sacred, nearly legal duty. She has reminded Barb of her ultimate obligation a bit earlier: "You're my daughter! I'm responsible for your eternal salvation!" Her obligation, her love and responsibility for her daughter, must keep them separated, for "time and all eternity," because Barb's form of coupling is not what Nancy has deemed appropriate enough to do the miraculous work of stepping outside time and into that most celestial sphere of loving eternity.

This episode of *Big Love* certainly portrays a family's impasse between quasi-competing notions of the afterlife and eternity that forms of coupling offer in various strands of the Mormon faith. It also disturbs one into a sense of how marriage and family, polygamous or not, religious or not, are relationships inflected by an overwhelming sense of worry about "forever." Just look at Google's most popular website in 2008 for wedding vows, "My Wedding Vows." I chose the nondominational examples to give you a sense of eternity's essentialness:

NONDENOMINATIONAL WEDDING VOW, SAMPLE 1:

I _____, take thee _____, to be my wife/
   husband.
To have and to hold,
in sickness and in health,
for richer or for poorer,
and I promise my love to you forevermore.

NONDENOMINATIONAL WEDDING VOW, SAMPLE 2:

I _____, take you _____, to be my wife/husband.
To share the good times and hard times side by side.
I humbly give you my hand and my heart
as a sanctuary of warmth and peace,
and pledge my faith and love to you.
Just as this circle is without end, my love for you is eternal.
Just as it is made of incorruptible substance,
my commitment to you will never fail. With this ring,
   I thee wed.

NONDENOMINATIONAL WEDDING VOW, SAMPLE 3:

Before our friends and those so special to us here,
on this wonderful day of gladness and good fortune,
   I _____ take
you _____ as my wife/husband, in friendship and
   in love,
in strength and weakness,
to share the good times and misfortune,
in achievement and failure, to celebrate life with
   you forevermore.[34]

Here we have eternity, and we need to stop and explain why
marriage vows no longer hinge on "till death do us part." Perhaps because we have property to inherit and wills to write, death
in marriage seems to not be so final: instead, there is a trend to
want marriage (and its trail of family making) to stop time, to
conceptualize the relationship as a relationship outside time,

confirming one of Lauren Berlant's more provocative formulations about conventional couplehood: that people "aspire to dead identities," by which she means "dead" as "in the rhetorical sense designated by the phrase 'dead metaphor.' A metaphor is dead when, by repetition, the unlikeliness risked in the analogy the metaphor makes becomes so conventionalized as to no longer seem figural, no longer open to history: the leg of the table is the most famous."[35] Berlant's part of the table, perhaps her favorite part of Marx's table, no longer seems to be open to time, and all that time can mean. The metaphor of the table having legs has become so common, so conventional, and so required that we fail to see that leggy table as alive. Have marriage and love and family, as they are necessarily cast by probate quandaries, become as dead as a leg of a table?

Never ending might mean never living. Or no longer living. ("The standing now" [and forever] of the table leg?) If we agree with Arendt's notion of eternity as I explained it in the previous chapter, and if we match her insights with Berlant's understanding of couple as a figuration for a death that hopes to belie history, then another version of everlasting love begins to take conceptual shape: the wish for the experience of eternity is a curious form of hoping for a death that isolates, one in which time and language and experience stop, or at least stop meaning conventionally. And if we then relate this conception of eternity to the kind of fetishism that preoccupied Marx, we have a version of eternal love as a kind of death that leaves us lonely "outside the plurality of men [and other humans]" with our things. Perhaps we can then grasp another layer of the secret the commodity keeps: alienation (*Entfremdung*) might also be about separating ourselves from ourselves as we obsess about the death of those we most love, opening ourselves up to an existence only with things rather than people (or we're left with people who must be construed as things that will be attached to one another). If we're not alienated, then we're thought to have some sort of control over the productions, the fruits of our labor (and our loins), where those things will go after we die, and also ourselves.

But love, families, and the death that circumscribes those sig-nificant relationships, those "Thing[s] significant," give us a dead-ening option for life:[36] the grand choice of a partner/spouse/wife/husband, which is the precondition of your family, only further alienates you because it leaves you lonely, separated, at the precise moment that you've chosen to believe you won't be alone. The family, that set of relationships most often presumed to not be so marred by capitalism, the place that has historically been considered the private household (which, as Arendt's work on eternity is trying to show off to be no longer private — but more on this idea in the next chapter), is stranding us in some "standing now." It's helping us feel alienated at the precise mo-ment when we're told that we shouldn't feel such things. This is the story of standardization that capitalism needs.

So here's a great big mystery about the commodity of a couple that morphs into families (the wedding ring?), which is also a mystery about you (and how well you'll negotiate your family's couple's social relations now and "forevermore"): if the couple's contract is one that is supposed to be sealed for time and all eter-nity (and if the coula will become things that can be sealed and resurrected in a very physical way in the afterlife), and if this is the logic that supports succession even if there is no legal instrument in place, then we're stuck in an alienating condition, one wed (and dead) to the kinds of mystical, religious fetishism Marx fa-mously explicates. Part of what the "theological niceties" such as love and marriage are doing, then, is locking people into the kind of couple/familial connections that are as reified and as hard as wood. We learn to stand still with each other, "identities not live, or in play, but dead, frozen, fixed, or at rest."[37] People seal each other with a kiss, as well as with a will, in order to be together through emotions as much as through property (in this life and the next). And then they have eternity, and its obsessive, often re-ligious, demands to endure in the face of a terror we cannot sur-vive. From this angle, the transcendence of sensuousness — the transcendence of the material conditions of this world — is a set of relationships we can see, as if in the "social hieroglyphic[s]," in the wills, the labors, of our love (and the property and things those wills negotiate as we struggle with ways to stay connected after death).[38] The tragic part of Marx's mystical table that I always forget: this religious thing stands on its head, generating some "grotesque ideas," but it does not dance, it is not that something dead figuratively becomes alive: it is the grotesque ideas that become "far more wonderful than if it were to begin dancing of its own free will." It's a grotesque version of property's (and by proxy your) afterlife, one with no free will (and I want all sorts of puns to jump to mind right now).

The point I'm trying to make is that as we start to strip away our own wonderful and grotesque ideas about love, marriage, death, and wills, religion, and Marx, we also need to start thinking of marriage and family commitments as wills in and of themselves, pondering the implications of making the family a supernatural relation of terror, longing, loss, and arrest. The Last Will and Testament that we are always making when we are in families, when we say, "I do," is shot through with a deep connection between love and property that keeps us wishing we could survive our deaths. The will as an explicit instrument of law and the probate court makes up for wills that might not be there, and this legal realm keeps describing, securing, transforming, and codifying the terms of the couple by way of the property of the person who will transcend the limits of her or his body, her or his "sensuousness," which means her or his body, but also the very tactile relationships she or he has with people, places, and things. The will is like a revelation: we're hoping that even when we become as dead as a table, there will still be a way to make our wills extend indefinitely into some eternal future. *Or* at least we're made to feel that our loves deserve this kind of commodity fetishism and that the couple, snaking its deadly way through families, is the only relation that gives us something religious, something we might even call "impossible," something like cheating death.

The lingering, ghostly question that haunts all of this book's pages: Is this cheating of the self necessary? By way of an answer, we have to seek protection from the probated couple. That means we have to seek shelter, go into a house, or at least underground, and hide while we strip away the dead wood of the deadening Two. Our carpenters (or architects): Ralph Ellison and Herman Melville. In our ears, a mantra of more words from Emily Dickinson: "Now — when I read — I read not — / For interrupting Tears — / Obliterate the Etchings / Too Costly for Repairs."

3

The Shelter of Singles

How often have I lain beneath rain on a strange roof,
thinking of home.
> WILLIAM FAULKNER, *As I Lay Dying*

Every ten meters or so along the seawall Geryon
could see small twined couples.
They looked like dolls.
> ANNE CARSON, *Autobiography of Red*

Home

This chapter is about two men, from two canonical pieces of
prose, from two centuries, who aren't lovers. Not with each other.
Not with anyone. They are a couple of men who won't couple. It's
precisely this rejection that stabs at the heart of what a single person can say to the couples of this world and the next: couples that
refuse, or are too fearful, to let a single person just be. In front of
us, we'll soon have Herman Melville's notoriously and delight-
fully enigmatic Bartleby. But first we'll wonder about Ralph Ellison's narrator-protagonist from his masterpiece, *Invisible Man*.
I use these two characters, after some twists and turns in the last
two chapters, to understand and propose what a single person
could give the world. On the remaining pages of this book, I will
theorize the "single," which requires stripping away those lonely
and impossible emotions that couples' culture displaces onto the
single who has no right to dwell happily as a single. Couples, as
we've seen in the past two chapters, clutter the picture, so we
need some *one* to clean some house.

Dwellings and architecture are important in this argument because protection and shelter from the awful affective forces I've
described in the previous two chapters are necessary, for every*one*.
Couples give singles the loneliness and impossibilities they feel as

they manage the paradoxically brittle and strong eternities they're constructing for themselves. So in this chapter we'll seek refuge from the storm of the couple form (even if you absolutely love your couple form, even if you credit it with all your happiness in the world). And we'll seek shelter in a strange place where people can be alone, can be single. And by *single* I mean outside partnering by virtue of luck, ban, or loss. Not singular, but single. Single, even if it's for a few moments out of a busy day being a spouse.

An ominous word of caution, a prophecy: these theoretical waters are treacherous. To be single in a world that won't permit you to be single makes being single an impossible thing to know with any precision. To try and know the single requires that we navigate something larger than what we're comfortable knowing. But there's greatness on the horizon: something epic. Remember, the point of Odysseus's adventures was not merely the return to his faithful Penelope, who was busy resisting all the other couples she could become. The point was the delay, the adventures that made Odysseus heroic — his striving to be immortal.[1] Greatness in many forms, and not just a marriage, is what we're after. And such grandeur is what the single can point us toward.

Couplism

So what can a single person say to a world that doesn't want anyone, ever, to be single? A world that can't simply even hear the single's voice? Before we ask Bartleby, we'll ask the invisible narrator from Ralph Ellison's *Invisible Man*. The novel is about an unnamed narrator, a bright, promising black man who encounters a series of misfortunes as he tries to come of age in a very segregated and racist mid-twentieth-century America. We follow him as he "wins" a scholarship to an all-black college in the American South; we are dismayed by his unfair expulsion; and we watch a series of catastrophes befall him as he tries to make it in New York, only to be undermined by political, cultural, and emotional forces that are imbued with the pathological destructiveness of invidious and hierarchical race distinctions between black and white. Sick of such tragedy and violence, the narrator goes underground, where he attempts to understand not only his place in the world but also what that world might mean. "Over and over again I've gone up above to seek it [cultural understanding] out," confesses the narrator. "For, like almost everyone else in our country, I started out with my share of optimism. I believed in hard work and progress and action, but now, after first being 'for' society and then 'against' it, I assign myself no rank or any limit, and such an attitude is very much against the trend of the times. But my world has become one of infinite possibilities."[2] After hundreds of pages of text about numerous, impossible, and racist situations, it's difficult to get a grasp of what kind of possibilities and insights this man has in mind. The narrator assures us that the phrase "infinite possibilities" is still "a good phrase and a good view of life, and a man shouldn't accept any other." The only concrete thing we have in these infinities is an odd address, underneath the concrete: "that much I've learned underground." The narrator, riffing off Dostoevsky's version of the philosophical sickness of the existential man underground, locates his shelter as a vantage point from which to see the good view of life: "Until some gang succeeds in putting the world in a strait jacket, its definition is possibility. Step outside the narrow borders of what men call reality and you step into chaos . . . or imagination. That too I've learned in the cellar, and not by deadening my sense of perception; I'm invisible, not blind" (576).

Although he learns something key about senses and perceptions, we're not permitted to share in his certainty. Yes, the hole is serving as a refuge from action, as a place to stop and think, but otherwise we're not sure what it is about this hole that gives him such a renewed sense of optimism, especially after his travels from being "for" and then "against" society. We're not even entirely sure what exactly he's running from. That's open to interpretation. But if society is increasingly thought of as the terrain of couples, a new series of insights are on the horizon.

It might escape one's sustained attention, as it did mine for many years, that there is no significant love plot for the narrator in the novel. He has no real romantic prospects for becoming part of a couple. But I want to note three minor moments of overt sexuality that envelop the narrator; each episode tropes on the encounter between the whiteness of the women and the blackness of the narrator. First, there's the burlesque performer very early in the novel: "The hair was yellow like a circus kewpie doll, the face heavily powdered and rouged, as though to form an abstract mask, the eyes hollow and smeared a cool blue, the color of a baboon's butt" (19). This hyperbolically white doll performs a dance that is quickly followed by a fighting match staged by white businessmen — a match between the aroused and ashamed young black men, who are blindfolded after having watched the striptease and who've been scared and lured into beating each other for fake money. Much later in the novel, the narrator sleeps with a woman who was interested in one of the narrator's speeches on "the Woman Question." She "glows as though consciously acting a symbolic role of life and feminine fertility" (409) and lures him to her bed by an offer to discuss ideology. Although he receives a retroactive approval from the woman's husband, the evening is one of confusing, guilt-ridden visions, so much so that the whole scene cannot be viewed with directness or precision: "I nodded, seeing her turn without a word and go toward a vanity with a larger oval mirror, taking up an ivory telephone. And in the mirrored instant I saw myself standing between her eager form and a huge white bed, myself caught in a guilty stance, my face taut, tie dangling; and behind the bed another mirror which now like a surge of the sea tossed our images back and forth, back and forth, furiously multiplying the time and place and the circumstance" (416). If we were to stop only here, it would be easy to think that the small episodes of sexuality in the novel are present only to illustrate yet another dimension of a world terribly refracted through racist visions that cannot offer helpful advice or insight on how to improve, let alone endure, so much bad faith and pathology. But near the very end of the novel, in one of the most important chapters that precedes the novel's race-riot crescendo, we dwell with Sybil.

Picture the scene one "hot dry August night" (516): disillusioned by an interracial organization that is only nominally committed to race and class struggle — the Brotherhood — our narrator has chosen to find out more information about the Brotherhood's secret objectives by seducing one of the white wives of the organization's leaders. The seduction has begun the night before, and because this married woman "was very lonely," the seduction "went very smoothly" (516). But even though his apartment promises a continuation of the smoothness of seduction — "I had neither itch nor etchings, but there was a vase of Chinese lilies in the living room, and another of American Beauty roses on a table near the bed; and I had put a supply of wine, whiskey, and liqueur, extra ice cubes, and assortments of fruit, cheese, nuts, candy and other delicacies from the Vendome" (516) — the date is a disaster. Not only does the narrator learn nothing about the Brotherhood, but he also has to endure a rapid descent into a drunken night of erotic role playing that involves an interracial rape fantasy that then transforms into something like a standard romance, where each participant clicks easily into the language and gestures of coupledom, underscoring the novel's damning assessment of love, sex, and romance. "'But I need it,'" pleads Sybil, "uncrossing her thighs and sitting up eagerly. 'You can do it, it'll be easy for *you*, beautiful. Threaten to kill me if I don't give in. You know, talk rough to me, beautiful'" (518). Of course, the racist implications are hard for the narrator to swallow, even as he tries to seduce. Yet the racist dimensions are wrapped up in euphemism, in silly *and* offensive figuration; something about Sybil's "prim" (517) delivery keeps the narrator (and the reader) engaged in her "modest proposal" (517). That proposal, inspired by a "friend's" story of her own experience, seems to define the mutually implicated symbolics of race and dangerous sexuality — what we could call "raciness." Outrages, rough talk, even racist talk, are stuffed into a destructive language of seduction, which trills around the terrible things one can say to another person after they've fallen into bed together: "'A really filthy name,' she said. 'Oh, he was a brute, with white teeth, what they call a 'buck.' And he said, 'Bitch, drop your drawers,' and then he did it. She's such a lovely girl, too, really delicate with a complexion like strawberries and cream. You can't imagine *anyone* calling her a name like that'" (518).

Obviously this is all Sybil can imagine, and the story helps her ruminate on the potentials of the exhilarating feeling — the threat of violence, death, and degradation — that she wants to "*really* feel" (519), with content that is not her own, and with a dangerous desire that begins to tell the story of intimacy that she wants to share immediately with the narrator. This kind of content is introduced to her seducer in a "whisper," and its communication "suddenly . . . drain[s] the starch" out of him (517). Yet he can't tear himself away — important work is happening here on this first night of coupling. Again, the scene of seduction has a dramatic racial figuration (like the previous sexual encounter of the narrator seeing himself in those two mirrors that "tossed our images back and forth, back and forth, furiously multiplying" whenever a black man must confront a white woman's bed): "'Lie back and let me look at you against that white sheet. You're beautiful, I've always thought so. Like warm ebony against pure snow — see what you make me do, you make me talk poetry. 'Warm ebony against pure snow,' isn't that poetic?'" (520).

When Sybil uses the word *against,* it's a crucial preposition because the warmth of the ebony still is *against* the "pure snow." As prepositions do, they locate our actions and us. Prepositions give us a kind of grammatical geography, which here matters not only because ebony is put into a spatial relation with "pure snow" but because the spatial relation is one of pure conflict. "Against" is the talk of Sybil's violent "poetry," which is a word Sybil quotes twice, unveiling what the rape fantasy condenses: warmth and beauty are brought into the world of this white sheet, brought into the world by a very localized antagonism whose content may be racial, and/or racist, but whose form is fundamentally about two who are divided, segregated, from one another. In one of his critical essays, Ellison writes: "Perhaps the most insidious and least understood form of segregation is that of the word. And by this I mean the word in all its complex formulations, from the proverb to the novel and stage play, the word with all its subtle power to suggest and foreshadow overt action while magically disguising the moral consequences of that action and providing it with symbolic and psychological justification. For if the word has the potency to revive and make us free, it has also the power to blind, imprison, and destroy."[3] Ellison is playing with the segregatedness of form in his novel, and it's helpful to think of Sybil's poetry as poetry of segregation's seduction — lyrical words that are always "against." Sybil confesses that she talks this kind of poetry because she "feel[s] so free" (520) with the narrator, and his response to this fantasy, this expression of poetry that makes awful things "beautiful," gets the reaction she desperately craves: an outraged look from her partner that deepens the desire for segregation's violence: "'That's it,' she said tightly. 'Look at me like that; just like you want to tear me apart. I love for you to look at me like that!'" (520).

Lest you dismiss Sybil's poetic desire as perversion, or something malignant in her character, I want to remind you, once again, about the ancient stories that, much like the narrator, might make us stay and linger with Sybil. It's not without all good reason that Hortense J. Spillers argues that Ellison's novel is very much a myth-making enterprise, which explains why she thinks it's "one of the most influential American novels of the twentieth century."[4] Most obviously Sybil's name alludes to those classical Sibyls, those prophetesses from the Greek and Roman world who spoke of the future, who spoke hard truths. Think of Virgil's famous Cumaean Sibyl from the sixth book of the *Aeneid*, who was at the entry to hell (Avernus), serving as Aeneas's guide to the underworld; Virgil's Sibyl points the way to an eternity among the dead. No wonder that the night of this scene is one when the gates of hell open up, when racial tensions uptown, in Harlem, swell into a terrible riot that quite literally leads the new couple into the underworld of simmering racist conflict. But more explicitly, Ellison offers an important architectural detail when he has the narrator reflect on the quality and kind of affection Sybil suddenly has for the narrator as they extract themselves from his apartment:

We tottered before an ancient-looking building, its windows dark. Huge Greek medallions showed in spots of light upon its façade, above a dark labyrinthine pattern in the stone, and

I propped her against the stoop with its carved stone monster. She leaned there, her hair wild, looking at me in the street light, smiling. Her face kept swinging to one side, her right eye desperately closed.

"Sure, boo'ful, sure," she said.

"I'll be right back," I said, backing away.

"Boo'ful," she called, "*my* boo'ful."

Hear the true affection, I thought, of the adoration of the Boogie Bear, moving away. Was she calling me beautiful or boogieful, beautiful or sublime . . . What did either mean? I am invisible . . . (529)

I want to put aside, initially, the permanent question about the nature of the sublime here (whether it's beautiful) and instead to focus on the propping up of Sybil against the ancient stoop (with the stone-carved monster) in order to interpret the description of her own façade — her face "swinging to one side, her right eye desperately closed" — as set against the segregated play of light and dark on the building, a description that offers sage statements about desire, and more importantly, the "love" Sybil so quickly and alarmingly has for the narrator. The desperation of having only one eye open, with her face swinging to one side, has come from her relations with the narrator. She feels rent in two, separated: her one-eyed-ness, her one-sidedness, casts oneness as a problem of stability. The ancient building where she calls out to her "boo'ful" love serves as a crutch, much like her feelings for the narrator that have crippled her by tearing her apart: "Look at me like that; just like you want to tear me apart. I love for you to look at me like that!" Indeed.

Once again, we have that hopefully too familiar Aristophanic kind of logic creeping in: love tears you apart, punishing you by ripping you in two. To cast Aristophanes' love using the terms of the novel: love, here as elsewhere, makes one fall in love with one's own segregation. The couples in this story don't tend to stay together, or don't get together, or don't really belong together, but they are placed together, as always apart — all the time *against*. In no time, really, they act like a couple that conforms by confronting one another. Listen to Sybil's pleas to repeat the erotic game playing (that the narrator lies he actually performed while Sybil was passed out, drunk):

> "Boo'ful," she said, blowing the word, "will you do it again sometimes?"
>
> I stepped away and looked at her. "What?"
>
> "Please, pretty boo'ful, please," she said with a wobbly smile.
>
> I began to laugh. "Sure," I said, "sure . . ."
>
> "When, boo'ful, when?"
>
> "Any time," I said. "How about every Thursday at nine?"
>
> "Oooooh, boo'ful," she said, giving me an old-fashioned hug. "I've never seen anyone like you." (525)

The rape fantasy quite effortlessly (perhaps because it doesn't have to be performed) transforms into a fantasy of sustained, if not standard, intimacy, with the promise of regular visits — every Thursday at nine. Sybil, with her old-fashioned hug, lapses into the familiar kind of romantic couple-cliché that is always busy finding uniqueness in the banality of two people getting close: "I've never seen anyone like you." Her sentiments are matched, coupled, just a few pages later by the narrator's own inappropriate aspirations: "I stared down the quiet street, feeling her stumbling beside me, humming a little tune; something fresh, naïve and carefree. Sybil, my too-late-too-early love . . . Ah! My throat throbbed. The heat of the street clung close" (528, ellipsis in original).

As we slide from racist rape fantasy into heavy romantic cliché, the doubles of couples feel like the doubles of race because Ellison thinks of couples as figures of segregation, of black and white that can't meet except in a violent confrontation with how they'll always be divided even as they attempt to unite. The way the narrator asks about what they're doing together tellingly alludes to D. W. Griffith's iconic pro-Klan film: "'What's happening here . . . a new birth of a nation?'" (522). Thus the violence of love, of being forced to be torn apart, then thrust back together, becomes even more apparent once the racist idiom is used to mediate the fantasies circulating between this new couple. And so, in this novel, the problems of racial conflict also articulate (among many other things) the problems of couples' conflict. One of the reasons I think Ellison uses the segregatedness of race in his tracking of failed love plots is that he wants to increase the scale of a critique of coupledom that his invisible single man provides. Segregation, with its hostile, highly spectacular injustices, offers a sense of physical separation that's always being torn down as people strain and hurt and hit their way into being closer; race, and more specifically the antagonism of race (racism), has a large sweep.

What this novel then prompts in me is a desire to think about race — an overdetermined analytic if there ever was one — as a figuration of two, which stands in for the multitudes that can't yet be, perhaps ever be, united. Read this passage carefully: "Between me and the other world there is ever an unasked question: unasked by some through feelings of delicacy; by others through the difficulty of rightly framing it. All, nevertheless, flutter round it. They approach me in a half-hesitant sort of way, eye me curiously or compassionately, and then, instead of saying directly, How does it feel to be a problem? they say, I know an excellent . . . man in town . . . At these I smile, or am interested, or reduce the boiling to a simmer, as the occasion might require. To the real question, How does it feel to be a problem? I answer seldom a word."[5] These words introduce W. E. B. Du Bois's canonical text on the African American condition in the United States, post-slavery but pre–civil rights. The minute I remind or reveal as much to you, a series of habitual assumptions about double consciousness, about life "born with a veil, and gifted with second-sight in this American world" (615), might obscure some of the ideas that also "flutter round" Du Bois's second-sight insight but are rendered mute by commonsensical assumptions about what race might mean. The giants of African American studies, Robert Stepto, Henry Louis Gates Jr., and Houston Baker (among many, many others), rightly see double consciousness as being at the heart of African American literary and critical production.[6] And so many have followed suit, faithfully reading the words that Du

Bois offered as his introduction to Black Folks' souls, finding and refining extraordinary and productive value in this concept of doubleness — that special kind of insight (and mistaken identity) that comes from knowing dominant *and* minority perspectives. These critiques can't help but be on the right track: they read Du Bois to the letter, so much so that race starts to take on the representational burden of the problem of doubles. Or to be more precise: race critique has become saturated with two-ness, so much so that race can almost be thought of as a problem of division that must always suggest Two (for instance, Black vs. White; North vs. South; Me vs. You — the House Divided).

Du Bois must shoulder the blame. Now read this fuller passage:

> After the Egyptian and the Indian, the Greek and the Roman, the Teuton and Mongolian, the Negro is a sort of seventh son born with a veil, and gifted with second-sight in this American world, — a world which yields him no true self-consciousness, but only lets him see himself through the revelation of the other world. It is a peculiar sensation, this double-consciousness, this sense of always looking through the eyes of others, of measuring one's soul by the tape of a world that looks on in amused contempt and pity. One ever feels his two-ness, — an American, a Negro; two souls, two thoughts, two unreconciled strivings; two warring ideals in one dark body, whose dogged strength alone keeps it from being torn asunder. (615)

Even though the Negro is the seventh son after a series of three couples, he is subject to a "peculiar sensation," the feeling of "his two-ness," and the ready-made divisions of the world so categorized in such an orderly, elegant manner: souls, thoughts, strivings, and ideals all come in twos. In a way, Du Bois partially answers his own question, "How does it feel to be a problem?," with a rhetorical flourish that quickly becomes fixation: it feels like two.

What I want to ask of you, then, is to think about the two-ness of race in Ellison's novel as a problem not of "singularity" (which can be quickly rendered as a collectivity of many, diverse strands) but of being "single" in the state-sanctioned couples' world that admires and enforces division, divisiveness, as the way we should fundamentally associate. Thinking of the "Negro" narrator as a *singular rather than single* figure of collective hope through which we'll overcome division through our attempts at unity doesn't quite fit the dynamic presented in the novel. Instead of the narrator serving as a synecdoche of the part of the whole that makes everything feel like two, let's think of the narrator as just a single part, freed of some grand representational burden of the multitudes' conforming unity disguised as coupledom. Rather than be a part, he's apart. If such unity is that which has been made predictably impossible by the two-ness of race, it is helpful to confront that two-ness by thinking about two-ness's most obvious antagonist: one-ness. Or, to put this battle in the terms of romantic coupledom that Ellison's novel surprisingly utilizes to great effect: I want to cast the conflict of race as a very familiar conflict: the couple versus the single, as well as, not so accidentally, the many versus the one, not to mention the public versus the private. Read this line from Du Bois again, but think of a grandmother, or overly concerned friend, asking the narrator (or you) about his love life: "They approach me in a half-hesitant sort of way, eye me curiously or compassionately, and then, instead of saying directly, How does it feel to be a problem? they say, I know an excellent . . . man in town . . . At these I smile, or am interested, or reduce the boiling to a simmer, as the occasion might require."

So why does Ellison want race to feel like a combat between two people, a couple, who, in turn, try to snare the single characters in its contagious conflict? Etienne Balibar offers some help. By refusing to see racism as just a particularizing force that locates people precisely in a subordinated, preassigned role that is pitted against a universal idea of humanity, Balibar argues for a much larger point, and as if he's taking up the spirit of Ellison's curious figurations about what race means, he clearly understands something that Spillers knows and writes about Ellison's novel. Spillers argues, "Frustrating the tendency to perceive a coterminous relationship between the symbolic boundaries of black and the physical, genetic manifestation named black, *Invisible Man* recalls *Moby-Dick* that stands Manichean orientation on its head."[7] To be sure, Balibar does not mention *Invisible Man*, but he similarly stands on its head the concept of racism, not least because he's calling racism a form of universalism, seeing in racism not just invidious and hierarchically arranged distinctions among groups of people. Much like Ellison, he is not content to rest with knowledge about local differences that are often offered as the more valuable, experiential knowledge that puts analytical pressure on appeals for larger, universal analyses. Racism has a capacious grasp; it's about where, who, and why you belong. "The more we become involved in discussions and militancy on the racist issue," writes Balibar,

> the more we are struck by the fact that racism embodies a very insistent *desire for knowledge*. It is not only a way of legitimating privileges or disqualifying competitors or continuing old traditions or reacting to situations of violence, it is a way of asking questions about *who* you are in a certain social world, *why* there are some compulsory places in the world to which you must adapt yourself, imposing upon yourself a certain *univocal* identity (something much more compelling than a *role*); and it is a way of asking and answering questions about *why* we are violent, why we find ourselves unable to resist the compulsion of violence going beyond the "rational" necessities of competition and social conflict.[8]

He doesn't make the connection as explicit as I'd like here: the desire to know, as we know, is often conflated with the desire for sexual knowledge. But biblical knowledge aside, that desire has a larger calling card if it's a kind of racism, and that kind of racism is, in Ellison, actually *couplism*.

So Ellison has racial conflict help sweep the couple into a larger, more capacious conceptual space. The racial conflict helps us picture our place, as couples, in the world. "I've lived a public life and attempted to function under the assumption that the world was solid and all the relationships therein," reveals the narrator. "Now I only know men are different and that all life is divided and that only in division is there true health. Hence again I have stayed in my hole, because up there's an increasing passion to make men conform to a pattern" (576). As we surely expect, the passion for the pattern we keep noticing is like the horrifying funhouse of race: "I have been surrounded by mirrors of hard, distorting glass" (3). Like the distorting mirrors, the narrator is quick to obscure or bend his insights. In the next paragraph, he gives us a snide sermon that makes even the consideration of race differences an impossible project because it's an enormous project — "Whence all this passion toward conformity anyway? — diversity is the word" (577). It sounds here as if he'll endorse, just like so many thinkers of the questions that preoccupy him, a "celebration of difference," a celebration of multiplicity, of multitudes, as the antidote to the "passion toward conformity." But he doesn't. Instead, he undercuts this celebration:

> Let man keep his many parts and you'll have no tyrant states. Why, if they follow this conformity business they'll end up by forcing me, an invisible man, to become white, which is not a color but the lack of one. Must I strive toward colorlessness? But seriously, and without snobbery, think of what the world would lose if that should happen. America is woven of many strands; I would recognize them and let it so remain. It's "winner take nothing" that is the great truth of our country or of any country. Life is to be lived, not controlled; and humanity is won by continuing to play in face of certain defeat. Our fate is to become one, and yet many — This is not prophecy, but description. Thus one of the greatest jokes in the world is the spectacle of the whites busy escaping blackness and becoming blacker every day, and the blacks striving toward whiteness, becoming quite dull and gray. None of us seems to know who he is or where he's going. (577)

The story of "infinite possibilities" that the narrator has come to understand in his hole is the story of "many strands" of America, unified. But we must be careful. "One, and yet many,"

America and its "multitudes," as Antonio Negri and Michael Hardt might phrase it, are capable of "an excess of value with respect to every form of right and law," but not necessarily in a good way. Negri and Hardt write:

> When the multitude works, it produces autonomously and reproduces the entire world of life. Producing and reproducing autonomously mean constructing a new ontological reality. In effect, by working the multitude produces itself as a singularity. It is a singularity that establishes a new place in the non-place of Empire, a singularity that is a reality produced by cooperation, represented by linguistic community and developed by the movements of hybridization. The multitude affirms its singularity by inverting the ideological illusion that all humans on the global surfaces of the world market are interchangeable. Standing the ideology of the market on its feet, the multitude promotes through its labor the biopolitical singularization of groups and sets of humanity, across each and every node of global interchange.[9]

Exuberant ideas here, flowing as if Gilles Deleuze and Félix Guattari had energetically joined with the authors in writing them, casting a set of radical reflections as a rhizome of utopian hope, for the rhizome, as Deleuze and Guattari described it, "is alliance, uniquely alliance."[10] But these theorists can't help too much with our reading of Ellison because what they articulate can't access the narrator's complicated presentation of the hope for the one-as-many. The narrator doesn't launch off on a romantic line of flight, skipping along a thousand plateaus of singular collectivities that revalue humans because they're not really required to become fungible in the "conforming pattern" of the marketplace. If anything, the narrator's experiences contradict the potentials and possibilities of alliance, especially alliances that seek racial and economic harmony. The novel's Brotherhood, like the novel's Black University supported by whites, doesn't inspire revolutions — just destruction: women, children, and men being ripped out of homes, expelled from college, and pushed out onto streets full of riots, loveless. What one should notice is that the narrator's hope for the multitude *qua* singularity is circumscribed by a tone that undercuts his sincerity: we have the insight of "becoming one, yet many" wedged between "But seriously" and "one of the greatest jokes in the world." We're not really offered a utopian vision of radical transformation of racial and economic harmony — "This is not prophecy, but description." The most salient details we have in this description are found within the novel's relentless scenes of confrontation with the multitudes. More precisely, we have figurations of the many pictured not as one but as two. We learn to understand the violent force of the multitudes by way of the couple — a couple that feels like a massive conflict of black against white, that seduces the whole world into joining the tiny battle between two.

Gimme Shelter

The bedroom of Ellison's narrator is the real location of the problem I want to consider now, especially as we move, at the novel's end, from that hot apartment into a hole. Thought to be most private, the bedroom — usually a "master bedroom" (with an ensuite if you're lucky and affluent) — is couples territory, which disguises its very public reach. The famous 1965 *Griswold v. Connecticut* Supreme Court ruling on the legalization of birth control attempts to define the precarious right of privacy not explicitly articulated in the U.S. Constitution. Its gushing about the intimacy and sanctity of the marital bedroom (which, now after *Lawrence v. Texas*, I think could be any couple's bedroom) feels almost as unrecognizable as it's disingenuous:

> Would we allow the police to search the sacred precincts of marital bedrooms for telltale signs of the use of contraceptives? The very idea is repulsive to the notions of privacy surrounding the marriage relationship.
>
> We deal with a right of privacy older than the Bill of Rights — older than our political parties, older than our school system. Marriage is a coming together for better or

for worse, hopefully enduring, and intimate to the degree of being sacred. It is an association that promotes a way of life, not causes; a harmony in living, not political faiths; a bilateral loyalty, not commercial or social projects. Yet it is an association for as noble a purpose as any involved in our prior decisions.[11]

Here's some convoluted logic we could pull out of these platitudes: the bedroom is the most private zone, yet more supreme than any law, so much so that it can hover celestially above the law, which means it's not really private, just in control. Ellison's novel, *avant la lettre*, serves as a kind of hyperbolic eye-roll at the ridiculousness of such trite and incoherent sentimentality. Instead of the harmony, intimacy, and nobility we find in the Griswold bedroom, we encounter only conflict in the narrator's. That conflict, moreover, tries to expose the exposures to the world that the private bedroom claims it avoids (yet mysteriously supersedes and directs). And as Ellison casts couples' love as race conflict, as antagonistic feeling that fuels that "increasing passion to make men conform to a pattern," he makes an argument about how the grand sweep of the couple's world has helped obliterate the small, secret places where we actually might resist these large forces of ontology, culture, violence, and belonging, while maintaining the erroneous conception that the privacy of those places remains intact. If you're in your bedroom, you're not alone; you have the weight of racism, brought by your relationship with another one, making you into a deadly grouping of two. The passion for conformity, then, is a passion for antagonism that helps erode the separations we only think we can overcome with love. The totalitarian logic of love, at least in its Platonic form, produces the sensation of relief when actually it erodes the privacy and protection one so desperately craves when one is held in a special someone's arms.

So at stake in this novel about a man hiding in a hole is a nagging question about privacy, and whether a single man (or woman) can achieve privacy. Such a concern is especially urgent because privacy seems to be mediated by various notions of privacy that offer no privacy at all. In addition to *Griswold*, I want to mention that two of the biggest Supreme Court rulings on privacy (so far) in the United States in the last thirty years, *Bowers v. Hardwick* and *Lawrence v. Texas*, were initiated by shady intrusions into bedrooms where two same-sex male couples copulated, with the interracial makeup of the latter couple being a suspicious element of the *Lawrence v. Texas* rationale.[12] The bedroom, we learn again and again, is where you "birth the nation," in the most standard, predictable ways.

"Privacy," according to Lauren Berlant, "is the Oz of America."[13] It's a utopian no-space that we desperately want to travel to, "a safe space" where we're not ravaged by the state, the imperatives of the public, and the violence and force of history — a history viscerally captured by the race plot. But rarely do we get to Oz, and if we approximate it, or dream about it, the lesson we're forced to learn is maddeningly repetitive: there's "no place like home." Following on the heels of volume 1 of Foucault's *History of Sexuality*, Leo Bersani years ago gave us our recent version of sex's "repressive hypothesis": "Our culture tells us to think of sex as the ultimate privacy, as the intimate knowledge of the other on which the familial cell is built. Enjoy the rapture that will never be made public, that will also (though it is not said) keep you safely, docilely out of the public realm, that will make you content to allow others to make history while you perfect the oval of a merely copulative or familial intimacy."[14] But our culture, as Berlant and Bersani know, is wrong, or at least lying: we think we're private when we're being intimate; we think we're in Oz, no place like home, but the "rapture" of the couple most certainly will appear in public, and a public that is in terrible disarray. As most of us surely understand on some frequency, you're never alone; you're never private when you're in a couple. In fact, you're exposed, out in public, without shelter.

So Ellison prompts us from the beginning of his novel to be very aware about the status, the character of the hole in which he hides, and whether it can offer protection that the narrator's bedroom (where he engages Sybil) cannot. The narrator nods to a history he doesn't want repeated when he reveals the age of the hole in which he now hibernates: "Now aware of my invisibility, I live rent-free in a building rented strictly to whites, in a section of the basement that was shut off and forgotten during the nineteenth century" (5-6). I like to think of this forgotten basement, one built during the era of Melville's Bartleby, in the context of what Walter Benjamin says about the emergence of the garish, accumulating rooms of the emerging "private individual" under the reign of the nineteenth-century French sovereign Louis-Philippe. In his 1939 version of "Paris, the Capital of the Nineteenth Century," we find this formulation: "For the private individual places of dwelling are for the first time opposed to places of work. . . . The private individual, who in the office has to deal with realities, needs the domestic interior to sustain him in his illusions" (19). This process of splitting the space between office and home creates a boundary that permits the home to then be a place of forgetting, thereby creating a divisiveness between the two spaces where individuals divide their time:

> The interior is the asylum where art takes refuge. The collector proves to be the true resident of the interior. He makes his concern the idealization of objects. To him falls the Sisyphean task of divesting things of their commodity character by taking possession of them. But he can bestow on them only connoisseur value, rather than use value. The collector delights in evoking a world that is not just distant and long gone but also better — a world in which, to be sure, human beings are no better provided with what they need than in the real world, but in which things are freed from the drudgery of being useful.[15]

Sisyphean because the private individual can't complete the task of stripping objects of their use value. Sisyphean because, as Benjamin subtly indicates, the divisions between the private and the public are forced in their futility if *escape* from the forces of the world is thought possible. The problem with the illusion is the misvaluation of the power of the small interior. The stripping of objects from the "drudgery of being useful" can't be successful;

even though, as Benjamin asserts, "the bourgeois has shown a tendency to compensate for the absence of any trace of private life in the big city," it does so by leaving traces "in the four walls of his apartment." The "liquidation of the interior" was swiftly disposed of "during the last years of the nineteenth century, in the work of the Jugendstil, but it had been coming for a long time."[16] What the century sets up, then, is, in the words of Benjamin, a home, a kind of muddled privacy, which develops as a "plastic expression of personality," one with dire consequences: "The attempt by the individual to vie with technology by relying on his inner flights leads to his downfall: the architect Solness [from Ibsen's *The Master Builder*] kills himself by plunging from his tower."[17]

A point to consider is what happens to the concept of the individual as she or he starts to collect things in those private spaces — those living rooms, usually occupied by another object collected: a partner, an Other. For one thing: the private individual, in that private room, has a tendency to become smitten with the sensation that she or he has shrunk the world from the large, abstract space it tends to be into a kind of manageability (much as Freud manages the oceanic feeling through the couple form in *Civilization and Its Discontents*). The inner flight that's posed to collect the world by virtue of collecting a relationship takes on the representational burden of the world; it makes us all too *(two?)* local in the place where we're bringing the whole world inside, containing and bounding its possibilities — with trinkets. It's an extraordinary coincidence that Benjamin festoons a quote from Virgil about Sybil's home address atop a subsection on the image of women in Baudelaire from an earlier version (1935) of the "Paris" essay where we learn about the private individual: "Easy the way that leads into Avernus [hell]."[18]

In *Invisible Man*, we see this inner flight not in the invisible man's escape to his hole but in his encounter with Sybil — in that hot, hell-like apartment (Avernus) where he has arranged, so easily, an encounter. Here Sybil finds odd comfort in immediately making her "Boo'ful" narrator into a kind of controllable object by virtue of a fantasy of mixed-race rape *and* domesticity that's supposed to snap her out of her already-collected, but boring, relationship with her husband, who has already been shrunken and belittled by his nickname, "Georgie." This exciting and violent drama of the bedroom has been circumscribed and scripted from the beginning, so much so that one too many drinks and a set of drunken lies allow the narrator to pretend that he has fulfilled his role properly. What seems important is the role the narrator is actually supposed to fill: scale down the emptiness that surrounds his and Sybil's life. Here's the exchange, occurring just moments before they first fall asleep together. Notice how the scale of small things that they can hold, literally, manages the large, sweeping feelings of terrible disquiet that storm in from the outside. Think about the language that filters everything into smaller vessels: wine glasses, arms. Take in how the grand notions of action and responsibility are smothered in the gestures of pouring drinks, drinking, and embracing:

> I looked at her out of a deep emptiness and refilled her glass and mine. What had I done to her, allowed her to do? Had all of it filtered down to me? My action . . . my — the painful word formed as disconnectedly as her wobbly smile — my *responsibility*? All of it? I'm invisible. "Here," I said, "drink."
> "You too, boo'ful," she said.
> "Yes," I said. She moved into my arms. (525-26)

Wine and wobbly smiles fill the void, the emptiness. The small world, responsibility cast as a "painful word," mutual drinks, uneven expectations are what fill the couple up rather than the love, honor, and action of a narrator who wants to do great things but keeps tripping into bed with associations of grandeur that lead usually to cringingly small attempts to fill the quiet. Although he thinks he's still invisible, he's not really invisible — he's actually figured as "All of it," so he inspires unrealistic, drunken devotion in Sybil, who can see him as some beautiful thing, only to call him "Boo'ful," over and over again — the abbreviated word that makes the great concept of the beautiful lose its wordy length and luster.

Here's the description of his private rooms I quoted above, but now I want to include the sentence that completes the description: "I had neither itch nor etchings, but there was a vase of Chinese lilies in the living room, and another of American Beauty roses on a table near the bed; and I had put a supply of wine, whiskey, and liqueur, extra ice cubes, and assortments of fruit, cheese, nuts, candy and other delicacies from the Vendome. I tried to manage things as I imagined Rinehart [a man that the narrator is mistaken for throughout the novel] would have done" (516). In this private dwelling, couples are "manag[ing] things" and each other as if they were as small and as tangible as things. The couple, in this inner asylum, is stripping things and people (especially themselves) of value by applying literally the local color closest to hand (Sybil's lipstick as well as the different colors of each character's body):

> my emotions locked, as I saw her lipstick lying on the table and grabbed it, saying "Yes, yes," as I bent to write furiously across her belly in drunken inspiration:
>
> SYBIL, YOU WERE RAPED
> BY
> SANTA CLAUS
> SURPRISE
>
> and paused there; trembling above her, my knees on the bed as she waited with unsteady expectancy. It was a purplish metallic shade of lipstick and as she panted with anticipation the letters stretched and quivered, up hill and down dale, and she was lit like a luminescent sign. "Hurry, boo'ful, hurry," she said. (522-23)

Sybil is surface here, with colorful writing that is claiming a violence that she has not and will not experience with the narrator — but the violence fits the pattern, so the difference between fantasy and reality really makes no difference. Lipstick sticks where she might want the lips of the narrator to stick, and it's marking her, containing her, all according to plan. Crucially, the message makes no real sense — why Santa Claus? Is the narrator giving her a gift? The idiom of this desire makes her seem small, like a kid waiting for a present she must have because others around her have had such a present before (and she's thrilled by the prospect of joining the repetition). Still, I don't think we can confidently assign too much meaning because the nonsense of the situation is what helps reduce her unique value — she's in this asylum-like funhouse in order to put herself in a violated position, for easy consumption. She's there to be collected by men (her husband, then the narrator). And the narrator makes clear what the words on her skin do not: "I looked at her, thinking, Just wait until George sees that — if George ever gets around to seeing that. He'll read a lecture on an aspect of the woman question he's never thought about. She lay anonymous beneath my eyes until I saw her face, shaped by her emotion, which I could not fulfill" (523). There's a movement from abstraction (the woman question, the repeated rape fantasy) to a kind of failing particularity, by which I mean the narrator cannot respond to her personal, not-anonymous, emotion that shapes her face after he colors her belly with a violent kind of attention in which he has been forced to engage. Local color (like the "lipstick") in this novel blocks the possibility of fulfillment in a violent world where so much cultural noise, racist fantasy beyond the narrator's and Sybil's bodies, informs nearly every gesture and emotion. Growing closer, growing away from anonymity, only gives the character the illusion of a closeness that can step outside of history, transcending and escaping the routine of one's own particular experiences. Black and white, man and woman — couples here don't fulfill each other; they just collect each other into a form of failure that makes the bedroom seem like any other situation where people can't relate and connect except through antagonism, as a larger couples market prefers because the desire and constant craving for more can never be satiated. The smallness of the bedroom stands in for the world that has been shrunk, ready for an unsatisfying game of consumption of the smallest gesture, the tiny glass of wine, and emotions that are not generous, just violent. Greatness, grandeur, and what I like to think of as abstraction (being something not specific, just unspecified) are not possible in a world that couples people in this manner. Can you exceed your marriage, which, like your race, is putting you in a very static place? Can you be large rather than small? Can you have the oceans of boundless connections when you fall into the arms of another? These are maddening questions we've encountered in my book's first chapter.

Michael Warner explains the complicated procedure of becoming abstract in various, sometimes-competing "mediating contexts of publicity." "We become the mass-public subject," writes Warner, "but in a new way unanticipated within the classical bourgeois public sphere. Moreover, if mass-public subjectivity has a kind of singularity, an undifferentiated extension to indefinite numbers of individuals, those individuals who make up the 'we' of the mass-public subject might have very different relations to it."[19] These thoughts might be quite true, but I don't see singularity in the spaces of publicity that are mixed up by culture's homogenization via the omniscience of the couple form. Instead, I want to characterize the public sphere as a destroyed public — destroyed by the totalitarian couple form — a form that disseminates a lonely, deadly, and impossible feeling that cripples even identification with something like an abstract mass of many unidentified individuals. The couple, not the abstract individual, transforms how we might conceive of our appeals to the public, and this couple cuts us all into two, reducing us to a romance with trifles, with the "phantasmagorias of the market, where people only appear as types," to use Benjamin's phrase.[20] And the only type in which you can appear to take mystical shape is the type-conjoined, the type-coupled — the ur-*Stereo*-type. The public, then, is nothing but very small moments, small things of the local, brought to your bedroom by the couple. It can't accommodate the abstract.

Benjamin, as Susan Sontag assures us, disliked marriage so much that he considered his own "'as fatal to himself.'"[21] Listen as he tells us about an image that spectacularizes a view of the public sphere that might be more helpful for our inquiry, a view that mourns the transformation of greatness into smallness:

The beginning of the nineteenth century witnessed those initial experiments in iron construction whose results, in conjunction with those obtained from experiments with the steam engine, would so thoroughly transform the face of Europe by the end of the century. Rather than attempt a historical account of this process, we would like to focus on some scattered reflections on a small vignette which has been extracted from the middle of the century (as from the middle of the thick book that contains it), and which indicates, although in grotesque style, what limitless possibilities were seen revealed by construction in iron. The picture comes from a work of 1844 [nine years before "Bartleby"] — Grandville's *Another World* — and illustrates the adventures of a fantastic little hobgoblin who is trying to find his way around outer space: "A bridge — its two ends could not be embraced at a single glance and its piers were resting on planets — led from one world to another by a causeway of wonderfully smooth asphalt. The three-hundred-thirty-three-thousandth pier rested on Saturn. There our goblin noticed that the ring around this planet was nothing other than a circular balcony on which the inhabitants of Saturn strolled in the evening to get a breath of fresh air."[22]

I want to think of those inhabitants as coupled as they walk all over the large and fantastical ring around Saturn, turning it into something more ordinary and standard such as an iron-clad balcony on which they can simply parade in the evening air. It's the inhuman goblin's job to notice Saturn's architecture; in fact he even melds into the balcony, becoming lost, becoming invisible, or perhaps part of the architecture, in the two successive references to this vignette in the two successive versions of Benjamin's "Paris, the Capital of the Nineteenth Century." The goblin drops out of the next versions, becoming, like Ellison's narrator, invisible over time, and all that remains are the remnants of the architecture — the balcony, which reveals people lost in a dream of abundant, if not absurd, phantasmagorias that are always proliferating and exhibited in the "universe of commodities."

Hobgoblin Highway to Saturn, scanned image from Jean-Jacques Grandville, *Un autre monde* (1844; repr., Paris: Editions Classiques Garnier, 2010).

People, in this view of the publicity, are not abstract — they're all too particular, stripped of grandeur. They walk on rings that are really balconies, protrusions from the private, interior dwellings of the private individual that emerge in the nineteenth century, the boxes, the "asylum" where people and things, "freed from the drudgery of being useful," are collected.[23] This is society's new, confused avenue of no shade or refuge, shabbily built upon the illusion of shade and refuge. Part of what has made the public so consumed by a standardizing culture is the affairs of the household, the affairs of the bedroom, which we should call "the affairs of the couple," that emerge into full public view to produce, not an aura of utopian abstraction, but a cacophony of crowding gossip, emotional assertion, correct behavior, regulated styles of appropriate identities and sexualities. Berlant and Warner give us a telling list of what appears in the public life of sex: "paying taxes, being disgusted, philandering, bequeathing, celebrating a holiday, investing for the future, teaching, disposing a corpse, carrying wallet photos, buying economy size, being nepotistic, running for president, divorcing, or owning anything

'His' and 'Hers.'"[24] There are innumerable balconies full of proud, arrogant couples, who might tell you about all the dates, details, and dynamics that have made their union superior to any of your single achievements, perhaps over a coffee, and maybe even at that proverbial coffeehouse.

To be most blunt: the mass-public subject is not a subject but a couple, and a couple that might drown you in its standardizing particularity rather than transcendent abstraction; in all its local, quickly understood, and antagonized color rather than in its stiff, colorless invisibility or inscrutability. Arendt puts this development humorously and harshly in her damning assessment of the French penchant for "*petit bonheur*" by focusing on France's alluring bedroom:

> Since the decay of their once great and glorious public realm, the French have become masters in the art of being happy among "small things," within the space of their own four walls, between chest and bed, table and chair, dog and cat and flowerpot, extending these things a care and tenderness which, in a world where rapid industrialization constantly kills off the things of yesterday to produce today's objects, may even appear to be the world's last, purely humane corner. This enlargement of the private, the enchantment, as it were, of a whole people, does not make it public, does not constitute a public realm, but on the contrary, means only that the public realm has almost completely receded, so that the greatness has given way to charm everywhere; for while the public realm may be great, it cannot be charming precisely because it is unable to harbor the irrelevant.[25]

Small things, many things, that seem trivial are what, in Arendt's estimation, now make up and so compromise the public sphere: the great public forum has now been reduced to a corner in a bedroom ("between chest and bed"). It's no wonder, then, that the French "empire," at the dawn of the new millennium, gave the world *Amélie* (dir. Jean-Pierre Jeunet). Arendt's quotation, now over a half-century old, is prescient: it's difficult to think about great moments of iconic abstraction in our new mediated contexts, especially since we're not dwelling and existing in a public that, in Arendt's stern estimation, cannot "harbor the irrelevant." I want to think about the trifling qualities of the couple form and imagine that we're strolling among the couples on Saturn's ring — that "long [Haussmann] stree[t] opening onto broad perspectives" that runs into so many small phantasmagorias "rendered in stone," which whisper, *sotto voce*, a terrible jingle: all we need is love. So much *petit bonheur.* So little greatness.

Arendt, as always, has her sights, almost obsessively, set on greatness. And her famous chapter from *The Human Condition*, "The Public and Private Realm," can still help us. Here's just a sliver of Arendt's argument.[26] The ancient divisions between household and *polis*, what we might consider the private and public realms, have collapsed. The basic provision of the necessities of living used to be the main aim and function of the household and family, which were shielded from public life. Such a barrier could enable one to then enter a public realm that was not riddled with necessity, and that, if properly constituted, could be a great place of politics, which once meant that "everything was decided through words and persuasion and not through force and violence," at least in its ideal formulations.[27] But over time, and no doubt because of the rise of modern industry and economics, the function and grasp of family and household extended into the public realm, radically transforming the purpose of the *polis*, which has resulted in the growth of what we now call society, a realm in which the organizational methods and forms of the household now shape all spaces. There's an extreme problem in this story of the human condition: behaviors are standardized, individuality and extraordinary achievement and character are devalued, and the prevalence of laboring rather than acting becomes constitutive of the common world. Political life, then, becomes the biopolitical activity of managing the necessities of life. Now the personal experiences of intimacy are what we think of when we think of the "public realm." And because the public/private divide has been "submerged" (69) into the social, there is then no place to hide, though a private realm used to serve in that capacity (or at least be the useful illusion of it). Consequently, then, there's now no location where a public could still exist, where the politics of speech and persuasion could create a city of the good life rather than an administration and fashioning of the maintenance of life.

In so many of her writings, Arendt obviously longs for and romanticizes the oldest forms of political association that, on the one hand, kept the concerns of home away from the concerns of politics and, on the other, permitted home to be that most private place, where one could hide. There are obvious shortcomings here, if not absurd political amnesias regarding, among other dark things, the economics of slavery and the acquisition of empires. But what I want to highlight is a generous offering of Arendt's: she craves property. Most pointedly, she is interested in the most important kind of property· real estate, shelter, or some kind of structure that permits a privacy that has otherwise been lost in the collapse between the public and the private. We might be annoyed with what we might consider Arendt's elitism here — politics hardly seem radical if they're predicated on home ownership as the condition needed to defend us against the totalitarian forces that standardize culture. But again I urge caution in resisting Arendt — she's arguing for a more antiquated but now annihilated understanding that there might be very good reasons why "there are things that need to be hidden and others that need to be displayed publicly" (73), and she wants us to consider that the desire for privacy, shelter, shade, is not the same thing as a desire for wealth (or even unequal accumulations of wealth). Wealth, for instance, does not have to be just about selfish acquisition; it can be about the preservation of substantial natural resources in a public commons that might otherwise tragically disappear through misuse. Such an "annoying" misunderstanding (61) makes some sense because wealth often enables the possibility of private property that gives one privacy, but the two conditions are by no means identical, and I'm convinced that what Arendt likes about the old forms of private property is not the extravagance of the structure but the ability of property to make the spheres separate — the thing that is important about privacy is "not the interior of the realm," but its giving us "an exterior appearance" in the form of the wall that separates things seen and things hidden. In other words, private property gives us a wall that is "actually a space, a kind of no man's land between the private and the public, sheltering and protecting both realms while, at the same time, separating them from each other" (63).

No wonder Arendt, in a footnote charged with etymological exuberance, points out that the ancient Greek word for law, *nomos*, "derives from *nemein*, which means to distribute, to possess (what has been distributed), and to dwell" (63). The law of the land is about land, and about how that land is divided to provide varying shares of privacy and shade through the property in which one dwells. Such divisions then also permit us to interact and encounter one another in ways that are *not* exposed, unhidden, and fragile. For our purposes, I'd like to pursue the concept of this dwelling, this boundary, this wall of the law, which shelters and hides, much to the consternation of those who'd prefer to storm and standardize.

But walls are hardly part of falling in love. Love does not grant you the privacy you think you're cultivating in that Oz you've been trying to make with someone else. Remember, you're not supposed to build walls between you and another person, especially your most significant other. Couples, in fact, are busy tearing down walls as they also cast that great illusion that they're making a world for just themselves in the rooms where they sleep. So in Ellison's Sybil chapter, after falling asleep, the narrator receives an alarming call: there's a race riot, which the narrator must join or witness. Suddenly, the walls of the narrator's apartment, in fact all of the novel's apartments, start to tumble down, Jericho style. The narrator flees his home with Sybil. He then tries to leave Sybil on the steps of the neoclassical structure. After a number of unsuccessful tries, he's able to release himself from her grasp, even though "She clung to me, and for an instant, I to her with a feeling immeasurably sad" (527). These private-but-really-in-public, previously and anciently scripted moments have prepared the narrator for what he's about to witness as he "tri[es] to reach the gray veil that now seemed to hang behind my eyes" (537). The passion for awful conformity that the segregated couple has inspired in him makes him nervous, and he carries this passion with him even after he's left her. No wonder he characterizes his decimated cityscape in terms that sound sexual as well as disorienting as he walks "slowly, smoothly into the dark crowd, the whole surface of my skin alert, my back chilled, looking, listening to those moving with a heaving and sweating and a blur of talk around me" (550). He's being robbed of something he's been trying to possess: "I was one with the mass, moving down the littered street over the puddles of oil and milk, my personality blasted" (550). But it's not really his personality; it's the personality that has been given to him as he's been on the "chase" that he's been on "all [his] life" (559): "Yet I knew with shattering dread that the uproar which for the moment marked the crash of men against things — against stores, markets — could swiftly become the crash of men against men and with most of the guns and numbers on the other side" (553). The clash of the mass is not just the enduring conflict of "individual versus society," nor is it about the individual giving in to the loss of individuality. This clash is the touch of a special, couples' kind. The narrator walks past all sorts of "silent houses" on his way through the riot, and he completes his flight into a metaphor that feels like an allusion to Noah's Ark (a hideous couples' parade if there ever was a more obvious one — I mean other than contemporary Gay Pride parades): "It was as though the tenants had vanished, leaving the houses silent with all the windows shaded, refugees from a rising flood" (554). The couples have left their crumbling homes, and now they are overflowing the streets, hands grasping: "They came toward me as I ran, a crowd of men and women carrying cases of beer, cheese, chains of linked sausage, watermelons, sacks of sugar, hams, cornmeal, fuel lamps. If only it could stop right here, here; here before the others came with their guns" (555). We can read the crowd then as a flood of emotions that are most poignantly described as being made articulate by the drama of couple love — the drama in which the narrator has finally participated.

As Ellison elaborates the flood imagery, the postcoital narrator comes upon an awful image of Sybil, who seems to be guarding, or at least swinging from, the gates of hell that bring him into the underworld in which he's now drowning:

> The moon was high now and before me the shattered glass glittered in the street like the water of a flooded river upon the surface of which I ran as in a dream, avoiding by fate alone the distorted objects washed away by the flood. Then suddenly I seemed to sink, sucked under: Ahead of me the body hung, white, naked, and horribly feminine from a lamppost. I felt myself spin around with horror and it was as though I had turned some nightmarish somersault. I whirled, still moving by reflex, back-tracking and stopped and now there was another and another, seven — all hanging before a gutted storefront. I stumbled, hearing the cracking of bones underfoot and saw a physician's skeleton shattered on the street, the skull rolling away from the backbone, as I steadied long enough to notice the unnatural stiffness of those hanging above me. They were mannequins — "Dummies!" I said aloud. Hairless, bald and sterilely feminine. . . . But are they unreal, I thought; *are* they? What if one, even *one* is real — is . . . Sybil? I hugged my brief case, backing away, and ran . . . (555-56, emphasis in original)

The fake Sybil-as-mannequin assumes the hideous posture of a lynched black body. Not one body — seven bodies, none of which are real, but all give us a sense of something generic. The body first seen and presumably the six others are "hung, white, naked, and horribly feminine," so here's a crucial reversal, much like Melville's reversal in making the symbol of evil in *Moby-Dick* a white whale. But the whiteness replacing traditional postures of blackness does not, here, reinforce the notion that whiteness is a race that can escape physical marking, racial profiling, terrible and subordinated embodiment — what Berlant describes as "the privilege that white Americans have to assume free passage within any public space they can afford to lease or own — such as a taxicab, a table in a restaurant, a private home."[28] These mannequins are not white in that conventional sense. They're quite obviously arrested. Even though they're hanged in what appears to be a protest, the fake lynched bodies are not the same thing as real lynched bodies. The meaning and anger of the symbol cannot be explained merely as the expression of a protester's desire for a reversal of racist roles — a reversal in which hierarchies are swapped by acts of dramatic race revolution. The narrator does not witness a traditional race conflict here. Instead, he thinks that one of the bodies might belong to Sybil. He personalizes the moment and then abandons it: poignantly, he flees rather than rescue her from her hanging there in the privately ravaged public space. It's not much longer before he finds himself in his infamous hole, which becomes his new home, where, all alone, he's finally free to empty himself of antagonistic color, or at least color's significance.

What's important about the mannequins' whiteness, and what that whiteness gives to the black narrator who sees it, is the adjective *stiffness.* Stiffness suggests something that the narrator has been resisting throughout the book. It's telling that the white mannequin gives him back the starch that he lost when he first heard Sybil's immodest proposal. I want to stare at this stiffness and track a similar stonelike feeling in Melville's Bartleby, because the adjective is revealing something about singleness — its lack of suppleness, its lack of warmth, its fear-inducing qualities, its utter refusal. Moreover, something about the unnaturalness of the stiffness enables the narrator to *not* return to his bedroom (and look for Sybil) and instead to flee into a privacy that the couple can't continue to destroy — a privacy where scripts, lipstick, fantasies, and the "passion for conformity" won't work so quickly to circumscribe the otherwise oceanic world that should never be collected and contained. I want to imagine that the single person points to the necessity of that Arendtian wall, which produces not supple and malleable intimacy but rather a surface that confounds and confuses the sphere that demands you remain limp in that tortured home of the couple, which demands that we relate in a terribly dual manner. For the single narrator knows that it's not all black and white. His walls allow him to know as much.

Sure, he's tempted to emerge from his hole: "I've sometimes been overcome with a passion to return into that 'heart of darkness' across the Mason-Dixon line" (579). And he almost ends the book with a series of incoherent declarations that seem to confirm the cliché that we just need what we already have: "but too much of your life will be lost, its meaning lost, unless you approach it as much through love as through hate. So I approach it through division. So I denounce and I defend and I hate and I love" (580). Even Arendt, who is so crucial in my theorizing of singleness, leans on the crutch of the couple when, in a letter to one of her lovers, she writes this hideous sentence: ""Believe me, my love, women must live inside the couple.'"[29] These ideas are hard to shake. The sing-song couples of Ellison's colorful rhetoric (denounce/defend; love/hate), however, combine to feel like that banal and passionate "pattern" for the "chaos (which insists on the primary feelings of love and hate)." When he's even admitted that he's "whipped it all except the mind, the *mind*" (580), he keeps coming back to twoness: the repetition of "the mind" leaves us with *two* minds that point to the way the world seems to be ordered only through a passion for division — for the Mason-Dixon line that illuminates the heart of darkness we all contain. It's hard to hold on to what the narrator is saying, which is why we're still arguing about what he's saying so many years after this novel was published. That's part of the point I want to make: he's insisting on the irrationality of couples, of dualism, of the conflict between black and white, in a world that forgets that "democracy," as Ellison puts it in that critical essay about segregated words, "is a collectivity of *individuals*,"[30] not a collectivity of couples.

So when the narrator sees Sybil as a mannequin, he knows that he can't rescue or embrace her: she's not accessible to him because he can't even know if it's her and what she'd want in that lifeless state. In a way, she's been hollowed out, emptied of all that bad erotic and romantic life that bounced her from one couple to the next. And the logic, or I should say, the color of the couple — the ability for color to even signify who she is, and where she belongs, and how she should relate and to whom — is now gone. Somehow, the narrator sees a horror hanging above him and refuses to be saved by that loving death. Rather than rescue her, he's inspired to hide in his new property's privacy, where he'll find four coupleless walls, and in those walls will learn to value a state of invisibility, where color and couples can no longer split and control the world.

The always quoted ending of this novel gives us some fantastic clues for understanding what Bartleby will soon tell us, so it requires repeating before we move to Melville:

Being invisible and without substance, a disembodied voice, as it were, what else could I do? What else but try to tell you what was really happening when your eyes were looking through? And it is this which frightens me:

Who knows but that, on the lower frequencies, I speak for you? (581)

The narrator tries to tell you things, but he cannot. So he ghosts himself, empties himself, as he hides himself behind a wall he's found in retreating from Sybil, his "too-late-too-early love." He has stiffened himself, hiding in a place we can't understand. He's hiding beyond that wall, ready to scare us. We often read the final, slightly accusatory question of the novel as a second-person address that speaks to the deeper parts of everyone. I want to add some nuance. Is it possible that the "you" he speaks of and for is your single you? Is that part of you a frightening mannequin, or a kind of ghost, that can keep colorful coupledom at bay? And can you live in a world without that kind of color?

Let's ask Bartleby.

I'd Prefer Not You

Just look at him. Yes, right there: "His face" is "leanly composed; his gray eye dimly calm. Not a wrinkle of agitation rippled him." And he's standing in front of you, so intriguing, so "unaccountably eccentric," that even though he's been lingering for a century and a half, he's impossible to resist.[31] "Bartleby, the Scrivener," Herman Melville's study of a stubborn, insubordinate law copyist and the lawyer who can't seem to fire him, cannot be discussed enough. The bare bones of the plot: a lawyer hires an employee, a scrivener, to help with all the paperwork that accumulates in his law office. Bartleby is an excellent scrivener but does only the very mechanical task he was originally asked to do: copy. He does not deviate from his job description (at least at first), and when asked to do more, or something else, he famously states, "I'd prefer not to." Throughout the course of the story, the lawyer attempts to engage Bartleby in all sorts of office tasks, and most requests are met with Bartleby's "I'd prefer not to." These engagements only make Bartleby and his motives more remote, and eventually Bartleby stops doing anything. Instead of dismissing him, the lawyer, incredulous, only becomes more curious: Who is this strange character? And why doesn't he prefer to do what's asked of him? Why does he stop doing anything? The lawyer puts it this way: "There was something about Bartleby that not only strangely disarmed me, but in a wonderful manner touched and disconcerted me."

Of course one can't tear down Bartleby's mystery, explaining his motivations or even his negative preference. Bartleby is full of so much potential meaning, potential refusal of any definitive, perhaps sovereign meaning, that philosophers and literary critics regularly use him as a figure of paradoxically strong passivity — Bartleby is passive but saturated with very aggressive ideas. Giorgio Agamben notably puts his name up in lights: "But the strongest objection against the principle of sovereignty is contained in Melville's Bartleby, the scrivener who, with his 'I would prefer not to,' resists every possibility of deciding between potentiality and the potentiality not to."[32] Hardt and Negri run with this idea but don't promote such an absolute bareness of life, which is too "*solitary*," "*tread[ing]*' too much "*on the verge of social suicide*": "*His refusal is so absolute that Bartleby appears completely blank, a man without qualities or, as Renaissance philosophers would say,* homo tantum, *mere man and nothing more.*

Bartleby in his pure passivity and his refusal of any particulars presents us with a figure of generic being, being as such, being and nothing more."[33] Slavoj Žižek focuses his "parallax" view vividly on Bartleby, describing his inaction, his figure as a key form of potential that opens a "new space outside the hegemonic position *and* its negation,"[34] one we should emulate as we engage in "Bartleby politics." And Gilles Deleuze takes fandom to ridiculous heights: "There is nothing particular or general about Bartleby: he is an Original," with his "I'd prefer not to" phrase, "a formula that carves out a kind of foreign language within a language."[35] This originality, this minor literature within a great literature, enables Bartleby to be an ultimate relation that will mediate and medicate everyone: "Bartleby is not the patient, but the doctor of Sick America, the *Medicine-Man*, the new Christ or the brother to us all."[36] Certainly it seems that many people can't resist taking Melville's narrator-lawyer's cue ("I began to reason with him" [12]), by reasoning with him — or, more accurately, reasoning around him, perpetually asking questions of Bartleby that won't be answered by the answer we know he'll give. There really is no way to silence those around Bartleby.[37] If I wanted to be flip, I could say that Bartleby is the new Antigone of political philosophy.[38] So he's open, or, as I'll insist, closed to interpretation, and thus he's available for any of our own peculiar readings, mine especially.

Odd, this fascination, because staring at him, staring at his one gray eye, is so much like staring at a wall. Melville insists that Bartleby, so "pale," so "silent"(10), so "pallidly neat, pitiably respectable, incurably forlorn . . . so singularly sedate" (9), has wall-like qualities; he says as much so frequently he risks overkill. And words about a wall, or anything having to do with stationary aspects and objects of the office, are the only kind of description that can surround him with any certainty, any stability, or at least any consistency, which is why most readers will make the association. The offices in which we find him are, of course, on Wall Street, with rooms that have windows that can look at nothing except other walls. And a flimsy cubicle-like wall hides Bartleby while he works: a screen for "his hermitage" where he indulges in "standing reverie[s]," "his great stillness" (17), which the narrator qualifies as "dead-wall reveries." As we read we learn that not only is he like a wall, he's like a building, like the structure of the space of the story. He's standing, yes, right over there, apparently there to remind you something about architecture. He's like a pale statue enclosed in a grand architectural ruin, and the years have eroded the statue's ancient color, leaving a figure of dull blankness you can't decipher.

Bartleby's absence of vivid color — especially given Manichean-obsessed Melville's penchant for writing about race in so many of his most famous stories — is why he is deeply curious to me. When I think of Bartleby's stiff stony visage, the wall he insists on not only becoming, but keeping between us, I affiliate Bartleby with Ellison's narrator, for they both occupy a color-dulled singleness that remains stiff, obscure, and confusing. Perhaps such befuddlement is why this single Bartleby is finally removed from the law office — quite literally driven outside the office of the law, made an outlaw, put into the walls of a prison, and remembered and memorialized, in vicious rumor, as someone who used to reside at the office of dead letters. This dead-letter office anecdote of Bartleby's previous employment, which the lawyer reveals at the very end of the story, inspires a malevolent imagining that closes the story: the lawyer's thought that Bartleby might have been sorting through the piles of letters that did not arrive where they were addressed when, one day, out of one of the dead folds of a dead letter's paper, an engagement ring appeared: "The pale clerk takes a ring — the finger it was meant for, perhaps, moulders in the grave" (39). Just one finger. Just one, pale Bartleby. Significantly, by the time the narrator tells us this bit, we've encountered dead Bartleby; he's the one who now moulders in the grave, ringless, his punishment for shunning conventional preferences. He appeared too soon in America to heed Beyoncé's advice.

Tellingly, Deleuze and, more recently, Branka Arsić suggestively call Bartleby a bachelor.[39] I want to follow their lead because Bartleby, the bachelor, befuddles the spheres in the nineteenth century and, in a way not unlike what Arendt sees happening in the twentieth century (and Benjamin in the nineteenth), marks this befuddlement with a quality of loneliness that is always thrust upon the single person who refuses coupledom. He lives in his hermitage, in the office of the law, which only confuses the status of the space. "Yes, thought I, it is evident enough that Bartleby has been making his home here, keeping a bachelor's hall all by himself" (19), concludes the lawyer after encountering Bartleby in the office on a Sunday. This realization instantly lurches into a description of Bartleby that reveals the desire of the lawyer to keep interacting with an employee he should otherwise fire: "Immediately then the thought came sweeping across me, what a miserable friendlessness and loneliness are here revealed! His poverty is great; but his solitude, how horrible! Think of it. Of a Sunday, Wall Street is as deserted as Petra; and every night of every day it is an emptiness. This building too, which of week days hums with industry and life, at nightfall echoes with sheer vacancy; and all through Sunday is forlorn. And here Bartleby makes his home; sole spectator of a solitude that he has seen all populous a sort of innocent and transformed Marius brooding among the ruins of Carthage!" (19). We have the kind of description of Bartleby that can't be trusted to give us any access to Bartleby because not only does he literally and figuratively resemble the blankness of a wall or some other architectural element, but his presence surrounds the space as a wall might, so that he now remains even in his absence. But alongside Bartleby, we have the swift, upsetting characterization of Bartleby as "forlorn," cruelly made by the lawyer, who desires so deeply to cure Bartleby of all sorts of imagined maladies — to cure him of the emptiness in which he finds him. It's the violation of the public office space by a hermitage that is also a home that encourages the lawyer to persist in trying to figure Bartleby out. Arendt's insights into the collapsing of the public and private spheres seem especially helpful here. And this drive for knowledge, which is drenched in illusions and projection, takes on the idiom of coupling, which has been present, but less obvious, throughout the tale:

"Will you tell me *anything* about yourself?"

"I would prefer not to."

"But what reasonable objection can you have to speak to me? I feel friendly towards you." (21)

Bartleby answers this answer with a gesture that says it all, but in a way the lawyer cannot see. "He [Bartleby] did not look at me while I spoke, but kept his glance fixed upon my bust of Cicero, which as I then sat, was directly behind me, some six inches above my head" (21). Sure, a bust of Cicero means something about the décor of the office, the appeal of having a figure of such glorious, ancient thought. But alongside the obvious reference to the time's neoclassical vogue (to which I'll presently return), we see Bartleby's frightening sight lines: he takes in two heads, which we're endlessly told must surely be better than one. He's looking at a couple, which indexes the kind of knowledge these two busts might want from Bartleby: his compliance, his intimacy, his insides, all splayed for a lawyer who wants the thing that all couples want: the eradication of a person's aloneness, which is construed as pathetic loneliness, but only so perched from the viewpoint of a culture that insists that people must be ringed into a divisive form of companionship. Listen to the exchange when the lawyer must convince Bartleby to leave the chambers that the lawyer has already left because Bartleby won't. After refusing the suggestions of a few occupations, all of which Bartleby rejects because he is "not particular," "Despairing of all further efforts, I was precipitately leaving him, when a final thought occurred to me — one which had not been wholly unindulged before. 'Bartleby,' said I, in the kindest tone I could assume under such exciting circumstances, 'will you go home with me now — not to my office, but my dwelling . . . ?'" (34). Bartleby, of course, rejects this offer, and the lawyer, as if heartbroken, flees the office, running up Wall Street, to Broadway no less.

Now, it would be impossible to know whether there are real romantic motives here, and although the lawyer was married in the original publication of the story in *Putnam's*, that detail of a

wife was dropped when the story was published again.[40] Deleuze
points out that this relationship has some whiffs of a mad, bad
romance: "Is it a case of shared madness, here again, another relationship between doubles, a nearly acknowledged homosexual
relation ('yes, Bartleby . . . I never feel so private as when I know
you are here . . . I penetrate to the predestined purpose of my
life . . .')?"[41] And that might make no difference — one desires all
sorts of couplings, even if, perhaps especially if, one is married.
To be honest, I could care less about the sexuality of the lawyer,
and whether a queer reading could ripple through the ambient
homosociality of the law office. I'm more interested in how the
consolidation of knowledge, the standardization of people, is
achieved through dwelling inside a home, or a home-office, together, intimately bound into two. The lawyer proposes, in a way,
to Bartleby, thereby only deepening his earlier, snide but genuine
insight after reading that period's version of self-help literature
(*Edwards on the Will* and *Priestley on Necessity*):

> I slid into the persuasion that the troubles of mine touching
> the scrivener, had been all predestined from eternity [a con-
> cept I think marks couples' time deeply], and Bartleby was
> billeted upon me for some mysterious purpose of an all-wise
> Providence, which it was not for me to fathom. Yes, Bartleby,
> stay there behind your screen, thought I; I shall persecute you
> no more; you are as harmless and noiseless as any of these
> old chairs; in short, I never feel so private as when I know
> you are here. At last I see it, I feel it; I penetrate to the pre-
> destined purpose of my life. I am content. Others may have
> loftier parts to enact; but my mission in this world, Bartleby,
> is to furnish you with office room for such period as you may
> see fit to remain. (29)

But that office space only becomes a shared dwelling in the
deepest, indulged desires of the lawyer. Providing an office or
a home for Bartleby, so he thinks, would solve the puzzle of
Bartleby, and thereby also solve the puzzle of the lawyer's own
mysterious reactions. The lawyer has wanted this understanding

almost from the beginning, and we're even given a floor plan that maps how the lawyer wants their relationship to develop:

> I should have stated before that ground glass folding doors divided my premises into two parts, one of which was occupied by my [other] scriveners [Turkey, Nippers], the other by myself. According to my humor I threw open these doors, or closed them. I resolved to assign Bartleby a corner by the folding doors, but on my side of them, so as to have this quiet man within easy call, in case any trifling thing was to be done. I placed the desk close up to a small side-window in the part of the room, a window which originally had afforded a lateral view of certain grimy backyards and bricks, but which owing to subsequent erections, commanded at present no view at all, though it gave some light. Within three feet of the panes was a wall, and the light came down from above, between two lofty buildings, as from a very small opening in a dome.
>
> Still further to a satisfactory arrangement, I procured a high green folding screen, which might entirely isolate Bartleby from my sight, though not remove him from my voice. And thus, in a manner, privacy and society were conjoined. (9-10)

The lawyer, in some way, perhaps in response to the layout of the rooms of his office, has been commanded by his God — one in a long line of gods — to bring Bartleby close, close to the window with a view of a wall but in a space that is still oddly lit: the light that shines down "as from a very small opening in a dome," a simile gesturing to a neoclassical detail that might reference the oculus of Federal Hall (built in 1842) on Wall Street, which, like its inspiration (its couple), the Pantheon in Rome, can so quickly look like "one gray eye" that stares at you, enticing you to gaze into its single soul. Bartleby must be close to the folding doors, which cut the law office into two, into a couple, and which the lawyer opens and closes "according to his humor"; the desk must have a view to a wall with a light afforded by an ancient architectural feature that isn't actually there.

Federal Hall's oculus, an eye to the heavens. Photo by author.

It is unclear why the lawyer keeps Bartleby, a scrivener, on his side of the divide away from the other two scriveners; it's unclear why Bartleby is singled out, except for the possibility that he's the only one who might be single (other than twelve-year-old Ginger Nut — but we'll never know!). So perhaps he's the only one available for the lawyer's special, personal attention, and for the assumption that the lawyer just might convert him and bring him into the world of the couple. If you think about it for a bit, this office, where privacy and society are conjoined, coupled, is a space that divides people into two, who are then instructed, from on high, that they must overcome that division in order to be united, divided, forever — at home, which is increasingly the world. The world, then, is rendered small. We're once again drawn apart in that maddeningly repetitive, ancient way here: split into two in

The Roman Pantheon's "one gray eye." Photo by author.

order to be reunified as a crippled unity, with the tiniest stage on which to play the very large drama of life. And this draw makes any "trifling thing" that might arise in this office, this home, this world, easier to handle, with the least disturbance possible. It takes two, quite literally, to break apart the rooms that will block any aspirations for grandness. "I am one of those unambitious lawyers who never addresses a jury, or in any way draws down public applause; but in the cool tranquility of a snug retreat, do a snug business among rich men's bonds and mortgages and title deeds" (3).

So yes, Bartleby, stay there behind your screen.

But the division the lawyer may want cannot be unified in the couple because Bartleby is a bad object choice: he's compared not only to a silent, noiseless chair but also to a "last column of some ruined temple," a strange chimera that sits on banisters ("'What are you doing here, Bartleby?'" "'Sitting upon the banister'" [33]). In fact, his most affirmative preference uttered is this one: "'I like to be stationary'" (34). He's not a couple-in-waiting; he's stubbornly single. Because he doesn't move, because he doesn't prefer to, and because the movements of his motives are never clear, we can encounter him only as inhuman abstraction. In Arendt's terms, and because he's so contiguous with architectural elements, Bartleby is figured as his own form of property: and not just one that gives him rights over himself or his will, but the property – the public/private wall — that blocks you from understanding what's behind his gray eye. He'll reveal nothing: he refuses everything "point-blank" (17); he is point-blank, and even when the lawyer later encounters Bartleby in prison, "standing all alone in the quietest of the yards, his face towards a high wall," the lawyer's consolations about the relative ease of the place are met with his characteristic blankness: "I know where I am" (36), and nothing more.

But people, in their intensely felt locality, are not supposed to be abstract. So how on earth can a person be abstract, or a figure of abstraction, especially in his or her most private (sheltered) self? What I want to suggest is that the single qualities of Bartleby, not unlike those of Ellison's narrator after him, render

Bartleby less than human, make him a surface upon which end-less, lonely mischaracterizations and affiliations can be postered, stapled, taped, by a maniacal band of people who insist that no one can be merely single — by an insistent chorus of couples that can't leave the singles they see well enough alone. And because all we have before us is this couple-dented surface of the single's blank architecture that is now only a palimpsest of mischaracter-ization, misvaluation, and malevolent euphemism, we can never really know the single except as a color-drained abstraction. We're literally hitting a wall here — the single as a wall — per-haps that wall of property that offers us something umbrageous, something that hides and shelters because it can't be particular-ized in an intimacy that divides everything into a snug "one size (size two) fits all" world. The wall is very much a shield, perhaps even a sword battling a terribly destructive form of standardizing publicity.

But this is not only a tragic love story. In fact, as all the neo-classical references I've been highlighting suggest, this story de-viates from the love story of Aristophanes for another kind of neoclassicism that belongs to the epic, or at least to the realm of ancient heroes (rather than lovers). I'd like to fix Bartleby in place by insisting that he's not another character of the lovers' phantasmagoria, not a charming thing to be ringed and brought home to that home that is a collector's asylum. His refusal is con-sistent and absolute. And instead of conjuring distracting charm, he never lightens the mood. Rather, he is great. He's full of fasci-nation, and we keep returning to the odd mysteries of this single, heroic character that has been emptied of any known or specific content but is fixed in a special kind of place. We could perhaps install him in the pantheon of historical figures that were mean-ingful to Benjamin: "His heroes — Kierkegaard, Baudelaire, Proust, Kafka, Kraus," writes Sontag, "never married."[42] Single, alone, and doing something large, something not-small, some-thing not at all irrelevant, something worthy of a public that we now find only hidden, commodified, in iron ruins. Arendt shares Benjamin's admiration for the single; she lauds the experience, even though she can't describe it. Tellingly, she concludes *The*

Human Condition by insisting that she thinks the greatest life of action (not labor, not work) is the life of the mind, in solitude, which is not lonely. For her, being single (even if she paradoxically thought women couldn't live without being in a couple) means being able to think, to ponder, to be self-possessed: "For if no other test but the experience of being active, no other measure but the extent of sheer activity were to be applied to various activities within the *via activa*, it might well be that thinking as such would surpass them all. Whoever has any experience in this matter will know how right Cato was when he said: . . . 'Never is he more active than when he does nothing, never is he less alone than when he is by himself.'"[43]

So Bartleby by himself is "oblivious to everything but his own peculiar business" (13). He's rapt in thought, wrapped and shielded in his own reverie. He's a figure sternly suggesting a vague sense of fullness that is monumentalized by the stone bust of his head, full and enclosed, not available to us in these days. A stone facade, with a wise gray eye, offering only a blank stare that won't let you in as it watches you, the couple. We could think of him (and all others such as him, regardless of gender) as a *flâneur* who won't share, who won't reveal secrets he has seen or thought about. And most importantly, Bartleby won't be budged into the intimacy implied and enforced in your dwelling.

So the single is not a useless distraction; it's a maddening one, with neoclassical designs that have heroic aspirations, on something larger than snug rooms charmed by the triviality of the couple. Anne Carson, while considering Homer, explains epic Being, epic constitutions, which she describes as "stable," where "particularity is set fast in tradition. When Homer mentions blood, blood is *black*. When women appear, women are *neat-ankled* or *glancing* . . . Homer's epithets are a fixed diction with which Homer fastens every substance in the world to its aptest attribute and holds them in place for epic consumption. There is a passion in it but what kind of passion?" Carson answers with a quotation: "'Consumption is not a passion for substances but a passion for the code,' says Baudrillard."[44] Bartleby's fixed diction, his tagline "I'd prefer not to," certainly fixes him in a stationary place. We could even affix epithets such as "Bartleby, standing," "Bartleby, staring," "Bartleby, refusing," "Bartleby, wall-like." What might this kind of standard code (quite different from the standardizing culture of Ellison and Arendt), which requires a *single* strong and abstract attribute, do to our acts of consumption? What passion do we have here other than one that is abstract, not given to us, or one that's distant from us? The thing that Carson does not highlight in her description is that this kind of epic consumption hardly wears out quickly; it's a form of consumption that doesn't destroy, doesn't conquer and divide, doesn't make the world small. It's a form of consumption that can only consume the code, as if it were a great statue, or a great wall, that might render our choices of painfully public private life (our life partner) less monumental in comparison.

The single, then, feels wall-like, like Bartleby, who becomes more statue than human as he freezes (friezes) in place. His singleness refuses the colorful details of all the couple's desire that the lawyer obsessively has had for him. But the fading of color (and even the death we all have to face, at some point in a place with a future that ends) is no punishment here. He's without strong color for a reason: his paleness, his marblelike whiteness, endows him with something grand even if he is emptied of recognizable affect. Instead, we near the end of the story with the image of Bartleby dying, slightly like a fallen classical soldier, divided emphatically from humanity by a coupled utterance of the couple-obsessed lawyer ("Ah Bartleby! Ah humanity!"), but with an image that cannot be contained by the rumor that follows it (the one about Bartleby opening the letter with the wedding ring). Our view of the single that dies in this public still finds a place in the cosmos that any immortal, from any antiquity, might find suitable.

Bartleby has been sent to a prison, where his ultimate transformation occurs:

The surrounding walls, of amazing thickness, kept all sounds behind them. The Egyptian character of the masonry weighed upon me with its gloom. But a soft imprisoned turf

Colorless single statue, up against a wall. Photo by author.

grew under foot. The heart of the eternal pyramids, it seemed, wherein, by some strange magic, through the clefts, grass seed, dropped by birds, had sprung.

Strangely huddled at the base of the wall, his knees drawn up, and lying on his side, his head touching the cold stones, I saw the wasted Bartleby. But nothing stirred.

I paused; then went up close to him; stooped over, and saw that his dim eyes were open; otherwise he seemed profoundly sleeping. (38)

The lawyer can't look into Bartleby's "dim eyes" because he can't ponder what secrets this single Bartleby refuses to share; he doesn't want to see into his eyes. But he can't resist the touch of Bartleby's skin, or is it stone? "Something prompted me to touch him. I felt his hand, when a tingling ran up my arm and down my spine to my feet" (38). The feeling of Bartleby shoots up and into the lawyer's back, stiffening him in place, putting him in place, on his two feet. And he's tingling, perhaps shivering, and feeling something not unlike what the narrator of Ellison's novel felt when he saw the mannequins. This stiff person before the lawyer, who is now more of an epic thing than possible partner, is no longer available for couples' consumption. And that is all the single can "tell" the lawyer: it's as if he's saying, "I'd prefer Not You." But all is not lost. Quite the contrary: "all" is what we might be able to find here with this one, who is not bounded by two. Bartleby, fixed in place, in his pale, wall-like grayness, is now available for epic consumption. Something unknowable and large tingles, captivates in this colorless, coupleless world. The voluminous quality of Bartleby criticism certainly suggests as much.

Melville has his lawyer close rather than color Bartleby's eyes. For a moment when he's with Bartleby's lifeless figure, the lawyer no longer insists on the color of his own love and thwarted desire for Bartleby. Instead, he describes Bartleby's death, his *telos*, with a biblical allusion (the first time the lawyer gets a description of Bartleby almost right). He quite literally puts Bartleby (at least for a moment before that gossip about him clutching on to an engagement ring ends the story) in an extraordinary pantheon:

after such a long struggle to rid himself of other people's couple-obsessed attention, Bartleby has assumed a prominent place on the wall of immortality — for Bartleby is not dead, he's asleep "with kings and counselors" (38), says the lawyer. The lawyer is on the right track, but he misses part of the point by chopping off the next line of this ancient scripture to which he alludes, chopping off the architectural details that Bartleby has been insisting on throughout the story, which make such greatness in the couples' world possible. The fuller quotation: "With kings and counselors of the earth / Who rebuilt ruins for themselves" (Job 3:14), says the Bible.

What we've learned, in our literary excursions into Ellison and Melville, is that the single can be a character or person who's like an architect, a builder, who rebuilds the ruins of lost privacy by stripping away the awful affect that conforms the world into divisions of color that domesticate in a segregated pattern. Put another way, the single freezes in its tracks that standardizing movement into intimacy, thereby making room for the single self in the rooms to which he or she is forced to flee. Emily Dickinson's words illuminate this hole, this prison that's actually an escape, in a poem about emptying out of one's heart the relationship one has with another person. Notice the recurring images of emptiness, oceans, questions of eternity, and death:

> Empty my Heart, of Thee —
> Its single Artery —
> Begin, and leave Thee out —
> Simply Extinction's Date —
>
> Much Billow hath the Sea —
> One Baltic — They —
> Subtract Thyself, in play,
> And not enough of me
> Is Left — to put away —
> "Myself" meant Thee —
>
> Erase the Root — no Tree —
> Thee — then — no me —

The Heavens stripped —
Eternity's vast pocket, picked [45]

We're picking eternity's pocket, making it as empty as a heart split into two. And it's this emptiness that will help us reveal the abstract roominess that's been hidden in plain sight: "the secret of immortality" of singleness that has been obscured by the couple's insistence on fragile, divisive eternities. With Ellison's narrator and with Melville's Bartleby, we've fixated on the walls of these isolated rooms. But the world is very large indeed, and the single is there to remind us that the world doesn't have to be divided into two. The single can give us much more — "infinite possibilities." To elaborate how the single can be so generous, in the next and final chapter we'll go to oceans so old they're now deserts. "Erase the Root — no Tree — ."

4

Welcome to the Desert of Me

Details are confusing. It is only by selection, by elimination,
by emphasis, that we get at the real meaning of things.
GEORGIA O'KEEFFE

Circumambulate the city of a dreamy Sabbath afternoon.
Go from Corlears Hook to Coenties Slip, and from thence,
by Whitehall, northward. What do you see? — Posted like
silent sentinels all around the town, stand thousands upon
thousands of mortal men fixed in ocean reveries.
HERMAN MELVILLE, *Moby-Dick*

straight lines over such great distances as one finds in Utah . . .
. . . .
there is something attractive about a mind
that moves in a straight-line —
MARIANNE MOORE, "People's Surroundings"

Unlovable

It's late 1990, and you're watching MTV. On the screen, you're
mesmerized by an undulating, very pale man, draped in an ill-
fitting black, diaphanously sheer shirt, which is almost always
about to fall or twist off, much to the titillation of his fanatical
fan base. Out of all the bewildering images, you might choose
now to pause and wonder why only one of his nipples is covered with a single band-aid. He's filmed alone in this Tim Broad
video, in Death Valley National Park, in the vicinity of its famous
Mushroom Rock. In a very recognizable, arch-baritone voice,
Morrissey croons about how "November Spawned a Monster."
From the swooping shots that track and attack him from all sides,
you become familiar with the brown and reddish desert landscape that Morrissey occupies. Here, by himself, he sways, hangs
off rocks, and stretches and gropes on the ground, making this

desert his showcase of sensual movement — and for no apparent reason.

Morrissey is undoubtedly one of the most iconic singles of the past thirty years, refusing to claim a sexual orientation or publicized or confirmed romances and relationships, so of course, like the lyrics he sings, he's here to be maddeningly enigmatic in his overt performance of sexuality. His words offer no clarity: you hear how the monster is loveless, desperate, and controlled. This monster, a "she," is twisted and ugly, probably disabled, in a wheelchair, not kissed on any part of her body. It's a somewhat sympathetic portrayal, yet Morrissey won't strip off the meanness of her description or fully celebrate her mild triumph at the song's end. He also parodies her by acting like a monster, lip-synching to the guttural, monstrous sounds made by Canadian singer-songwriter Mary Margaret O'Hara. You're not sure what he wants to say, but that's hardly the point of anything sung by Morrissey. The visuals of the video confirm as much — they are

Morrissey, with one bandaged nipple, in the desert. Screen capture from "November Spawned a Monster" (dir. Tim Broad, 1990).

Author, in the style of Morrissey, in Utah in November 2009. Photo by Shelley White.

not literally interpreting the lyrics. As is the case with so many of his songs (from his solo career or the band that made him famous, the Smiths), the lyrics create a soundscape offering a luxurious melancholy, a delicious *tristesse*, that needs no specific content. Specifics might interrupt the easy transferability of the melodrama of the anxiety of self-pitying adolescence, or even the glib and clever snideness of postadolescence, that all his songs consistently offer to the knowing band of listeners who adore his music. Who hasn't felt "ugly, so ugly"? Who hasn't felt like a monster? Perhaps felt like Carson's red Geryon? And for those of you Scorpios who are lucky enough to have been born in November (desert monsters indeed), Morrissey has come to celebrate you and your sadness (and his sadness) with the movements of his hips. And not just Scorpios, but everyone. You should delight in your monstrosity. He delights in his abstractness.[1]

Close to four minutes into the video, you experience a very compelling and protracted tracking shot (which elaborates an earlier, similar shot, but this time from an eye-level angle, and for longer): the camera travels at a quick speed, from left to right over the red sand, approaching Morrissey, who is frozen in a statuesque pose with his shirt half off, revealing his muscular upper chest with that one nipple bandaged. His hands are in his pockets. As the camera gets closer (and just before you pass him), you notice that his neck is contorted toward your left, as his mouth, seen in profile, has been stuffed, roasted-pig style, with a large, red apple.

There's something both sacrificial and defiant in this stance, and again, we're not sure what any of this might mean. But the visual image is stunning, and it's the only occasion in the video when Morrissey does not move. It's a Bartleby moment (in the sense I described in the previous chapter). He's standing still, wall-like, refusing sense, understanding, and intimacy as he frustrates your desire. (We could even go too far and draw comparisons between Bartleby's one eye and Morrissey's one bandaged nipple, but I'll resist.) Assertively, Morrissey won't let you in; he won't let you get to know him intimately.

Defiant Morrissey with apple, Bartlebyesque. Screen capture from "November Spawned a Monster" (dir. Tim Broad, 1990).

Perhaps more importantly, he's brought you to this desert, in a national park, to sing about a monster and her lack of love and partnering and, through his resolutely single stance, to blend this performance into the scenery of the desert, making it as fascinating as him. What differentiates Morrissey from Bartleby and the narrator from *Invisible Man* is that he's showing off the wide-open spaces of the single rather than its hidden and heavily walled-off places. It's this gesture, as we'll learn, that further clarifies the great potentials of the single's powers of abstraction, which have designs on immortality rather than eternity. The single can surely be more than the scapegoat for or the local color-stripping antidote to the poisons of couples culture. We'll follow him to the desert and see what we can see in locations much like Morrissey's dancing place. It's a trek that's as old and familiar as any in Christendom: "Then Jesus was led up by the Spirit into the wilderness to be tempted by the devil," only to find the truth of the word of God.[2] But instead of the devil in our ear, we often have a partner.

In the desert, we'll learn to resist the partner's tempting words. And immortality, that special kind of grand emphasis, will be in our sights.

The Last Temptation of the Single

I'm going to begin this journey with myself by myself, in what this chapter's title locates as "the desert of me." The cartoon version of deserts, the ones I remember watching on reruns of *Sesame Street,* include vast sand dunes, with some hopeless, stranded person, crawling on the ground, dying of thirst, often tricked by mirages that offer no quenching relief. But any journey to a desert will reveal the extreme distortions of this portrait. Deserts are full of jaw-dropping beauty and intriguing life. Deserts are only called deserts because of their aridity — on average, only ten inches of rainfall per year is the measurement that grants a place its deserted status. Life is certainly less abundant because water is scarcer than other places, but life lives in the desert, and in such a place, it must want to be there. Life, as a result, is not crowded. Perhaps that's what persistently draws people to this landscape in order to gain insight. Hannah Arendt, quoting a medieval author from the twelfth century, calls the desert the destination of the contemplative way of life: "The contemplative way is sheer quietness . . . the contemplative [life takes place] in the 'desert.'"[3]

Although I'm punning on the deserted quality of deserts to impress upon you the importance of spending time alone, the pun will go only so far. I need to give you a less barren sense of this climate so it can help us contemplate a notion of the single's desertion from couples culture that is not lifeless, not without its infinite pleasures. So I'll start by telling you about a hike I first did in the summer of 2008 in Capitol Reef National Park in southern Utah, one of Utah's least-visited national parks. On this five-hour hike in the middle of August, at the height of midday, in 104-degree Fahrenheit heat, I encountered no one. It's the closest I have ever been to being truly alone. Let's orient you in this desert with some historical, geological, and trivial detail about the place — an orientation, by the way, that won't continue to matter

Rocks that look like the dome of the Capitol Building: politics name nature. Photo by author.

as we learn to look at the desert. The details and differences will be framed and phrased away, making historicism irrelevant as we indulge the pathetic fallacy, projecting all sorts of our human emotions onto these breathtaking landscapes.

Capitol Reef, a relatively new addition to the national park system, covers 378 square miles and receives about 650,000 visitors each year (Zion National Park has around 2.5 million).[4] Its most distinctive feature is an enormous one-hundred-mile-long rock upthrust in the earth's crust called the Waterpocket Fold, which was once covered by an inland sea that retreated nearly two hundred million years ago. This park was so named because the domelike rock formations of Navajo sandstone along the top of the fold resemble the dome of the U.S. Capitol Building.

The earliest inhabitants of the region were the indigenous Americans who made up what now has been termed the Fremont people. White settlement began in the mid-nineteenth century with the arrival of persecuted, polygamous Mormons, looking for territory outside the United States where they could be free to practice their religious beliefs. One of the main canyons and front-country hiking trails, Cohab Canyon, is so named, we're told, because it would serve as a hiding place for these polygamous families who were breaking the law by unlawfully cohabiting with more than one wife. Out of the park's three Mormon settlements, only Fruita remains, in historically managed ruin: remnants of buildings and fruit orchards along the Fremont River are maintained by the National Park Service and Mormon volunteers. Inside another canyon, Mormon settlers would stop to carve their names onto a part of the canyon walls that is now called "the Pioneer Registry" and is located along one of the easiest and most accessible hikes in the park (drawing larger numbers of visitors than most of the other easily accessible trails). The park is still considered remote, even though Utah Highway 24, built in 1962, drives right through its middle, connecting the small towns of Hanksville, Torrey, and Caineville. You can also travel to the park along Highway 12, a scenic state byway officially designated an "All American Road" by the U.S. Department of Transportation and described by the *New York Times* as one of the "country's most stunning" stretches of road.[5] Franklin Roosevelt set large portions of this area aside from economic development by declaring the area a national monument, but it wasn't until the early 1970s, after a variety of typical struggles over farming, cattle ranching, and water rights were "resolved," that Congress could designate the area a national park.[6]

When you visit the national parks that feature wilderness (such as the system's marquee parks in the West) rather than the National Park Service's historical sites (such as the birthplace of Theodore Roosevelt in New York City), you're visiting a highly administrated and manufactured experience of nature, bursting with a complicated history of bureaucracy, infrastructure, landscape design, and management. The NPS is always struggling with how to preserve and conserve parklands while also keeping them accessible and tour-friendly for the visitors that pay for them (with taxes, entrance fees, and the direct and indirect costs of not allowing these lands to develop and produce other types of privately generated revenue).[7] Welcome centers, groomed hiking trails in the front country, camping facilities, staff-housing units, utilities, gift shops, lodges, tours, films, and extensive roads for cars and buses inevitably mediate the experience of the wilderness. Even if you're the intrepid adventurer, embarking on long hikes or mountain bike and kayaking excursions in the backcountry, you still need to acquire permits and to pay fees. Such is the case with most land developments; there are hordes of competing interests and attitudes guiding park maintenance and development. The unnaturalness of this nature experience is an extensively discussed topic and surely can't be a surprise to parkgoers themselves — it is a park after all. Luckily, even amid all the obvious "interference" of the government and the public in these locations, there is still an abundance of wildlife and scenery to enjoy, offering up an orchestrated occasion with "nature" that features all sorts of "natural encounters": you can, for instance, easily get injured, be attacked by wildlife, overexert yourself, run out of water, get lost, fall victim to a flash flood, or fall victim to a fall. The parks are too vast, and the resources just too limited, to be utterly "safe" and "civilized," and there's never a first-aid center, restroom, outhouse, water fountain, or park ranger exactly when you need one.

So what attracts us to these places is not merely the wilderness experience (you could certainly find more wild and remote places) or simply an easy form of tourism — inconvenience is inevitable even in the most convenient of these wilderness parks. What might attract us most is the scenery. The *New York Times*, for example, implants the desire to travel to this remote part of Utah so we can "navigate a series of mind-bendingly beautiful mesas and wild canyons in Capitol Reef National Park, in almost near solitude."[8] Frederick Law Olmstead Jr., the son of the father of American landscape architecture, and one of the key figures in the history of the United States' national park system, offered up this assessment: "The National Parks are set apart primarily in order to preserve to the people for all time the opportunity of a peculiar kind of enjoyment and recreation, not measurable in economic terms and to be obtained only from the remarkable scenery which they contain — scenery of those primeval types which are in most parts of the world rapidly vanishing for all eternity before the increased thoroughness of the economic use of land."[9] This aesthetic and "peculiar form of enjoyment and recreation" relies on a crucial frame of focus: the vista. Andrew Jackson Downing, in his *Treatise on the Theory and Practice of Landscape Gardening,* offered crucial concepts that nearly defined the early days of park development, concepts highly influenced by British Romanticism and English garden landscape traditions — scenery, vista, enframement, and sequence. And it seems that the vista was particularly essential. In his well-documented visit to the pleasure grounds of a Hudson Valley estate, Montgomery Place, Downing provides us with an account of what was so moving about a walk in the garden: "Halfway along this morning ramble, a rustic seat, placed on a bold little plateau, at the base of a large tree, eighty feet above the water [of a river], and fenced about with a rustic barrier, invites you to linger and gaze at the fascinating river landscape here presented. It embraces the distant mountains, the sylvan foreground, and the broad river stretching away for miles, sprinkled with white sails."[10] The landscape, obviously situated in an impressive scenic setting, has a point, literally a vantage point, which a rambling walker will find after passing through a sequence of other, perhaps less dramatic natural features, only to come to a perfectly situated, rustic "bench" that has framed the shot where the beautiful distance can count as a significant view, inviting the walker to rest and reflect on the landscape. This kind of framing intensifies the scenery; it becomes a vista because it is framed, and watched from the seat that positions one's eyes, making the land into a picture. The vista is intensified focus, a view with a very important point: a grand scene to be brought to the one who is there to take "it all in."

On the morning of my first long hike through Capitol Reef, it struck me that over years of hiking there always seemed to be some particular location that served as a goal of the hike: a waterfall, a mountaintop, a lake, an arch, a land bridge. In other words, there had to be a particularly important vista, achieved after a variety of diverse sights, and a trail would bring me there, purposefully. So I had another plan. I drove my rental car down a large wash, appropriately called Grand Wash, which brought me to the trailhead of a hike that would take me to the top of Cassidy Arch. I was in the process of ignoring the cautionary advice on the park information sheets given to me at the mid-twentieth-century Mission 66-style Welcome Center at the entrance of the park, which urgently cautioned, "Never hike alone!" (Singles can never get a break.) I was also about to ignore the advice of a park ranger, who urged me to not be tempted, once I got to the arch, to then go on to the adjacent Frying Pan Trail because it would be too hot by the time I reached it. "It's not called 'Frying Pan Trail' for nothing," she said, smiling. The reason I wanted to keep venturing on was to give myself a sense of a hike that had multiple prominent vistas, which would require a trail that would lead into another trail — I'd have at least two ultimate vistas, which would shortchange each other's primacy. My expressed reason, at that point, was to hike without the hierarchy of one destination, which so often manipulates and marks the experience of a hike. Trails can't help but have a *telos*, and the sensation of achievement, or the arrival at that all-important vista, can permit you to ignore all the other scenes that have been sequenced for you. What do I inevitably miss while I'm walking toward that vista? What am I not seeing as I search for some chosen sight? Could I just enjoy wandering along these paths?

This impulse was ruined because I had failed to realize that I am always interrupting my hikes with all sorts of vista-making moments: I usually take my digital camera so I can keep recording the astonishing scenes I'm seeing, which makes me stop and take in all sorts of sights as if they are those framed vistas. Obsessed with posterity, or perhaps just with the desire to record and remind me of what I've seen and how that scene moved me, I always already chop up my hikes with endless, minor discoveries that just have to be captured. A case in point: I spent a good thirty minutes that morning taking pictures of cairns, piles of stone that have been stacked by hikers (or, in this case, park rangers and volunteers), often in a conical shape, to orient hikers. Cairns are crucial guides, especially in parts of trail that traverse the abundant slick rock in southern Utah, where there are no discernible signs of erosion that would typically index the pathway. After some time, the cairns were the bread crumbs in my midday Hansel and Gretel fantasy, a fantasy that charmed me to no end, and so I took at least seventy pictures of these ubiquitous rock formations.

Cairns, which carefully curate a hike in nature. Photo by author.

Capitol Reef welcomes you to the desert. Photo by author.

Eventually that passion subsided and was replaced by an overwhelming fear about a hypothetical mountain lion attack, implanted in me by the placard outside of the Welcome Center, advertising a ranger talk that night on "Mountain Lions in Capitol Reef National Park." If I were to come upon one of these creatures (suddenly each site was a potential hiding place), what, exactly, was I supposed to do? I had once heard that you had to smack the lion on the nose, but that was not sounding wise at that point in my paranoia. Had I dreamt that up? Also, since I hadn't done this hike before, I was wondering if I really had brought an adequate water supply: I had at least a gallon on me in various packs and containers, but was this really enough? And should I have taken a picture of that beautiful canyon a few yards back, or was this point a better view? Are any of these pictures ever going to do me any good? (Maybe I'll one day include them in a book.)

I think that, in part because I was putting myself into peril by not being with anyone else, I was feeling menaced by how I was to be connected to the experience, to the world, and to my own sense of survival. It's unnerving to not run into another soul for many hours in the hot desert sun. Your mind can go wild, which is upsetting. So how could this experience not become a parable that illustrates the case for the soothing, predictable comfort of coupledom? I'd have some kind of support in a partner: he or she would be there to relieve me or confirm me in these anxieties, and I would be "saved."

So my hike was proceeding like so many of my solo hikes, chattering, full of worries, tyrannical details, technological fixations, and an obsession with water supply, intensified by my fear of the solitude I had sought. But then, near the end of four hours, I encountered the last vista on my path. It stretched into an exhilarating distance, with a vibrant collection of colors, beautiful sky — so much so that my mind gathered all the typical clichés: breathless, amazing, incredible, and so on. I had known that this would happen, and I had done my best to resist the experience by hoping to avoid the primacy of the moment by crowding vistas, hiking contrary to the big vista, the "money shot," that had been chosen for me by landscape architects, hikers from years ago, and park officials. And yet, here I was, astonished and gushing, and all the specifics of the hike — the chopped-up moments I thought I had wanted to relish, the ones I thought I always missed — vanished, and I felt released. The history of Fruita. The history of Capitol Reef. The specific dimensions to my hike. The frightening aloneness of wandering in the hot sun alone. None of these thoughts, facts, feelings mattered in the least. They melted away as I stared at the reds, blues, greens, and browns of the view. Despite my inclination toward atheism, I muttered, "Jesus Christ," which surprised me.

Something about gorgeous vistas occasions a "peculiar form of pleasure" and aesthetic arrest, which begs for the kind of description that cannot, will not, describe: something like the sublime meets romantic clichés about nature meets New Age spiritualism, which will utterly fail to capture the view. So we're left straining

A vista of the single you. Photo by author.

to express the grandeur we're seeing and feeling. What's more, my affect had been anticipated, expected, solicited. It's nearly astonishing to note how similar the expressions of landscape appreciation tend to be. Just read the following farrago of examples: early references to Eden and Milton defended the need for establishing Yosemite, inspiring generations to "inves[t] it with spiritual qualities."[11] Orson Pratt, just after he was one of the first Mormons to descend into Utah's great basin on July 21, 1847, wrote these words: "After issuing from the mountains among which we had been shut up for many days, and beholding a moment such an extensive scenery open before us, we could not refrain from a shout of joy which almost involuntarily escaped from our lips the moment this grand and lovely scenery was within our view."[12] Utah naturalist Terry Tempest Williams, in her introduction to the cookbook from southern Utah's only Zagat-rated restaurant, the extraordinary Hell's Backbone Grill, writes the way people seem to always write about Utah's red rock wilderness; it's a "landscape of imagination," where we "are changed on a cellular level and begin to see the world differently. We remember why the desert is holy, a place for pilgrims in search of peace."[13] Edward Abbey's 1968 book of memories of his time as a park ranger in Arches National Park outside of Moab, Utah (where I not-so-coincidentally bought his book at the Arches gift shop), *Desert Solitaire: A Season in the Wilderness*, is considered a sacred desert tome; he calls the desert an "elegy," and "a tombstone," a "bloody rock."[14] Abbey feels guilt for being here because "this sweet virginal primitive land will be grateful for my departure and the absence of the tourists, will breathe metaphorically a collective sigh of relief — like a whisper of wind — when we are all finally gone and the place and its creations can return to their ancient procedures unobserved and undisturbed by the busy, anxious, brooding consciousness of man."[15] Robert Redford, who might be Utah's most famous preservationist, proclaims: "This place in the mountains, amid nature's casualness toward death and birth, is the perfect host for the inspiration of ideas: harsh at times, life threatening in its winters of destruction, but tender in attention to the details of every petal of every wildflower resurrected in the spring."[16] The National Park Service's guide to Zion National Park inflicts the following paragraph from a section called "Wrought by Water": "Immutable yet ever changing, the cliffs of Zion stand resolute, a glowing presence in late day, a wild calm. Melodies of waters soothe the desert-parched ears, streams twinkle over stone, wren song cascades from redrock cliffs, cottonwood leaves jitter on the breeze. But when lightning flashes waterfalls erupt from dry cliffs, and floods flash down waterless canyons exploding log jams, hurling boulders, croaking wild joyousness, and dancing stone and water and time. Zion is alive with movement, a river of life always here and always changing."[17] Finally, Ken Burns's twelve-hour PBS miniseries, *The National Parks: America's Best Idea*, may devote eight of its hours to repeating similar romanticisms. The series' companion illustrated history trumpets that national parks *"preserve cathedrals of stone"*[18] and quotes a young doctor in 1851, who relates the view from the western slopes of the Sierra Nevada: *"I said with some enthusiasm . . . 'I have seen the power and the glory of a Supreme Being; the majesty of His handy-work is in that "Testimony of the Rocks."'"*[19]

So the desert landscape tempts people into all sorts of gasping pathetic fallacies, into nearly nauseating metaphorical excesses — excesses that quickly slide into clichés wrangling life, nature, love, transformation, and, especially, the dangers of death and extinction. And these desert journeys are expressed with a rhetorical coherence we predictably could call "religious." Frank Lloyd Wright tries to convey the power of the desert, which he returned to each winter as an escape from the cold winters of Wisconsin, by beginning with a quotation: "Victor Hugo wrote: 'The desert is where God is and Man is not.' Arizona desert is like that."[20] It's stunning how often all sorts of people share in Wright's decision to claim a sacred quality for the desert. One can't resist, it seems, pursuing God at his home address, in God's own terms. This language, however, is relentlessly unspecific, even if you feel that the place is great, even if you feel something spiritual, even if you're not spiritual. Abbey knew what all who come to this region seem to know, you "can't get the desert into a book," or a phrase, or even an idea. "The desert is a vast world, an oceanic world, as deep in its way and as complex and various as the sea. Language makes a mighty loose net with which to go fishing for simple facts, when facts are infinite."[21] But there's always an effort to describe and capture the experience, because it "changes you," and there is often a desire to make that landscape and the effect it has on you legible enough so you can share the good news of the gospel of the new you. Can you describe that vast and holy desert, a desert that is so old that it once was the sea? No, you can't. But does that stop you? Never.

Originality is not the point. There were sensations of the "beautiful as such," and when I was staring out on the horizon, by my standing in that place I transformed it into something like a great work of art. And here, at this vista, in front of this picture, made legible and perhaps unique by my relenting to the sacred quality invoked by the cliché sensations and utterances, is where we can see the stretch of horizon that the single can offer us. Because we're literally in nature, in solitude, it's hard not to classify this experience as an encounter with the sublime — as Kant put it, "It [the sublime] must be nature or be thought of as nature."[22] I'm not going to take a strong side on whether I prefer Burke's or Kant's notion of the sublime; I'm going to wimp out and have all conceptions of the sublime — whether empiricist or formal — as the background ambience of this chapter.[23] The sublime or the beautiful, however, is not where I want to pursue, explicitly, the process of theorizing singleness — even though surely, like nature, it's always in the background. Here's what I want to claim, as we gush about the sacred qualities of the natural world: there is something theological, or, to be more precise, *rhetorically* theological that happens when we encounter our vistas by ourselves. I want to think about why the God talk on a vista is necessarily cliché talk, and how that cliché enables us to dwell within some deep pathetic fallacies for which we're not entirely responsible, thereby perhaps encouraging our gaze to take in the view. An uninspired language is evoked to grasp a moment of "inspiration," which oddly carves out some banal and generic space for self-extension. It's a form of abstraction that evacuates all the terrorizing details and upsetting proximities that bind us to a couples context at the expense of ourselves.

To help us paint this theoretical picture, I want us to consider two artists — other, much more impressive "me's" in the carefully cultivated desert, who were both known to be "loners" and who made the abstraction of singleness's vistas signatures of their formidable paintings: Georgia O'Keeffe and Agnes Martin.[24] These two women share similar biographical details, which, like the details of Capitol Reef National Park, are not going to matter in any lasting way for my argument. O'Keeffe herself insisted, "Where I was born and where and how I have lived is [*sic*] unimportant."[25] But through biography, she and Martin are easily grouped together. At roughly similar times, they moved from consuming art world activity in New York to regions of the New

Mexico desert that aren't too far from one another (the Abiquiu-Ghost Ranch region and Taos), an area that locals (or at least my tour guide at the Georgia O'Keeffe Museum) call "O'Keeffe Country." Both women are thought to have lived mostly alone in these desert homes and studios (although these facts are debatable). O'Keeffe's twenty-year relationship with the influential gallerist-photographer Alfred Stieglitz is famous, even inspiring an insipid 2009 Lifetime Network made-for-television movie on their affair, *Georgia O'Keeffe* (dir. Bob Balaban), starring the ordinarily terrific actors Joan Allen and Jeremy Irons.[26] We're told that it was only after Stieglitz's death that O'Keeffe was single enough to move to New Mexico full time. Agnes Martin's love life, on the other hand, is said to have been queer, and her relationship with her friend the American "fiber artist" Lenore Tawney is particularly noteworthy. She left New York (and whatever intimacies she might have held in her heart), the Abstract Expressionist scene centering on her studio on the Coenties Slip in Lower Manhattan, to live her famously hermitic lifestyle alone (although it's unclear how alone she was, especially as she aged and required assistance). Both O'Keeffe and Martin attained varying levels of great artistic success, and they share a narrative, a legend, of self-sufficiency, of going to the desert by oneself and cultivating a single lifestyle, that led them to become two canonical painters from the American twentieth century. These loners' lives are indeed fascinating and can fill many books and imaginations ("Were they, indeed, lovers?"), but the part of the story beyond the biography I want to draw attention to, even beyond their quasi-single-in-the-desert status, is both painters' devotion to abstract art, to certain tenets of abstraction, and the particular view on abstraction that I think of as a very single kind of view of the world.

Although Georgia O'Keeffe is most known for her flowers, her large, garish colors, and a notorious sensuality (quite purposefully engineered by her husband, especially after his choice to show a collection of nude photographs he took of her), her abstract lines are why she intrigues me, and why she helps us understand what we could call the single's perspective. She made herself into a "representational painter," so we're told, after the critical response to her earlier abstract work, which considered such forms emblematic of her sexuality. But her devotion to abstraction is something that the Georgia O'Keeffe Museum is careful to impress alongside the iconic flowers, skulls, and natural landscapes that saturate both O'Keeffe's oeuvre and people's imagination of her oeuvre: in its large coffee-table book celebrating the tenth anniversary of the museum, the volume's author, Barbara Buhler Lynes, writes: "Abstraction was always her preferred language. . . . It remained the underpinning of her art. But for over a quarter of a century, with few exceptions, she made clear the sources of her abstractions. . . . She discontinued this practice in the late 1950s, when she was in her 60s, preferring again to work directly with abstraction almost exclusively until failing eyesight ended her career in 1984."[27] Perhaps this is why the book highlights her more abstract work, as in the first section of "themes" in which the volume organizes her long career. More recently, a major exhibition from September 2009 to September 2010, called quite simply *Abstraction,* appeared at the Whitney Museum of American Art, the Phillips Collection, and the O'Keeffe Museum. As I walked through this show in Santa Fe, I again and again had the sense that the contemporary curatorial work around O'Keeffe desperately seeks to encourage a larger audience to look beyond the sexual imagery so often read into her flowers and to see a major practitioner of something like Abstract Expressionism. In other words, instead of vulvas, she was painting lines, exquisite forms, intriguing colors that could exist outside of immediate representational sense. To insist that the arc of her career never abandoned the alluring vertical and horizontal lines (such as those in her series of 1916 black and blue line paintings) is to also insist that her gestures toward verisimilitude and prominent imagery are mere distractions. In fact, my museum guide spent a great deal of time encouraging all of us in her tour group to look for repetitive shapes in her paintings: Canyons were V-shaped, right? Why did O'Keeffe paint that door on her adobe home in Abiquiu so frequently? What was it about the black rectangle that intrigued her so much? We were being directed to abstract O'Keeffe's abstraction even from the houses, canyons, deserts, and flowers we knew to be part of the ubiquitous imaginary that accompanies the impressive popularity of America's most successful woman painter.

I applaud this curatorial obsession because I appreciate abstract art, especially since we're usually overloaded by the Georgia O'Keeffe industry: so much is presumed to be known about her art before you even encounter it. Indeed, before going to the O'Keeffe Museum in Santa Fe, I thought I hated O'Keeffe — those garish, pastel petals one could find in any college dorm room, next to a Monet poster or Gustav Klimt's *The Kiss*. I had a conversion experience similar to that of Terry Castle, who in a *London Review of Books* essay, "Travels with My Mom," relates a trip she made to New Mexico, seeking O'Keeffe and Martin — "An Artistic Pilgrimage."[28] She describes her qualms about O'Keeffe in her characteristically acerbic essay style:

> Rightly or wrongly, I can't help associating O'Keeffe's work – colourful, vegetal, Modernist yet compromised, endlessly reproduced on tatty notecards, posters, and datebooks — with my mother's abstracto-feminine creations. Like the beetle-browed Frida — you know the one I mean — O'Keeffe has become a sentimental icon, the culture heroine of a generation of (now increasingly elderly) female amateur artists. After all, it's said, she was a feminist of sorts: earthy and independent; muse to a host of eminent men (Stieglitz, Paul Strand, et al.); lived almost for ever. Best of all, she is supposed to have celebrated — fairly unabashedly — something called "female sexuality." Who can contemplate those swelling pink and purple flowers — or the roseate canyon-wombs opening up within them — without thinking of the plush, ding-donging joys of female genitalia? Georgia, by god, must have had orgasms to spare. Until the 1990s — when the Asian-minimalist spa aesthetic finally took over — there was hardly a hippy-dippy hot-tub establishment between Baja and Mendocino that didn't have an O'Keeffe poster (or several) decorating the premises. The fact that the

artist seems to have been a frightful old harridan who ended up leaving her entire $50 million estate to an unsavoury boy-toy sixty years her junior is seldom allowed to tarnish the legend. Oh, and by the way — to judge by the famous Stieglitz snaps, she looked JUST LIKE A MAN.[29]

Castle's dead-on commentary permits the transformation that can occur in the O'Keeffe Museum to seem like a conversion experience:

But something odd is also happening. The paintings, when I get to them, are not, I notice, as huge and blowsy as I was expecting. Several in fact are quite small. Not Vermeer small, but definitely smallish. And one or two, I have to admit, are pleasing — especially the pre-New Mexico ones from the 1910s and 1920s. Hmmm. Addled connoisseur-brain starts gently powering up again — trying to process the unanticipated subtleties of the situation. Okay, they're all still flowers, but aren't some of them at least as good as ones by those American Modernists you like so much? You know: Marsden Hartley, Arthur Dove, Charles Demuth? If you didn't know they were hers, wouldn't you be impressed? Aren't you being hard on her — as is your perverted wont — because she's a woman? I keep looking round for more of the expected monstrosities — lewd river basins, vaginal canyons — but have only intermittent success.[30]

I read this essay after my first trip to the museum and was happy to find so many uncanny correspondences with my own experience — Castle's overcoming of her distaste for O'Keeffe (and her admiration of Agnes Martin) could have come from pages of my diary (if I had ever kept a diary). The shapes, lines, colors, and technique steal the show away from the mainstreaming of O'Keeffe, and you're brought someplace strange and interesting (much as you are by a Martin painting, as I'll discuss below). Castle seems to channel my own admiration when she singles in on one of my favorite paintings ever: "loathe all the

famous pictures but sort-of-like some of the more obscure ones
(*My Last Door*, from 1954, could almost be a Malevich [a painter
whom Castle genuinely admires])."[31] *My Last Door* features
that patio door I mentioned above, a frequent object O'Keeffe
painted throughout her life. Absent of vivid color, it features
bright whites, deep blacks, and soothing grays that pull you into
a deep consideration of the imperfect rectangular shapes of the
adobe structure, the black door, and the patio tiles that make
a dotted line underneath the famous door. I like to think that
I could spend hours staring at this painting: it transfixes you,
strands you in place, and illuminates why staring at the outlines
of recognizable things (such as a door, or a house) can send you
into untoward meanings that go beyond the sense that you're seeing a representation of a house, or a door. The lines are as important as what they are enclosing.

What's especially striking about this painting are the whiffs
of a repetitive effect O'Keeffe creates in a number of her works.
To notice this effect requires that you find the imaginary horizon line — the place where sky touches the earthly world in a
field of vision, rather than the "true" horizon (where sky touches
earth, and you can imagine vanishing into infinity). The adobe
house, near the top of the frame, serves as the horizon line, and
because it appears near the top, with very little sky painted (also
just a strip of color), you have a sense that you're very close to
the building. Yet capturing the imaginary horizon often requires
distance rather than proximity. So we have a flatness that brings
distance close. In the Georgia O'Keeffe Museum's anniversary
volume, while discussing the 1940 painting *Untitled (Red and
Yellow Cliffs)*, Lynes writes, "The cliffs . . . dominate the com-
position, allowing almost no room for sky. This implies that the
viewer is very close to them, but in order to see the green trees
near the lower edge of the painting in the scale and proportion
in which they occur in the painting, the viewer must be very far
away from the cliffs. Thus, O'Keeffe combined two very different
points of view into a single painting whose spaces are both close
and distant, or as she called it, the 'faraway nearby.'"[32] Certainly
My Last Door's faraway imaginings are not as dramatic as the red

and yellow cliffs, but the play with perspective captures a quality of flatness that's there to remind you that something distant like the horizon is not so very far away. And manipulating this horizon line creates this flatness. Bringing distance into closeness — being able to make distance part of intimacy — might not be an extraordinary contribution to art per se (certainly photography, as we're told by Lynes, can flatten spatial depth quite adeptly). But it is a crucial technique of looking at the world that I think can illuminate the power of a single's perspective.

In 1977, Georgia O'Keeffe wrote in her biography, "[I try to capture] the unexplainable thing in nature that makes me feel the world is so big and far beyond my understanding — to understand maybe by trying to put it into form. To find the feeling of infinity on the horizon line or just over the next hill."[33] In her last "unassisted painting," which she completed in 1972, *The Beyond*, O'Keeffe pursues this desire to capture the infinity of the horizon by creating a very abstract painting that might be a landscape or an oceanscape (or both, where land meets ocean).[34] The colors suggest ocean and sky: dark blues nearer the top of the painting get lighter and lighter as they reach a strip of strong white, only to then meet a strip of milky gray, then a gray-greenish blue, then stronger blue again, and then a very sharp line of pronounced black, which dominates the bottom of the painting, suggesting land. These pronounced strips bring her closer, perhaps more than most of her inventions, to the grid-obsessed work of Martin, who famously made strips of horizontal and pale color, often separated by faint graphite lines, the subjects of her paintings for the bulk of her life (or at least the paintings she did not destroy). We can see in O'Keeffe's *The Beyond* an obsession with these strong lines, these lines of infinity, these lines of horizons. How do you suggest so much beyond our usual understandings of the world we look upon? Gazing at the vista of the horizon, or multiple horizons, seems to be an important clue O'Keeffe is providing.

She's hardly alone in what she sees in her solitary, deserted landscapes. Here's what happens to Freud when he climbs a hill: "I was already a man of mature years when I stood for the first time on the hill of the Acropolis in Athens, between temple ruins, looking out over the blue sea. A feeling of astonishment mingled with joy."[35] In the next major work, *Civilization and Its Discontents*, as we've already learned, Freud elaborates the "oceanic feeling" that has been washing up on all the shores of each of my book's chapters. Unbounded qualities, those "religious" feelings, have, it seems, a pictorial vantage point, which requires bringing the faraway nearby. A contemporary of Freud's, Benjamin, also relies upon a vista to make an important point. His elusive and famous concept of the aura is most thoroughly illuminated by a dramatic view: "We define the aura . . . as the unique phenomenon of a distance, however close it may be. If, while resting on a summer afternoon, you follow with your eyes a mountain range on the horizon or a branch which casts its shadow over you, you experience the aura of those mountains, of that branch."[36] Miriam Hansen, who has, shockingly, clarified the myriad of possible tricky meanings the aura in Benjamin possesses, is shrewd to move the conversation beyond posing the aura as simply a romantic concept, something like the "beautiful semblance" or the antisocial sublime, a lyrical past that will only disintegrate with the passing into more mechanized and alienated forms of modernity. The aura, instead, is a capacious concept, a "sleight-of-hand," as Hansen phrases it, which "allows him [Benjamin] to preserve, without having to explain, the esoteric nature of the concept."[37] So much can be sheltered in the concept of the aura — there's so much room for all kinds of meaning in this concept that feels like the complexity, the richness, of singleness.

While Hansen explores a number of these esoteric qualities, she reminds us of another example of looking out at a vista, this time from Georg Simmel: "All art brings about a distancing from the immediacy of things: it allows the concreteness of stimuli to recede and stretches a veil between us and them just like the fine bluish haze that envelops distant mountains."[38] Certainly a mountain scene quickly pictures distance (that's certainly how I portrayed it as a child in grade school — two rounded mountain peaks, with a sun rising or setting between them), and distance becomes, at least for Kant, a requirement for achieving safety and pleasure in sublime encounters.[39] Distance, like the aura, is not merely sublime. Art, disenchantment, representation, the arbitrariness of the sign, nonidentity, assertions of difference all require some assertion of distance. But mountains, from afar or from their tops, do have a persistent place in essential aesthetic questions. We keep seeing something repetitive and insistent in these scenes that estrange our proximity by calling attention to a predictable and legible vastness we crave to bring closer to us. Benjamin's aura, according to Hansen, most certainly is a response to all sorts of spiritualist, occultist, theological, theosophist, and Kabbalistic accounts of self-alienation and connection to which Benjamin, however reluctantly, was attracted.[40] So why do mountains and branches create these large, distance-full sensations that people want to call "divine," or "religious," or "holy," or "spiritual," especially when those people don't believe in a religious or spiritual faith? How does the predictability of these statements reduce the grand experience but produce a reduction that actually frees one up for literally other, perhaps multiple, things rather than just one other thing (or love object)?

Hansen's reading of Benjamin's aura helps here (and it does speak to the "oceanic" in Freud), because she argues that he adapted a very generic, religious concept like the aura so it could become a nebulous and heterogeneous analytical tool that "reimagine[s] the possibility of experience in mass-mediated modernity."[41] Hansen, like Benjamin, is concerned with the mediation of "experience" through technology and film. I, however, want to wrestle Benjamin away from film and let his aura speak to the person, struggling to "reimagine" experience as a single, after touring through other social landscapes that insist that you should never be on your own, that you must always relate as two. I have no interest in insisting that these moments, in which one is in a way removed from society, staring out on something blue and majestic, are the more real and important moments of a life that we all should aspire to. Instead, I want to suggest, hypothesize, what could be at stake in these moments of singleness and what they might offer all of us who are otherwise confronted by the couples that swarm our day-to-day public sphere.

Benjamin's obsession with mass culture, his obsession with processes of standardization and mechanization and how those processes transform our senses, our capacities for perception, clues us into what to do with a particular kind of isolation. Just after he describes his auratic vista, he explains "the increasing significance of the masses in contemporary life. Namely, the desire of contemporary masses to bring things 'closer' spatially and humanly, which is just as ardent as their bent toward overcoming the uniqueness of every reality by accepting its reproduction. Every day the urge grows stronger to get hold of an object at very close range by way of its likeness, its reproduction."[42] Wonderfully, Benjamin is never quite clear if this is a good or bad development, so we're invited to play with his concepts. So, for now, here's what I want to read into what's happening in this moment in the "Work of Art" essay: when we see a vista and experience "something big and distant," we only sort of want to capture it, often reaching for the most typical words for a scene so "mind-bendingly beautiful" ("it's holy," "it's divine," etc.); we're reaching for a mass form of communication in the sense that's it's not a unique utterance or a peculiar and arcane expression — we're reaching for a mass-form of likeness. And we're safer than we think, being in a desert in a park, or on a ranch, or in an adobe home we built for ourselves. So we're grasping for domesticated clichés, not wild utterances, about the distance — the largeness, greatness, and sublimity of the situation. And by infusing the carefully presented or reached vista with our "oceanic," unbounded feelings, we're bringing it closer, making it intimate by calling it by the most typical of names. Generic spirituality, all-inclusive religious energy, an unboundedness that fills one with a greatness all help us shrug off the other kinds of attachments, terror, and fear that accompany those who are *not* single in the world. In these vista moments, I think we start to reverse Freud's version of development that requires that we grow up, bound ourselves (often by binding ourselves to a couple that starts to represent and stand in for all sorts of relational quandaries and fear), and learn to become limited and sad. And we thus seem to be evacuating out of the scene before us all its rocky, changeable, erosive particularity in the service of making it, and we who want to bring it so close, generic. All the park history, the geological fascination, the local color, and the stories of the love lives of O'Keeffe and Martin melt into a feeling of grandeur, expansiveness.

The Beyond inspired me to seek out Martin's paintings. Castle's essay features a side-excursion to Taos, New Mexico, to pay homage to Martin's work. The main attraction in Taos: seven Martin paintings in a permanent, octagon-shaped gallery lit by the soft light from an oculus that casts a serene glow on four yellow benches designed by Donald Judd. We're prepared for a "religious" experience of sorts by the museum's website about this gallery: "Scholars have compared the Harwood Museum's Agnes Martin Gallery to the Matisse Chapel and Corbusier's Ronchamp Chapel in France and the Rothko Chapel in Houston."[43] Castle glowingly describes the experience that I, inspired by Castle, repeated, almost to script, in my own August 2010 pilgrimage (although, unlike Castle, without a girlfriend or mother or anyone in tow):

> The space is bijou — only about fifteen feet across — white-walled, octagonal and windowless, with the same low light Tate Britain has in its Blake room. Seven paintings are on display, one on each wall; you go in through the eighth side of the octagon. Though plain and unadorned the space is the opposite of austere. The pictures seem alive and sentient and even to be regarding one another across the space — enjoying each other's company in a friendly familial way. It's a tiny orgone box of a room — full of faintly pulsing energy currents, but also strangely full of grace, a promise of contact. . . . The paintings are from 1993-94 — a late period as extraordinary, in its own quiet stone-butch way, as that of Titian, Milton or Yeats. You'd call it a flowering except there aren't any flowers; just the same old pencil lines and stripes. But the lines and stripes have become positively floral in their glow and poise and breeziness. Most of the pictures are pink and

blue — the same pale hues used to indicate sex in the world of baby clothes and Sippee Cups. The familiar stripes have been laid out precisely and painstakingly. . . . Martin never minded repeating titles: she saw nothing wrong with using one she liked over again or giving a new picture a title very similar to that of an earlier one. But in the late work this repetition becomes almost rhapsodic, at times even oddly sexual. Martin's last paintings all have names like *Beautiful Life, Lovely Life, An Infant's Response to Love, A Little Girl's Response to Love, I Love Love, Loving Love, I Love the Whole World.* Though Martin seems to have banished any hint of the erotic from her life — at least in her hermit years — Stein and her work again come to mind: the babyish, burbly and hypnotic love-language, say, of "As a Wife Has a Cow: A Love Story," dedicated to Alice B. Toklas."[4]

In my own prolonged reverie in the space, I stared at my arbitrary favorite (the second painting from the left once you enter, which is quite similar in feel, although not color, to O'Keeffe's *The Beyond*). I tried to recall the Rothko Chapel that I had visited ten years earlier. *Spiritualism* is a word *always* associated with Martin's work, perhaps because she gives you such serene, content-less work (other than the lines and colors). In 2009 the Guggenheim Museum in New York held an impressive show on the influence of Asian art and religious belief on modern and contemporary American art, *The Third Mind: American Artists Contemplate Asia, 1860-1989.* The show's catalogue, in the section on the period in which we historically group Martin, grasps what's at work in work such as Martin's: "The calligraphic brushstroke was an approach to abstract painting that focused on the spontaneous gesture of the artist's hand and was informed by the non-mimetic brush work of the East Asian art of calligraphy. The tradition of metaphysical speculation, particularly of Zen Buddhism but also other Asian religions . . . provided artists with a conceptual basis for the understanding and representation of the spiritual and universal potential of abstract art."[45] Spontaneous brushstrokes are not part of surviving Martin paintings, but the focus on lines, metaphysics, and especially Zen Buddhism is certainly in great abundance. Martin, as Alexandra Munroe's essay in the same catalogue notes, is hard to pin down; she's divided between two major schools of postwar American art:

> It is often remarked that Martin's grid paintings occupy an uncertain territory between Abstract Expressionism and Minimalism. From the early 1960s, living alone in the expansive desert of New Mexico, Martin developed her signature paintings of light graphite lines hand-drawn over pale oil washes, unprimed linen surfaces. . . . While she shares reductiveness, repetition, geometry, and an allover, unitary composition with her minimalist contemporaries, Martin's intentionally imperfect, slightly off-center, and weightless execution of those compositional practices compels a divergent reading. . . . Significantly, both views cite Martin's sustained interest in Asian contemplative philosophies, her friendships with [Ad] Reinhardt and [Richard] Tuttle (who was already deeply engaged with Japanese Zen Buddhist aesthetics when they met in 1963), and her affiliation with Betty Parsons, who encouraged an understanding of abstraction as an amalgam of Eastern and Western logics.[46]

So one is prone to look in Martin's work for some mysticism, something that feels like an "amalgam of Eastern and Western logics," a feeling that doesn't seem too different from the mystical insights of those desert wanderings I described above. In Taos, I felt something as I stared at the pale stripes in the Agnes Martin Gallery. The paintings were different from the faint grids I had seen most of my adult life — these were newer works. And when you get close enough, and have enough time, and especially when you can compare multiple Martin paintings right next to each other, you can obsess about her technique, especially the light graphite lines that delicately bring out the shape of the colored space between the lines. The artist Richard Tuttle, on Martin's ninetieth birthday, tries to capture what he sees and feels in front of her art and rightly fixates on her strong lines, which he considers her primary "vehicles for the most tender expressions": "When I think of an Agnes Martin painting, I see bundles of lines spread out vertically to make a horizontal line. A certain painting in the collection of the Museum of Modern Art often comes to mind. The general impression is of horizontal bands varying from white to gray to white again and so on until the entire square is filled. At this moment, the gray seems to subsume every aspect of the painting — its structure, dynamic, and pictorialism. It makes us look at the line as an afterthought, even though, upon reflection, it becomes obvious that the line is what makes it all happen."[47] No brushstrokes — but exquisite lines, which can vanish from your thinking unless you stop and consider them, unless you have the time to meditate, in a deserted gallery, in the desert, where Martin's work has brought you. The tenderness is an amalgamated mysticism straining to communicate something large and abstract that can barely be communicated, illustrated.

What I want to emphasize, and what I certainly felt as I was nearly touching each slightly wavering graphite mark with my one squinting eye, is the power of the horizontal lines. Even in her more traditional graph paintings, the darker marks tend to be the horizontals. They are, in fact, imaginary horizons that perhaps make each line feel especially available as a vehicle of tender emotion, a tenderness that happens to the single who has the time and room to look and reflect. Ned Rifkin, in a catalogue for an exhibition on Martin's later work, insists on the centrality of the horizon line, especially since he includes a poem by Edwin Hirsch, "The Horizontal Line (Homage to Agnes Martin)," to introduce the collection. Rifkin, who immediately locates her work in the realm of the "ineffable," dissects her technique: "The tracery of pencil lines drawn at consistent increments of space reveals an irregular hand, one that stops and restarts to span the width of the canvas, using a simple ruler to guide each line's implicit parallel relationship to the edges of the top and bottom of the canvas. Martin's compositions are symmetrically divided around a central horizontal divide. This balanced approach to dividing the painted area of the canvas discloses the artist's propensity for geometric order. Yet it is the irregularities within this context of geometric order and symmetry that uncover the humanity of the artist's touch."[48] Humanity, in Rifkin's use, is evidence of imperfection — the implication that perfection is not human, maybe something a machine or a god might be capable of, but definitely not an artist with some perspective that stirs your sense of the really big, unknowable questions. Tellingly, he quotes an oft-quoted sentiment of Martin's: "'I hope I have made it clear that the work is *about* perfection as we are aware of it in our minds,' the artist said in 1973, 'but that the paintings are very far from being perfect — completely removed in fact — even as we ourselves are.'"[49] So to paint about perfection is not the same as the painting being perfect, and Martin's technique (straight lines that aren't straight, that aren't consistent) impresses as much. In fact, the painting's wishes deepen our understanding that we can hold a view of ourselves that has been "removed" from perfection. Alienation and enlightenment, however, are not the names for this particular artistic effect; instead, the meditation is on separation from the aspiration for the achievement of perfection. You start to feel that the horizon is there to make you consider separations, and, as I want to suggest, separations between perfection (immortality) and imperfection (mortality). And in spite of these lines between the heavenly and the earthly, and the impossibility of reaching them (the horizon is always growing away from you), Martin's work encourages the aspiration of striving for perfection, for a spiritual awareness that exceeds the regular earthly world, which is perhaps what makes her art so compelling for so many.

In one of her best-known poemlike essays, "The Untroubled Mind," Martin's reveries about her desert inspire an important formal innovation:

> I used to paint mountains here in New Mexico and I
>   thought
> my mountains looked like ant hills
> I saw the plains driving out of New Mexico and I thought
> the plain had it
> just the plane.

If you draw a diagonal, that's loose at both ends
I don't like circles — too expanding
When I draw horizontals
you see this big plane and you have certain feelings like
you're expanding over the plane."[50]

Her decision, by way of horizontals and grids, to develop the abstract, flat planes as her method to capture some quality of the plains in her desert view is more than a preference for one kind of shape over another. Martin assures us that she sees great freedom in the abstraction of planes, and in order to explain such release she develops a theory of impersonality that we can associate with the theories of Leo Bersani and Adam Phillips in their shared work *Intimacies*, where they propose "alternatives to the violent games of selfhood," especially through the elaboration of an idea of "impersonal intimacy" in which people don't destructively overpersonalize and territorialize their relations with each other, enabling, instead, "an experience of exchange, of intimacy, of desire indifferent to personal identity."[51] They're writing about generic interpersonal relating (ideas I've been building upon, but without their focus on the interpersonal exchanges). Martin articulates something similar:

If a person goes walking in the mountains that is not
        detached
and impersonal, he's just looking back
Being detached and impersonal is related to freedom
That's the answer for inspiration
The untroubled mind
Plato says that all that exists are shadows
To a detached person the complication of involved life
is like chaos
If you don't like chaos you're a classicist
If you like it you're a romanticist."[52]

Here she is in a way developing a notion of classicism's perfection — its ideals, which she pits against the context of human imperfection. "Classicism," for Martin, "is not about people / and this work is not about the world. . . . It represents something that isn't possible in the world / More perfection than is possible in the world / It's as unsubjective as possible."[53] Moreover, this inhuman perfection, not available on this earth, has a particular kind of temperature that removes it from the stumbling passions of romanticism, if not romantics more generally: "The classic is cool / a classical period / it is cool because it is impersonal."[54] Not hot, not impetuous, not violent. Cool, calm, but not collected: like Bartleby perhaps. Not passion, but something else — from the distant past; the distance that has no specific past; the distance of the plane.[55]

The divisions between the domains of perfection and imperfection, especially in the ideas Martin names as classical, do indeed amalgamate Eastern and Western logics. But she's doing more. Rosalind Krauss's early essay on Martin and other artists of the grid rightly argues for a more capacious understanding of what story might be told in an image of geometric space: "In the cultist space of modern art, the grid serves not only as emblem but also as myth."[56] I choose to read the classical myth of Martin's grid, understood structurally, as one about the intensified focus on the split between perfection and imperfection — or, in mythical parlance, what we could call the split between heavenly and earthly realms. This classical division is different, I want to suggest, from the mythical division that love makes between people who are then obsessed with overcoming that division by falling violently in love; Martin, indeed, doesn't like the circle. Her classicism is more like the heroism I referred to in the last chapter. Her work on division is the horizon where sky touches earth and where all those figurative, historical, and mythical connotations of sky and earth (divine and human) can be gathered as an alternative to the violence of Aristophanes' violent cut — the line drawn through large beings that were being punished for being too grand, too divinely imitative. Christopher Gill's translation of Plato's *Symposium* brings out quite a visceral dimension to this crucial image of couples' love, which highlights centrality of perspective in Aristophanes' speech: "As he [Zeus] cut each one, he told Apollo to turn the face and the half-neck attached to it toward the gash, so that humans would see their own wound and be more orderly[.]"[57] That's the sum-total horizon of the lover's look: the gash, which is replaced by the representative of that gash: the other, missing half, originated by the punishment of the gash — the other half of the dying couple. Your lover. The frame of the world fills up with the punishing and regulating control of your other's face, which is a gash at which you must forever stare (it's your punishment for aspiring to greatness). Martin's classical reference point, however, insists on a much less intimate point of view, with a larger, less subjective and subjugating sense of what will stand in to represent the world. For Martin, the gaze is turned away from the gash that the other marks through and among you. Instead, you "see this big plane and you have certain feelings like you're expanding over the plane." You look at the horizon, which marks where heaven and earth (not two people) meet.

This redirection of your gaze is what my whole book has been preparing you for. Leo Bersani, while glossing Freud's 1914 essay on narcissism, provides some helpful language: "The loving subject projects onto the loved one his own idealized and now lost infantile ego."[58] Freud associates the "oceanic feeling" with infantile narcissism — but the single's gaze onto the ocean, or even the ancient ocean (a desert), projects one's own sense of unboundedness onto the plane, the vista, rather than the loved one, who will fail to express everything, forever. The single, however, is not reducing the loved one, with its gashed and controlling narcissism — she or he is letting the loved one off the hook. It's a generous rather than neurotic kind of narcissism (to use Freud's terminology, but only if that works for you). In many ways, I like to think that the single — not self-centered but self-horizoned (if you will) — can take the weight of the world off the shoulders of the couple: from this perspective, the single alleviates the pressure of relation. This perspective can encourage you to return you to yourself, making you into something like a vista rather than a gashed and ghostly spouse. Sure, this view is impossible to achieve fully — you're obviously not a vista, you're bounded, restricted, and you don't have the landscape's endurance. But it's a crucial theoretical gesture that imagines yourself to be an empty fullness like what the desert implies. It's something akin to what Rei Terada inspiringly claims while discussing Freud's *Civilization and Its Discontents* at the end of her book on "looking away": "Bringing this figure [of combined utopian plenitude and its dystopian figure of analytical negation] back to the critical debate about whether or how to think about impossible projects, though, may help to clarify why, for a reservation that seems both too small and too large to be spoken, an unconditional space is a better idea than the few seconds of tolerance we usually give ourselves."[59] In my take on Terada, I imagine the single self, looking not away exactly but far away into the distance. The single is a *flâneur* figure with an impossible thought project — one who stands in a way of existence that is as unconditional as the vista she surveys, who can tolerate herself for much longer, much larger, than the couple's chopping block ordinarily permits.

In other words, the single is trying to resacralize itself by removing the face of the other. The single goes to this "holy" place and doesn't just see the painful, standardizing culture of couple control: instead, she or he sees something very abstract that has only an unspecific language of cliché but nevertheless opens up an extremely important panorama on the grand, distant, oceanic, deserted world. "That's religion / solitude and independence for a free mind," proclaims Martin.[60] We could say that the horizon points us toward striving for our immortality rather than for eternity. The single stares at a vast, oceanic, and religious distance. So whether you have religion or not (I don't), I offer you a generic beatitude that will purposefully not capture all that's in our sight lines: blessed is the single, for she or he stares at God. Or something like God.

The Secret I Can't Keep

"The single, watching god" is the heroic vision that the pilgrimage to the desert can inspire. This insight reverberates through a variety of works that have the courage to present the perspective of the single who, by all rights, is thought not to have any. Virginia Woolf ends her own story of a painting, *To the Lighthouse*, with an Agnes Martin twist — we finish the novel with a single person, horizon obsessed. Lily Briscoe, a painter, struggles throughout the novel to complete a portrait for the novel's patriarch, Mr. Ramsay:

> "He must have reached it," said Lily Briscoe aloud, feeling suddenly completely tired out. For the Lighthouse had become almost invisible, had melted away into a blue haze, and the effort of looking at it and the effort of thinking of him landing there, which both seemed to be one and the same effort, had stretched her body and mind to the utmost. Ah, but she was relieved. Whatever she wanted to give him, when he left her that morning, she had given him at last . . . Quickly, as if she were recalled by something over there, she turned to her canvas. There it was — her picture. Yes, with all its greens and blues, its lines running up and across, its attempt at something. It would be hung in attics, she thought; it would be destroyed. But what did it matter? she asked herself, taking up her brush again. She looked at the steps; they were empty; she looked at her canvas; it was blurred. With a sudden intensity, as if she saw it clear for a second, she drew a line there, in the centre. It was done; it was finished. Yes, she thought, laying down her brush in extreme fatigue. I have had my vision.[61]

Her gift to Mr. Ramsay, which the completion of the painting might represent, is unspecified. And that's not really the point of the painting. This painting is not a gift for only one person — in fact, we don't know who will see it in the offing: it may be "hung in attics" or "destroyed." The painting's subject is, of course, Mr. Ramsay's destination, the lighthouse. But the lighthouse is becoming invisible, melting into abstraction. And as she paints, Lily's self, her details, become obscure — she's stretching and expanding body and mind as she stares into the expansiveness. These transformations are not about what she's gazing at per se, or about who or what she might be claiming as her deepest concern. It's all about the canvas, which draws her and asks her, somehow, to finish her work. So Lily completes her vision, her own painting of an ocean that has required that she work through an artistic desert of sorts — this time, instead of a desert, an ocean represents the "oceanic." Woolf's book ends with the drawing (not painting) of a line, which I can't help but think of as a horizon line (that's my reading). As in O'Keeffe's *The Beyond*, the blues and greens of the water create multiple lines, graphs, producing a blurry intensity that suggests clarity, a clarity that by virtue of being expressed in the painting we can't see in the novel remains undisclosed in Lily's mind. Nothing in the canvas is described clearly, which is noteworthy in a Woolf novel, where the sparest of gestures can be unpacked with extensive and impressive meaning. This abstraction, moreover, leads to the horizon, the line that divides the mortal and immortal worlds rather than people trapped in the awful commandment to build all the intimacy in their lives while facing one other person. Lily draws a line, in the sand as it were, and decides that that is the vista she wants to insist upon and will give to the world: an abstract scene of striving for the completion of a painting — a work full of grandeur, which might, wherever it lands, impress upon those who see it the unspecified power she's felt, all alone, inside.

Although she is one, it's difficult to think of Lily as a hero. She's an odd character who is tricky to get a critical hold on because she's not moored in our field of vision by a partner. She makes me think of another one of Woolf's single women, from *Mrs. Dalloway*: Miss Kilman, the historian who is devoted to religion and who desperately loves Clarissa's daughter, Elizabeth. Over tea, Miss Kilman tries to detain young Elizabeth, using her knowledge and ideas to flirt, to possess this precious person. ("She had lent her books. Law, medicine, politics, all professions are open to women of your generation, said Miss Kilman."[62]) The desperate feelings of the couple can't help but slice through Miss Kilman: "She was about to split asunder, she felt. The agony was so terrific. If she could grasp her, if she could clasp her, if she could make her hers absolutely and forever and then die; that was all she wanted" (132). Elizabeth doesn't stay, and the mediated voice that focalizes Miss Kilman's feelings describes her in nearly monstrous terms: "The thick fingers curled inwards" (132); "Beauty had gone, youth had gone. . . . She got up, blundered off among the little tables, rocking slightly from side to side" (133). As an antidote to the loss and to the overwhelming feelings of disquiet that cast her as grotesque, Miss Kilman goes to the abbey, where she seeks a more generous kind of religious insight (more generous than the controlling morality that she wields against Elizabeth and Clarissa and uses to repress herself). She presses her hands together in prayer:

> But Miss Kilman held her tent before her face. Now she was deserted; now rejoined. New worshippers came in from the street to replace the strollers, and still, as people gazed round and shuffled past the tomb of the Unknown Warrior, still she barred her eyes with her fingers and tried in this double darkness, for the light in the Abbey was bodiless, to aspire above the vanities, the desires, the commodities, to rid herself both of hatred and of love. Her hands twitched. She seemed to struggle. Yet to others God was accessible and the path to Him smooth. Mr. Fletcher, retired, of the Treasury, Mrs. Gorham, widow of the famous K.C., approached Him simply, and having done their praying, leant back, enjoyed the music (the organ pealed sweetly), and saw Miss Kilman at the end of the row, praying, praying, and, being still on the threshold of their underworld, thought of her sympathetically as a soul haunting the same territory; a soul cut out of immaterial substance; not a woman, a soul. (134)

The "deserted" Miss Kilman, "a soul haunting the same territory," is here watched by two other people who do not form a couple with each other (Mr. Fletcher might have a spouse, but we don't know; Mrs. Gorham is a widow), but these two souls can access an easier "path" to religious feeling. Their impression of Miss Kilman's immateriality, her place on this earth, however, is transformed, at least in the estimation of Mr. Fletcher:

But Mr. Fletcher had to go. He had to pass her, and being himself neat as a new pin, could not help being a little distressed by the poor lady's disorder; her hair down; her parcel on the floor. She did not at once let him pass. But, as he stood gazing about him, at the white marbles, grey window panes, and accumulated treasures (for he was extremely proud of the Abbey), her largeness, robustness, and power as she sat there shifting her knees from time to time (it was so rough the approach to her God — so tough her desires) impressed him, as they had impressed Mrs. Dalloway (she could not get the thought of her out of her mind that afternoon), the Rev. Edward Whittaker, and Elizabeth too. (134)

She can't be known, she has a tough exterior, but she's full of something ("largeness," "robustness," and "power") that makes an impression. Much like Bartleby's lawyer, this retired man can't help being fascinated by Miss Kilman's abstract qualities, which are not qualities so readily detected in one who is kneeling in prayer. Her body, not her soul, convinces him that she has something like a more material soul, enclosed in its vibrancy, replete with urgency of hard desire, that gets into one's head. In fact, Miss Kilman is unforgettable to those around her, even if they're not sure why, or what she's done. She's a presence as she yearns to overcome the trifling details of her life, the divisive emotions of love and hate, the vanities, the desires, the commodities. This prayer, this reverie, this robust struggle leaves its mark. Here's a solitary soul, uncoupled, unloved, who cannot leave your mind. It's as if the oceanic feeling had swelled within her, allowing for her to achieve something impressive we're not permitted to know as she "tents" her face from our view.

Miss Kilman is pushing herself toward that horizon line, so to speak, trying to imagine a world beyond her fatal love for Elizabeth. It's not a particular religious devotion she's practicing as much as an aspiration for more kindness, for a calmer set of desires — for a more peaceful path out of her sense of desertion (by Elizabeth) and into a feeling that will help her aspirations to rise "above" the vanities she sees in all the beauty in the world that leaves her once the youthful Elizabeth makes her choice to leave. Miss Kilman is asking for more than a pretty face to shield her from the difficulties of the world. Instead, she is pictured reforming herself, reversing her binds as she strives, regardless of the difficulty, *for more*, "praying, praying." To put this most simply, Miss Kilman is learning to be heroic in her singleness — and she succeeds, at least from the point of view of Mr. Fletcher, Reverend Whittaker, and yes, even her beloved object of deadly devotion, Elizabeth. Miss Kilman has a vision of herself, as do Lily, O'Keeffe, and Martin, stretching above and beyond her circumstances.

So the secret of immortality I'm revealing is just on the horizon, where we can imagine relation beyond the supremacy of the couple. It's about striving to be heroic without killing those we most love. In front of you is immortality on the horizon instead of a face. Don't worry, that face you love might be next to you, helping rather than hurting, encouraging rather than compromising. Or there might even be many faces of friends, families, communities, or animals. Or there might be just you. And as we stare at the horizon line, we can be encouraged in the knowledge that the way to be heroic, or "religious" (and I must insist on religion's metaphoricity because belief is of no necessary consequence here), is to be not in a couple, or at least a couple that is predicated on an eternity that encircles you in the terrible metaphorics of death.

I want to end this book by returning to the other novel I discussed in the first chapter: Anne Carson's *Autobiography of Red*. Geryon, like Miss Kilman (and the other deserted figures from this chapter), is single, recovering from the couple. Once Herakles leaves Geryon, "Water! Out from between two crouching masses of the world the word leapt," and so it "was raining on his face. He forgot for a moment that he was a brokenheart / then he remembered. Sick lurch / downward to Geryon trapped in his own [or Morrissey's?] bad apple. Each morning a shock / to return to the cut soul."[63] What to do with this natural element, these raindrops, the tears (he's always crying) erupting from the battle between two masses? How to heal the cut, the gash? It helps that time and distance intervene. Herakles leaves, so Geryon wrestles in "a numb time" (72), which sounds like another phrase for a "couple's eternity," but eventually he must bring this concept of time back to earth: "'What is time made of?' is a question that had long exercised Geryon" (93). So in the chapter "Distances," we watch as he returns "time" and other great mysteries to the human world, which he now surveys in his occupation as a photographer, bringing the "faraway nearby" in frozen moments. More concretely, he travels to photograph South America. And we are permitted to see our little monster have a deep feeling of pleasure, which he's not had since Herakles left:

> Then a miracle occurred
> in the form of a plate of sandwiches.
> Geryon took three and buried his mouth in a delicious
>   block of white bread
> filled with tomatoes and butter and salt.
> He thought about how delicious it was, how he liked
>   slippery foods, how
> slipperiness can be of different kinds.
> I am a philosopher of sandwiches, he decided. Things good
>   on the inside.
> He would like to discuss this with someone.
> And for a moment the frailest leaves of life contained him in
>   a widening happiness.
> When he got back to the hotel room
> he set up the camera on the windowsill and activated the
>   timer, then positioned
> himself on the bed.
> It is a black and white photograph showing a naked young
>   man in a fetal position.
> He has entitled it "No Tail!"
> The fantastic fingerwork of his wings is outspread on the
>   bed like a black lace
> map of South America.
> (97)

The camera's timer can materialize time by freezing time, picturing the advent of Geryon's own sense of distance: the "widening of happiness," the "wings outspread" from the fetal young man (no longer only a monster) are steps toward making small Geryon's cut-apart self large again, so large that he can represent the world (or, in this moment, a map of South America) without being "tailed" by the couple that made him feel especially small and monstrous.

But Geryon makes real progress when he re-encounters Herakles during his South American travels. At this point Geryon is dating Ancash, who interrupts the eternity of Geryon and Herakles, making it harder for Geryon to be pulled back into the myth of Herakles, even when they travel as a threesome together, and even when Geryon and Herakles have sex again. Certainly, while "Geryon sat in the back watching the edge of Herakles' face" (131) and in "the space between them / developed a dangerous cloud" (132), Geryon is all too aware that he can't be pulled back to the old days: he "knew he must not go back into the cloud. Desire is no light thing" (133). Carson, in this chapter, twice refers to Geryon watching the "edge," the "side" of Herakles' face, recalling the formal dangers of the desire to couple with his chopped-off half. Even when Geryon slips "And I want to be in love with someone" — a sharp emotion arrives with haste and violence: "This too fell on him deeply. It is all wrong. / Wrongness came like a lone finger / chopping through the room and he ducked" (136).

And Ancash is now hanging around, making the threatening twoness seem even worse. He has a current claim on the foolish but devilishly handsome Herakles, so his eternity comes into violent contact with Geryon's recurring past. Infuriated by Geryon's sleeping with Herakles after all these years, Ancash confronts, quite violently, the red monster:

> So what's it like — Ancash stopped. He began again. So
>   what's it like fucking him now?
> *Degrading,* said Geryon
> without a pause and saw Ancash recoil from the word.

I'm sorry I shouldn't have said that,
said Geryon but Ancash was gone across the garden. At the
    door he turned
Geryon?
Yes.
There is one thing I want from you.
Tell me.
Want to see you use those wings.
(144)

And so in kind, Geryon does something an immortal might
do: he wants to give Ancash a gift, perhaps out of guilt for fucking
Herakles, but also perhaps because Ancash has saved him from
his death in the couple. Geryon wakes up his dormant wings, and
does what only he can do, alone (and single):

He has not flown for years but why not
be a black speck raking its way toward the crater of
    Icchantikas on icy possibles, why not rotate
the inhuman Andes at a personal angle and retreat when it
    spins — if it does
and if not, win
bolts of wind like slaps of wood and the bitter red
    drumming of wing muscle on air — he flicks Record.
This is for Ancash, he calls to the earth diminishing below.
    This is a memory of our beauty. He peers down
at the earth heart of Icchantikas dumping all its photons out
    of her ancient eye and he smiles for the camera: "The
    Only Secret People Keep."
(145)

This moment of flying by one's self has brought Geryon to
a vantage point, the necessary distance that we might call the
classicism of a single's perspective — not unlike Clarissa watching her neighbor, and not unlike Freud, who characterizes the
oceanic feeling of religion by quoting Schiller, "Let him rejoice
who breathes up here in the roseate light!" (Freud, 21). Geryon

gives us a memory of our beauty by way of an image of beauty's horizon, which includes Ancash, Herakles, himself, and perhaps all us mortals who are striving to be great, grasping, and flying high above this big red earth.

In the final section of the romance, "THE FLASHES IN WHICH A MAN POSSESSES HIMSELF," Geryon has finally learned to no longer be in a couple. After this vision quest, Geryon walks with Ancash and Herakles, and suddenly, they each turn around and look, not at each other, but at a bakery oven, in a wall, a "Volcano in a wall":

> Did you see that, says Ancash.
> *Beautiful,* Herakles breathes out. He is looking at the men.
> *I mean fire,* says Ancash.
> Herakles grins in the dark. Ancash watches the flames.
> We are amazing beings,
> Geryon is thinking. We are neighbors of fire.
> And now time is rushing towards them
> where they stand side by side with arms touching,
>   immortality on their faces,
> night at their back.
> (146)

We are left with these precious insights: the arms of neighbors touching; an endurance in the space of rushing time; and the beautiful, majestic insights of a single who can lift himself up quite high. Certainly, if you choose, you can fall in love, get married (to one wife or many), make a will, share a bedroom if you want. You can also go underground; prefer not to; go to the desert and paint some pictures; go to a national park to dance and hang off rocks; go for a hike; or refuse to let your grandma or Beyoncé scare you into no longer being a single lady. Geryon, having found the strength of his wings again, is here to show us the simple but forgotten fact that "We are amazing beings," capable of striving for and arriving at great heights, great views of the wide expansive world. A romantic, perhaps silly romantic notion, but a romance that belongs to one rather than two and a romance that's not necessarily easy, or pleasurable (being single is very difficult indeed). Yet it's a romance that is not marked for tragedy, fatality, and failure from its beginning. Instead of dead cattle, we have fire, a connection, and a sense of a large, great feeling that can burn our faces with something like immortality — a kind of red complexion befitting us desert monsters all. Geryon is urging us to have less love, more "religion." And I can see no earthly reason I should resist his advice.

Notes

Introduction

The chapter epigraph of Charles Baudelaire's "Paysage" ("Landscape") is taken from *The Flowers of Evil,* ed. and trans. James McGowan (Oxford: Oxford University Press, 1998), 166 – 67. The epigraph of Roland Barthes's *A Lover's Discourse* is taken from *A Lover's Discourse: Fragments,* trans. Richard Howard (New York: Hill and Wang, 1978), 1.

1 In my understanding of Freud's definition of melancholia, there is an internalization of the lost attachment, which cannot be mourned (and thus be a loss that can be worked through). What I'll be suggesting, in the sentimental logic of the couple, is that internalization is not necessarily the most helpful way to think about couples' reliance on a logic of threatening loss for so long that the couple is already ghostlike from the beginning. In fact, the loss of the significant other is a literalization of what has been there all along: a specter that is your loving companion. The physical death is certainly awful and challenging, but it doesn't mean that the metaphorics of emotional place in the person's psyche (heart) has been internalized any more than years before the loss. So I'm resisting melancholy's internal metaphorics not because Freud's definition is incorrect but because I want the outside of the partner's loss to be a figuration that we don't abandon because the partner has died. See Sigmund Freud, "Mourning and Melancholia," in *The Standard Edition of the Complete Psychological Works of Sigmund Freud,* vol. 14 *(1914 – 1916),* ed. and trans. James Strachey (London: Hogarth Press, 1961), 239 – 58.

2 Candace Bushnell, *Sex and the City* (New York: Time Warner Books, 2001), ix.

3 Ibid., x.

4 See "Weddings: Vows, Candace Bushnell, Charles Askegard," *New York Times,* July 7, 2002, www.nytimes.com/2002/07/07/style/weddings-vows-candace-bushnell-charles-askegard.html.

5 Bushnell, *Sex and the City,* 243.

6 *Bridget Jones's Diary,* dir. Sharon Maguire, 2001.

7 Bella M. DePaulo, *Singled Out: How Singles Are Stereotyped, Stigmatized, and Ignored, and Still Live Happily Ever After* (New York: St. Martin's

Press, 2007). DePaulo writes, "T[he] stigmatizing of people who are single — whether divorced, widowed, or ever single — is the twentieth-century problem with no name" (2). I'd say the problem goes back further, but I heartily agree with the sentiment.

8   Christopher Stewart, Terius Nash, Kuk Harrel, and Beyoncé Knowles, "Single Ladies (Put a Ring on It)," on the album *I Am Sasha Fierce* (Columbia, 2008).

9   For an example of this important line of inquiry, see Michael Warner, *The Trouble with Normal* (Cambridge, MA: Harvard University Press, 2000).

10   A slew of studies, memoirs, and essays about singleness have been appearing recently. New ones appear all the time, so I could never hope to be comprehensive. I especially appreciated the excellent titles suggested by the anonymous reader of my book for NYU Press; some I had already known, but together they produce a compelling archive of how people are writing about singleness: Sara Maitland's *A Book of Silence*, Vicki Mackenzie's *A Cave in the Snow*, Jenny Diski's *Stranger on the Train*, Admiral Byrd's *Alone*, Captain Joshua Slocum's *Sailing Alone around the World*, Anthony Storr's *Solitude*, and Adam Sharr's *Heidegger's Hut*. My book, however, differs somewhat from these writings in that it proposes how to think the single, not just as an aberration from the couple, but as a necessary political, theoretical, literary, and philosophical intervention into the hierarchy that privileges the couple.

11   Thomas Dumm, *Loneliness as a Way of Life* (Cambridge, MA: Harvard University Press, 2008), 26.

12   David Riesman with Nathan Glazer and Reuel Denney, *The Lonely Crowd, Revised Edition: A Study of the Changing American Character* (New Haven: Yale University Press, 2001).

13   I'm taking the term *stranger-intimacy* from Georg Simmel via Mark Seltzer, *Serial Killers: Death and Life in America's Wound Culture* (New York: Routledge, 1997), esp. 41 – 45.

14   Eric Oakley, "David Riesman: *The Lonely Crowd*," Yahoo Associated Content, November 16, 2005, www.associatedcontent.com/article/13832/david_riesman_the_lonely_crowd_pg2.html?cat=38.

15   Barack Obama, *Dreams from My Father: A Story of Race and Inheritance* (New York: Three Rivers Press, 1995, 2004), 91.

16   Ibid., 140.

17   Ibid., 124.

18   Ibid., 127.

19   Ibid., 439.

20   Ibid., 440.

21   Ibid., 442.

22   Robert D. Putnam, *Bowling Alone: The Collapse and Revival of American*

Community (New York: Simon and Schuster, 2001); John T. Cacioppo and William Patrick, *Loneliness: Human Nature and the Need for Social Connection* (New York: Norton, 2009).

23 Nathanael West, *Miss Lonelyhearts* (New York: New Directions, 1962), 1, 179.

24 Henry David Thoreau, *Walden: Or, Life in the Woods,* in *The Norton Anthology of American Literature,* 4th ed., vol. 1, ed. Nina Bayn et al. (New York: W. W. Norton, 1994), 1790.

25 Dumm, *Loneliness.* I like very much Dumm's impulses in this book to not eschew but embrace the pain and difficulty of loneliness.

26 Ibid., 168.

27 Cacioppo and Patrick, *Loneliness,* 5.

28 Ibid., 12.

29 Ibid.

30 See my *God Hates Fags: The Rhetorics of Religious Violence* (New York: New York University Press, 2006).

31 Laura Kipnis, *Against Love: A Polemic* (New York: Pantheon, 2003), 26. Subsequent citations to this work are to this edition and are given parenthetically in the text.

32 Hannah Arendt, *The Origins of Totalitarianism* (1951; repr., San Diego: Harcourt, 1976), 478. Subsequent citations to this work are to this edition and are given parenthetically in the text.

33 Thoreau, *Walden,* 1789.

34 See all of Lauren Berlant, *The Queen of America Goes to Washington City: Essays on Sex and Citizenship* (Durham: Duke University Press, 1997).

35 DePaulo, *Singled Out,* 2.

36 Thornton Wilder, *The Bridge of San Luis Rey* (1927; repr., New York: Harper and Row, 1986), 18.

37 Kathryn Bond Stockton, *The Queer Child, or Growing Sideways in the Twentieth Century* (Durham: Duke University Press, 2009), 10.

38 Eve Kosofsky Sedgwick, *Epistemology of the Closet* (Berkeley: University of California Press, 1990), 72.

39 Judith Butler, *Precarious Life: The Powers of Mourning and Violence* (London: Verso, 2004), 139.

40 I'm thinking of figures of loneliness and problematic coupling in Eve Kosofsky Sedgwick, "Jane Austen and the Masturbating Girl" and "A Poem Is Being Written," from *Tendencies* (Durham: Duke University Press, 1993); Leo Bersani, *Homos* (Cambridge, MA: Harvard University Press, 1995); and, in a way, Lee Edelman, *No Future: Queer Theory and the Death Drive* (Durham: Duke University Press, 2004). Sedgwick's focus on the ways that the witnessing of masturbatory desire can teach us much about modern sexual identities is, typically, excellent. I'd like to resist, however, a reliance on sexual desire in my preliminary investigations of loneliness.

41 Leo Bersani and Ulysse Dutoit, *Forms of Being: Cinema, Aesthetics, and Subjectivity* (London: British Film Institute, 2004), 67.

42 Ibid., 67–68.

43 Ibid., 67.

44 Sedgwick, "Jane Austen," 129.

45 Walter Benjamin, "The Work of Art in the Age of Mechanical Reproduction," in *Illuminations*, ed. Hannah Arendt, trans. Harry Zohn (New York: Schocken Books, 1968), 223.

46 Ibid., 223.

47 Benjamin, "On Some Motifs in Baudelaire," in *Illuminations*, 193.

48 Ibid., 194.

49 Thomas Laqueur, *Solitary Sex: A Cultural History of Masturbation* (New York: Zone Books, 2004), 23.

50 Giorgio Agamben, *Homo Sacer: Sovereign Power and Bare Life,* trans. Daniel Heller-Roazen (Stanford: Stanford University Press, 1998), 47.

51 Sigmund Freud, "On Narcissism," in Strachey, *Standard Edition of the Complete Psychological Works,* vol. 14, trans. James Strachey (London: Hogarth Press, 1961), 85.

52 Thanks to Debra Fried for turning this phrase for me during a lecture at Cornell University, November 2009.

53 Anne Carson, "Every Exit Is an Entrance (A Praise of Sleep)," in *Decreation* (New York: Alfred A. Knopf, 2005), 20.

54 Arendt, *Origins of Totalitarianism,* 474.

1. The Inevitable Fatality of the Couple

The epigraph to *Romeo and Juliet* is from act 5, scene 3, line 169. The epigraph to Sappho is from fragment 42, in *If Not, Winter: Fragments of Sappho,* trans. Anne Carson (New York: Alfred A. Knopf, 2002).

1 The interviews appended as extras to the DVD edition of the film recount this story of the film and the writer's postrelease success. See *Love Story* (dir. Arthur Hiller, 1970; DVD, 2001).

2 Melinda Henneberger, "Author of 'Love Story' Disputes a Gore Story," *New York Times,* December 14, 1997, http://query.nytimes.com/gst/fullpage.html?res=9801EED9163FF937A25751C1A961958260&n=Top/Reference/Times%20Topics/People/G/Gore,%20Tipper.

3 The discussions of American deathbed sentimentality are long and varied, especially those concerning *Uncle Tom's Cabin.* See, for instance, Leslie Fiedler, *Love and Death in the American Novel* (1960; repr., New York: Avon, 1992); Jane Tompkins, *Sensational Designs: The Cultural Work of American Fiction, 1790–1860* (New York: Oxford University Press, 1985); Ann Douglas, *The Feminization of American Culture* (1977; repr., New York: Avon, 1978); Nancy Armstrong, "Why Daughters Die: The Racial Logic of American Sentimentalism," *Yale Journal of Criticism*

7, no. 2 (1994): 1–24; Hortense J. Spillers, *Black, White, and in Color: Essays on American Literature and Culture* (Chicago: University of Chicago Press, 2003); and Lauren Berlant, *The Female Complaint: The Unfinished Business of Sentimentality in American Culture* (Durham: Duke University Press, 2008).

4 Georg Simmel, "The Isolated Individual and the Dyad," in *The Sociology of Georg Simmel,* ed. and trans. Kurt H. Wolff (London: Free Press of Glencoe, 1950), 124.

5 Plato, *The Symposium,* ed. and trans. Alexander Nehamas and Paul Woodruff (Indianapolis: Hackett, 1989), 25 (189E). Subsequent citations to this work are to this edition and are given parenthetically in the text.

6 See Leo Bersani's chapter "Sociality and Sexuality," in his *Is the Rectum a Grave and Other Essays* (Chicago: University of Chicago Press, 2010), 117–19.

7 I'm referring to Joy Division's iconic song "Love Will Tear Us Apart" (prod. Martin Hannett and Joy Division, 1980).

8 Sigmund Freud, *Civilization and Its Discontents,* ed. and trans. James Strachey (New York: W.W. Norton, 1961), 10–11. Subsequent citations to this work are to this edition and are given parenthetically in the text.

9 Virginia Woolf, *Mrs. Dalloway* (1925; repr., San Diego: Harcourt, 1981), 126–27. Subsequent citations to this work are to this edition and are given parenthetically in the text.

10 Anne Carson, *Autobiography of Red* (New York: Vintage, 1998), 70. Subsequent citations to this work are to this edition and are given parenthetically in the text.

11 Carson uses this poem at the beginning of the romance section of *Autobiography of Red,* 22. From *The Complete Poems of Emily Dickinson,* ed. Thomas H. Johnson (Boston: Little, Brown, 1955), no. 1748.

12 Pat Benatar, "Love Is a Battlefield," lyrics by Mark Chapman and Holly Knight.

13 Hannah Arendt, *The Human Condition* (1958; repr., Chicago: University of Chicago Press, 1998), 20. Subsequent citations to this work are to this edition and are given parenthetically in the text.

2. The Probated Couple, or Our Polygamous Pioneers

The epigraph is from *The Complete Poems of Emily Dickinson,* ed. Thomas H. Johnson (Boston: Little, Brown, 1955), no. 360.

1 See my *God Hates Fags: The Rhetorics of Religious Violence* (New York: NYU Press, 2006).

2 Quoted in Norman Mailer, *The Executioner's Song* (New York: Vintage International, 1979), 568–69.

3 Wallace Stegner, *Mormon Country* (1942; repr., Lincoln: University of Nebraska Press, 2003), 171.

4   Ibid., 173.

5   Mark Twain, *Roughing It* (1872; repr., New York: Penguin, 1971), 139 – 40.

6   "Republican Party Platform of 1856," from *National Party Platforms,* rev.
    ed., vol. 1, *1840-1956,* comp. Donald Bruce Johnson (Champaign: Univer-
    sity of Illinois Press, 1978), 27-28, www.columbia.edu/itc/history/foner/
    civil_war/linked_documents/republican_platform.html.

7   Fanny Stenhouse and Harriet Beecher Stowe, *Tell It All: A Woman's Life
    in Polygamy* (1875; repr., Whitefish, MT: Kessinger, 2003), vi.

8   Frances E. Willard, introduction to *The Women of Mormonism: Or the
    Story of Polygamy as Told by the Victims Themselves,* ed. Jennie Anderson
    Froiseth (Detroit, MI: C. G. G. Paine, 1886), i.

9   Mailer, *Executioner's Song,* 572 – 73.

10 Oliver Wendell Holmes Jr., *The Common Law* (1881; repr., New York:
    Barnes and Noble, 2004), 216.

11 Ibid., 212, 217.

12 Karl Marx, *Capital,* vol. 1, introd. Ernest Mandel, trans. Ben Fowkes
    (1859; repr., New York: Vintage, 1976), 164 – 65.

13 Ibid., 165.

14 See Jacques Derrida, *Spectres of Marx: The State of Debt, the Work of
    Mourning, and the New Internationalism,* trans. Peggy Kamuf (New York:
    Routledge, 1994).

15 Utah State Legislature, Utah Code, 2008, title 75, Utah Uniform Pro-
    bate Code, chapter 2, Intestate Succession and Wills, http://le.utah.
    gov/~code/TITLE75/htm/75_02004.htm, accessed January 29, 2008.

16 To assert as much is almost axiomatic. For a fascinating read on the rise
    of common law, and the problems of dividing and representing power
    and legal force, see Bradin Cormack, *A Power to Do Justice: Jurisdiction,
    English Literature, and the Rise of Common Law* (Chicago: University of
    Chicago Press, 2008).

17 If only I had found the following article before I wrote this section
    and published a version: William R. Handley, "Plural Marriage, Gay
    Marriage, and the Subversion of the 'Good Order,'" *Discourse* 26, no.
    3 (2004): 85 – 109. We make similar arguments when we evaluate two
    similar cases from the nineteenth century in the Utah Territory, with
    differing but by no means opposed conclusions. I encourage reading the
    Handley article for a deeper treatment of my subject, and because the
    author has a particular ancestral stake in the debate.

18 Quoted in 137 U.S. 682, 682.

19 Quoted in 137 U.S. 682, 686.

20 137 U.S. 682, 685.

21 137 U.S. 682, 685.

22 137 U.S. 682, 687.

23 U.S. 682, 689.

24 U.S. 682, 685.

25 See all of Gayle S. Rubin, "Thinking Sex: Notes for a Radical Theory of the Politics of Sexuality," in *The Lesbian and Gay Studies Reader*, ed. Henry Abelove, Michele Aina Barale, and David M. Halperin (New York: Routledge, 1993), 3–44.

26 The mission statement of the conservative (and primarily evangelical) Family Research Council has become emphatic about making sure that we understand the "true" meaning of family: "Properly Understood, 'families' are formed only by ties of blood, marriage, or adoption, and 'marriage' is a union of one man and one woman." www.frc.org/marriage-family, accessed January 2, 2008.

27 U.S. 145, 165.

28 Marx, *Capital*, 163.

29 Ibid.

30 Ibid., 163–64. For a fascinating take on this table, see Bill Brown, *A Sense of Things: The Object Matter of American Literature* (Chicago: University of Chicago Press, 2004), 8–12.

31 Marx, *Capital*, 165.

32 Harold Bloom, *The American Religion: The Emergence of the Post-Christian Nation* (New York: Touchstone, 1993), 82.

33 For a critique of futurity I'm not fully comfortable with, but which is astonishingly productive of all sorts of great discussions, see Lee Edelman's *No Future: Queer Theory and the Death Drive* (Durham: Duke University Press, 2004).

34 "My Wedding Vows: Non-Denomination Wedding Vows," n.d., www.myweddingvows.com/traditional-wedding-vows/non-denomination-wedding-vows, accessed February 1, 2008.

35 Lauren Berlant, *The Queen of America Goes to Washington City: Essays on Sex and Citizenship* (Durham: Duke University Press, 1997), 60.

36 I'm referring here to the Dickinson poem epigraphically cited above.

37 Berlant, *Queen of America*, 60.

38 Marx, *Capital*, 167.

3. The Shelter of Singles

The chapter epigraphs are from William Faulkner, *As I Lay Dying* (1935; repr., New York: Vintage, 1990), 81, and Anne Carson, *Autobiography of Red* (New York: Vintage, 1998), 130.

1 I've learned a great deal about the usefulness of delay from Kathryn Bond Stockton. See her *The Queer Child, or Growing Sideways in the Twentieth Century* (Durham: Duke University Press, 2009).

2 Ralph Ellison, *Invisible Man* (1947; repr., New York: Vintage, 1990), 576.

3 Ralph Ellison, "Twentieth-Century Fiction and the Black Mask of Humanity," in *Shadow and Act* (1953; repr., New York: Vintage, 1972), 24.

4 Hortense J. Spillers, *Black, White, and in Color: Essays on American Literature and Culture* (Chicago: University of Chicago Press, 2003), 67.

5 W. E. B. Du Bois, *The Souls of Black Folk*, in *The Norton Anthology of African American Literature*, ed. Henry Louis Gates Jr. and Nellie Y. McKay (New York: W. W. Norton, 1997), 614. All subsequent citations to this work are to this edition and are given parenthetically in the text.

6 See Robert Stepto, *From behind the Veil: A Study of Afro-American Narrative* (Urbana: University of Illinois Press, 1979); Henry Louis Gates Jr., *The Signifying Monkey: A Theory of Afro-American Literary Criticism* (New York: Oxford University Press, 1987); and Houston A. Baker Jr., *Blues Ideology and Afro-American Literature* (Chicago: University of Chicago Press, 1984).

7 Spillers, *Black, White*, 67.

8 Etienne Balibar, "Racism as Universalism," in *Masses, Classes, Ideas: Studies on Politics and Philosophy before and after Marx*, trans. James Swenson (New York: Routledge, 1994), 200; emphasis in original.

9 Antonio Negri and Michael Hardt, *Empire* (Cambridge, MA: Harvard University Press, 2000), 395.

10 Gilles Deleuze and Félix Guattari, *A Thousand Plateaus: Capitalism and Schizophrenia*, trans. Brian Mussumi (Minneapolis: University of Minnesota Press, 1987), 25.

11 U.S. 479, at 485, 486.

12 For a helpful history of these two cases, see David A. J. Richards, *The Sodomy Cases: Bowers v. Hardwick and Lawrence v. Texas* (Lawrence: University Press of Kansas, 2009).

13 Lauren Berlant, "The Subject of True Feeling: Pain, Privacy, and Politics," in *Left Legalism/Left Critique*, ed. Wendy Brown and Janet Halley (Durham: Duke University Press, 2002), 113.

14 Leo Bersani, *Homos* (Cambridge, MA: Harvard University Press, 1995), 165–66.

15 Benjamin, "Paris, the Capital of the Nineteenth Century" (1939), in *The Arcades Project*, ed. and trans. Howard Eiland and Kevin McLaughlin (Cambridge, MA: Harvard University Press, Belknap Press, 1999), 19.

16 Ibid., 20.

17 Ibid.

18 Ibid., 10.

19 Michael Warner, *Publics and Counterpublics* (New York: Zone Books, 2002), 171.

20 Benjamin, "Paris," 14.

21 Susan Sontag, *Under the Sign of Saturn* (New York: Picador, 1972), 128.

22 Benjamin, "Paris," 885.

23 Ibid., 19.

24 Lauren Berlant and Michael Warner, "Sex in Public," *Critical Inquiry* 24 (Winter 1998): 555.

25 Hannah Arendt, *The Human Condition* (1958; repr., Chicago: University of Chicago Press, 1998), 52.

26 I'm indebted to my colleague Sara Salih: we wrote a joint presentation for a conference at Napier University in 2007. Parts of the following discussion are extracted from my contribution to that work, and the points and analysis were refined by our separate arguments.

27 Arendt, *Human Condition*, 26.

28 Berlant, *The Female Complaint: The Unfinished Business of Sentimentality in American Culture* (Durham: Duke University Press, 2008), 108.

29 Quoted in Julia Kristeva, *Hannah Arendt,* trans. Ross Guberman (New York: Columbia University Press, 2001), 23.

30 Ellison, "Twentieth-Century Fiction," 28.

31 Herman Melville, "Bartleby, the Scrivener," in *Bartleby the Scrivener and Benito Cereno* (1853; repr., London: Hesperus Classics, 2007), 35. Subsequent citations to this work are to this edition and are given parenthetically in the text.

32 Giorgio Agamben, *Homo Sacer: Sovereign Power and Bare Life,* trans. Daniel Heller-Roazen (Stanford: Stanford University Press, 1998), 48.

33 Hardt and Negri, *Empire,* 203 – 4; emphasis in original.

34 Slavoj Žižek, *The Parallax View* (Cambridge, MA: MIT Press, 2006), 381.

35 Gilles Deleuze, "Bartleby, the Formula," in *Essays Critical and Clinical* trans. Daniel W. Smith and Michael A. Greco (New York: Verso, 1989), 83.

36 Ibid., 90.

37 I'm obliquely referring to Dan McCall's lament about the "Bartleby Industry" in his *The Silence of Bartleby* (Ithaca: Cornell University Press, 1989). I can only imagine McCall's irritation at reading Branka Arsić's *Passive Constitutions or 7½ Times Bartleby* (Stanford: Stanford University Press, 2007).

38 I'm thinking of the rich usages of the figure of Antigone for all sorts of philosophy, which led Judith Butler to write an entire book on Antigone. See *Antigone's Claim: Kinship between Life and Death* (New York: Columbia University Press, 2002).

39 Deleuze, "Bartleby, the Formula," 75; Arsić, *Passive Constitutions,* 109 – 31.

40 See Arsić, *Passive Constitutions,* 109 – 31.

41 Deleuze, "Bartleby, the Formula," 75.

42 Sontag, *Under the Sign,* 128.

43 Arendt, *Human Condition,* 325.

44 Anne Carson, *Autobiography of Red* (New York: Vintage, 1998), 4.

45 Emily Dickinson, *The Complete Poems of Emily Dickinson,* ed. Thomas H. Johnson (Boston: Little, Brown, 1955), no. 587.

4. Welcome to the Desert of Me

The chapter epigraphs are from Georgia O'Keeffe, a quotation attached to the wall of the Georgia O'Keeffe Museum in Santa Fe, NM; Herman Melville, *Moby-Dick* (New York: Penguin, 1972), 93 – 94; and Marianne Moore, "People's Surroundings" (1935), in *Complete Poems of Marianne Moore* (New York: Penguin Classics, 1994), 55 – 58.

1 Morrissey fan and biographical literature is as capacious as the Internet, and it can't help me try to fill in the details that Morrissey leaves unsaid — especially romantic details. Morrissey is infamous for toying with the press and manipulating his image, and even published biographies can't fully capture the details Morrissey would prefer to have obscured. For two points of reference, if you can't resist Morrissey, see Mark Simpson's love-letter biography, *Saint Morrissey: A Portrait of This Charming Man by an Alarming Fan* (New York: Touchstone, 2003), and Johnny Rogan's *Morrissey and Marr: The Severed Alliance* (London: Omnibus Press, 1993).

2 Matt. 4.1 (New Revised Standard Edition).

3 Hannah Arendt, *The Life of the Mind* (1971; repr., San Diego: Harcourt, 1977), 6.

4 National Park Service, "Zion: Park Visitation Statistics," www.nps.gov/zion/parkmgmt/park-visitation-statistics.htm, and www.nps.gov/archive/care/visit.htm, both accessed November 5, 2008.

5 "31 Places to Go This Summer," *New York Times,* June 1, 2008, http://query.nytimes.com/gst/fullpage.html?res=9E06E3D9143BF932A35755C0A96E9C8B63&sec=&spon=&pagewanted=2, accessed November 5, 2008.

6 Many of the historical descriptions paraphrase the basic details available on the National Park Service website for Capitol Reef, "Capitol Reef: History and Culture," January 10, 2007, www.nps.gov/care/history-culture/index.htm. Other details were provided by my own travel and research on the park.

7 Two helpful histories of the national park's development are Linda Flint McClelland, *Building the National Park: Historic Landscape Design and Construction* (Baltimore: Johns Hopkins University Press, 1998), and Ethan Carr, *Mission 66: Modernism and the National Park Dilemma* (Amherst: University of Massachusetts Press, 2007).

8 "31 Places to Go This Summer," *New York Times,* June 1, 2008, http://query.nytimes.com/gst/fullpage.html?res=9E06E3D9143BF932A35755C0A96E9C8B63&sec=&spon=&pagewanted=2.

9 Frederick Law Olmstead Jr., "The Distinction between National Parks and National Forests," *Landscape Architecture* 6, no. 3 (1916): 115 – 16. This passage is also quoted in McClelland, *Building the National Park,* 10 – 11.

10 Andrew Jackson Downing, "A Visit to Montgomery Place," 1847, quoted in McClelland, *Building the National Park,* 17.

11 Mark Stoll, "Milton in Yosemite: *Paradise Lost* and the National Parks Idea," *Environmental History* 13 (April 2008): 238.

12 Quoted in Leonard J. Arrington, *Brigham Young: American Moses* (Urbana: University of Illinois Press, 1986), 144.

13 Terry Tempest Williams, "Prayer Flags in the Desert," in *With a Measure of Grace: The Story of Recipes of a Small Town Restaurant,* by Blake Spalding and Jennifer Castle with Lavinia Spalding (Santa Fe, NM: Provecho Press, 2004), 9.

14 Edward Abbey, *Desert Solitaire: A Season in the Wilderness* (New York: Ballantine Books, 1968), xii.

15 Ibid., 334.

16 Sundance Resort, "Our Story," n.d., www.sundanceresort.com/about/story.html, accessed April 7, 2009.

17 National Park Service, *Zion National Park Guide,* brochure, on file with author.

18 Dayton Duncan and Ken Burns, *The National Parks: America's Best Idea* (New York: Knopf, 2009), xxii; emphasis in original.

19 Ibid., 2; emphasis in original.

20 Frank Lloyd Wright, *An Autobiography* (1943; repr., San Francisco: Pomegranate, 2005), 309.

21 Abbey, *Desert Solitaire,* x.

22 Quoted in Frances Ferguson, *Solitude and the Sublime: Romanticism and the Aesthetics of Individuation* (New York: Routledge, 1992), 3. The quotation, as Ferguson explains, comes from Kant's "Deduction of Judgments and Taste" (sec. 42) in *Critique of Judgment,* trans. J. H. Bernard (New York: Hafner, 1951).

23 See all of Ferguson, *Solitude and the Sublime.*

24 Of course, many biographies of O'Keeffe can be consulted. O'Keeffe penned her own, *Georgia O'Keeffe* (New York: Viking Press, 1976). Laurie Lisle's *Portrait of an Artist: A Biography of Georgia O'Keeffe* (Albuquerque: University of New Mexico Press, 1986) is a good starting place. Martin's life has inspired less ink, and much comes from scholars doing critical assessments of her work. Martin's own writings provide scholars with much direction: Agnes Martin, *Writings,* ed. Dieter Schwarz (Winterthur: Kuntsmuseum, 1992). Some great critical sources are Ann C. Chave, *Agnes Martin: On and off the Grid* (Ann Arbor: University of Michigan Museum of Art, 2004); *Agnes Martin,* ed. Barbara Haskell (New York: Whitney Museum of American Art, 1992); Gavin Butt, "How New York Queered the Idea of Modern Art," in *Varieties of Modernism,* ed. Paul Wood (New Haven: Yale University Press, 2004).

25 Georgia O'Keeffe Museum wall quotations; also in O'Keeffe, *Georgia O'Keeffe,* unpaginated.

26 See also *Georgia O'Keeffe and Alfred Stieglitz: Two Lives: A Conversation in Paintings and Photographs,* ed. Alexandra Arrowsmith and Thomas West (New York: Callaway Editions, 1992).

27 Barbara Buhler Lynes, *Georgia O'Keeffe Museum: Celebrating Ten Years 1997–2007* (New York: Abrams, 2007), 14.

28 Terry Castle, "Travels with My Mom," *London Review of Books,* August 16, 2007, www.lrb.co.uk/v29/n16/terry-castle/travels-with-my-mom.

29 Ibid.

30 Ibid.

31 Ibid.

32 Lynes, *Georgia O'Keeffe Museum,* 232.

33 Georgia O'Keeffe Museum wall quotations; also in O'Keeffe, *Georgia O'Keeffe,* unpaginated.

34 Lynes emphasizes that O'Keeffe was unassisted here as she describes the sometimes-assisted work that she undertook late in her long life (*Georgia O'Keeffe Museum,* 62).

35 Sigmund Freud, "The Future of an Illusion," in *The Standard Edition of the Complete Psychological Works of Sigmund Freud,* vol. 21 *(1927–1931),* ed. and trans. James Strachey (London: Vintage, 2001), 25.

36 Walter Benjamin, "The Work of Art in the Age of Mechanical Reproduction," in *Illuminations: Essays and Reflections,* ed. Hannah Arendt, trans. Harry Zohn (New York: Schocken Books, 1968), 222–23.

37 Miriam Hansen, "Benjamin's Aura," *Critical Inquiry* 34 (Winter 2008): 351.

38 Georg Simmel, *Philosophy of Money,* trans. Kaethe Mengelberg, Tom Bottomore, and David Frisby, 2nd ed. (1900/1907; repr., London, 2004), 473, quoted in Hansen, "Benjamin's Aura," 353.

39 Ferguson's *Solitude and the Sublime* has an excellent discussion of this feature in Kant, especially on 27.

40 See all of Hansen, "Benjamin's Aura."

41 Ibid., 375.

42 Benjamin, "Work of Art," 223.

43 Harwood Museum, "Agnes Martin Gallery," n.d., www.harwoodmuseum.org/exhibitions/view/59, accessed August 25, 2010.

44 Castle, "Travels with My Mom."

45 Bert Winther-Tamaki, "The Asian Dimension of Postwar Abstract Art: Calligraphy and Metaphysics," in *The Third Mind: American Artists Contemplate Asia, 1860–1989,* ed. Alexandra Munroe (New York: Guggenheim Museum Publications, 2009), 145.

46 Alexandra Munroe, "Art of Perceptual Experience: Pure Abstraction and Ecstatic Minimalism," in Munroe, *Third Mind,* 291.

47 Richard Tuttle, "What Does One Look at in an Agnes Martin Painting? Nine Musings on the Occasion of Her Ninetieth Birthday," *American Art* 16 (Autumn 2002): 92.

48 Ned Rifkin, "Agnes Martin — The Music of the Spheres," in *Agnes Martin: The Nineties and Beyond,* ed. Ned Rifkin (Ostfildern-Ruit, Germany: Hatje Cantz, 2001), 25.

49 Quoted in ibid., 26.

50 Martin, *Writings,* 37.

51 Leo Bersani and Adam Phillips, *Intimacies* (Cambridge, MA: Harvard University Press, 2008), 122.

52 Martin, *Writings,* bilingual ed. (Ostfildern-Ruit, Germany: Hatje Cantz, 2005), 37 – 38.

53 Ibid., 37.

54 Ibid.

55 For an interesting discussion of distance and "dissident subjectivity," see David R. Jarraway, *Going the Distance: Dissident Subjectivity in Modernist American Literature* (Baton Rouge: Louisiana State University Press, 2003).

56 Rosalind E. Krauss, "Grids," *October* 9 (Summer 1979): 54.

57 Plato, *The Symposium,* introd. and trans. Christopher Gill (New York: Penguin Classics, 1999), 23.

58 Leo Bersani, "The Will to Know," in *Is the Rectum a Grave? And Other Essays* (Chicago: University of Chicago Press, 2009), 159.

59 Rei Terada, *Looking Away: Phenomenality and Dissatisfaction, Kant to Adorno* (Cambridge, MA: Harvard University Press, 2009), 204.

60 Martin, *Writings,* 40.

61 Virginia Woolf, *To the Lighthouse* (1927; repr., San Diego: Harcourt Brace Jovanovich, 208 – 9. Subsequent citations to this work are to this edition and are given parenthetically in the text.

62 Virginia Woolf, *Mrs. Dalloway* (1925; repr., San Diego: Harcourt, 1981), 130. Subsequent citations to this work are to this edition and are given parenthetically in the text.

63 Anne Carson, *Autobiography of Red* (New York: Vintage, 1998), 70. Subsequent citations to this work are to this edition and are given parenthetically in the text.

Index

Note: Page numbers in italics indicate illustrations or photographs.

Abbey, Edward: *Desert Solitaire*, 172, 173
abortion issue, 17
Aeneid (Virgil), 111, 124
affirmative action issue, 17
African American double consciousness, 114–15
Against Love (Kipnis), 18–19, 22
Agamben, Giorgio, 31–32, 140
Allen, Joan, 175
aloneness: aesthetics of distance, 30; Arendt on, 19–20; in desert, 162, 167, 170; loneliness differentiated from, 15, 37–38, 144; modern difficulty of, 28–30; privacy and, 55–57; topic of, 30; value of, 15–16, 33
Amélie (film), 131
aneu logou, concept of, 66
Anti-Polygamy Act (1862), 84–85
Arendt, Hannah, 14; on desert as destination for contemplation, 162; eternity differentiated from immortality, 65–66, 67, 100, 101; on French happiness with "small things," 131–32; *The Human Condition*, 132–34, 150–51; on immortality through creative work, 38; *The Origins of Totalitarianism*, 19–21, 28–29, 30, 32; on retreating from public sphere, 39, 133–34,

137, 143, 149; on women's need for coupledom, 138, 151
Aristophanes' speech in Plato's *Symposium*, 33, 46–48, 50–51, 53, 112–13, 150, 190
Aristotle, *aneu logou* concept, 66
arrheton, concept of, 66
Arsić, Branka, 142
art's distancing effect, 39, 175, 181–82
Askegard, Charles, 4
"aura" concept of Benjamin, 18–19, 181–83
Austen, Jane, 28, 80
Autobiography of Red (Carson), 33, 105, 169; dynamics of coupledom in, 59–67; falling in love as tragedy, 51; recovery from coupledom in, 197–202

Baker, Houston, 114
Baker, Nicole K., 72–74, 77, 78–81
Balaban, Bob, 175
Balibar, Etienne, 116–17
Barthes, Roland: *A Lover's Discourse*, 1
"Bartleby, the Scrivener" (Melville), 36–37, 105, 122, 139–56; alterations to, 144–45; architectural detail in, 146–47, 149; Bartleby described, 139–40; Bartleby in prison, 149, 152, 154; Bartleby labeled "bachelor," 142–44; Bartleby's death, 154–55; Bartleby's fixed diction, 151–52;

14–15, 33, 42–51, 100; domesticity
and, 130–32; dyad concept and,
45; "each" in, 61–62, 65; eternity
concept and, 34–35, 53, 62–65,
66–67, 89–103, 145, 156, 197, 199–
200; family attachments, 69–70,
83; formal terror of, 57–59; as
foundation of Western society,
17–18, 19, 31; fragility of, 33–34,
38, 44–45, 63; ideology of, 30,
49–51; immortality and, 51–55;
intensity of, 41, 42–43; light and
dark, 111–12; loneliness and, 15,
16, 22, 41, 47, 48–49, 194–95; loss
of individuality in, 29, 34, 124;
loss of privacy and, 122–23, 134;
Noah's Ark and, 135; "Other"
and, 25–26, 31; portrayed in
Godard's Le mépris, 26–28; race
and, 109–11, 113–14, 116–18, 122;
restraints of, 183–84; security felt
in, 12–13; shelter from, 105–6, 118;
as shrinkage of greatness, 53–55,
67, 106, 124–28, 147, 149, 190–91;
singles seen as scapegoats, 35–36,
161; society's valuation of, 1–3,
5–8, 18, 26; stability and, 19, 51;
totalitarianism of, 130–31; ubiquity of, 24–25; values voters and,
17–18
"couplism," 117

Death Valley National Park, 157
Deleuze, Gilles, 119, 141, 142, 145
Denney, Reuel: The Lonely Crowd
(with Reisman and Glazer), 9, 10
DePaulo, Bella: Singled Out, 6, 15, 22,
203–4
desert: alone in the, 37–38, 162–70,
186, 189; heroic vision in, 192–93;
Jesus' temptations in, 161; Mor-
risey in the, 157–58, 160–62; National Park Service and, 164–66,

172; "sublime" and, 170–74,
188–89
Desert Solitaire (Abbey), 172, 173
dialectics, twoness of, 20, 24–25
Dickinson, Emily, 59–60, 69, 103,
155–56; on immortality through
creative work, 38
Dostoevsky, Feodor: Notes from Underground, 107
double consciousness, 114–15
Downing, Andrew Jackson: Treatise on the Theory and Practice of
Landscape Gardening, 166
Dreams from My Father (Obama),
11–13
Du Bois, W. E. B., 14, 114–15
Dumm, Thomas: Loneliness as a Way
of Life, 9, 14–15, 205n13
Dutoit, Ulysse: Forms of Being (with
Bersani), 26–28
dyad concept, 26, 45, 65, 69, 77

Edelman, Lee: No Future, 205n28
Edmunds-Tucker Act, 85–86
Ellison, Ralph: Invisible Man, 36, 37,
103, 105, 106–39. See also Invisible Man
Emerson, Ralph Waldo, 13, 14
emptiness: abstract art and, 175–92;
desert vistas and, 162–74; Dickinson on, 155–56; distancing
effect of, 198–99; loss and, 59; as
refuge in "Bartleby," 139–56; retreat to in Invisible Man, 133–34;
topic of, 30, 37–38
epistemology of coupledom, 24–26
Epistemology of the Closet (Sedgwick), 24–25
eternity, concept of: coupledom
and, 34–35, 53, 62–65, 66–67,
77–80, 89–103, 145, 156, 197, 199–
200; Freud on, 52–53; in Greek
philosophy, 66;